D1484002

The Natural History of
WEASELS
& STOATS

Christopher Helm Mammal Series
Edited by Dr Ernest Neal, MBE, former President of the Mammal
Society

Already published:
The Natural History of Antelopes
C.A. Spinage

The Natural History of Badgers
Ernest Neal

The Natural History of Otters
Paul Chanin

The Natural History of Squirrels
John Gurnell

The Natural History of Whales and Dolphins
P.G.H. Evans

The Natural History of Deer
Rory Putman

Forthcoming titles include:

The Natural History of Moles
Martyn L. Gorman and David Stone

The Natural History of Rabbits
David Cowan

The Natural History of Seals
Nigel Bonner

The Natural History of
WEASELS
& STOATS

CAROLYN KING

COMSTOCK PUBLISHING ASSOCIATES
A division of CORNELL UNIVERSITY PRESS
Ithaca, New York

© Carolyn King
Line illustrations by Larry Douglas

All rights reserved. Except for brief quotations in a review, this book or parts thereof, must not be reproduced in any form without permission in writing from the publisher. For imformation address Cornell University Press, 124 Roberts Place, Ithaca, New York 14850.

First published 1989 by Christopher Helm Ltd. and Cornell University Press.

Library of Congress Cataloging-in-Publication Data

King, C.M. (Carolyn M.)
  The natural history of weasels / Carolyn M. King.
  p. cm. – (The Natural history of mammals series)
  Includes bibliographical references.
  ISBN 0–8014–2428–3
  1. Weasels. I. Title. II. Series.
  QL737.C25K58 1990
  599.74′4477–dc20

Photoset by Opus, Oxford
Printed and bound in Great Britain by Billing and Sons Ltd, Worcester

Contents

Colour plates

Figures

LIST OF FIGURES

Tables

Acknowledgements

I could not hope to be able to remember and thank everyone who has helped me in various ways over the long years of my fascination with weasels. I compile this list with some hesitation, trusting that those who find themselves absent from it will already know how much their help was appreciated.

First, I thank Dr H.N. (Mick) Southern, my supervisor at Oxford, and Dr J.A. Gibb, Director of DSIR Ecology Division in Lower Hutt, New Zealand, for their thoughtful care during my years under their direction. Then I thank all the fellow students and researchers, gamekeepers, wildlife, forestry and National Parks rangers who helped me to collect material or to make sense of it. I thank the librarians who tracked down obscure references, the secretaries who typed my MSS over and over (before I got my PC), and the referees whose searching comments taught me to write. I owe much to the eagle eyes and razor-blade minds of D.G. Dawson, M.G. Efford, B.M. Fitzgerald, J.E.C. Flux, P.J. Moors, and M.R. Rudge. I thank Larry Douglas for his superb weasel drawings, and all those who lent me original data or illustrations or granted permission to reproduce copyright material: Cornell University Press, The Game Conservancy, the Zoological Society of London, the British Museum of Natural History, the New Zealand Science Information Publishing Centre (DSIR), G. Caughley, C. Vispo, P. Sleeman, S. Tapper, M. Weber, and H. Grue. Many readers of *The Shooting Times* and *The Field* responded to my request for information, and I have quoted from some of their helpful letters here. I have always wanted to at least partly discharge my debt to these people by writing down for them some of the things I have learned about these fascinating little animals.

It is a daunting task to read the entire MS of a book with sufficient attention to make constructive criticisms of it, and I am very grateful to E.G. Neal, H.V. Thompson, R.A. Powell and two anonymous publisher's reviewers for finding the time to undertake this valuable service.

Family responsibilities have complicated and long delayed the preparation of this book. I am very grateful for the apparently endless patience of Jo Hemmings and Ernest Neal at Christopher Helm, and for the resigned forbearance of my husband and son, Joe and David Miller.

Series editor's foreword

In recent years there has been a great upsurge of interest in wildlife and a deepening concern for nature conservation. For many there is a compelling urge to counterbalance some of the artificiality of present-day living with a more intimate involvement with the natural world. More people are coming to realise that we are all part of nature, not apart from it. There seems to be a greater desire to understand its complexities and appreciate its beauty.

This appreciation of wildlife and wild places has been greatly stimulated by the world-wide impact of natural-history television programmes. These have brought into our homes the sights and sounds both of our own countryside and of far-off places that arouse our interest and delight.

In parallel with this growth of interest there has been a great expansion of knowledge and, above all, understanding of the natural world — an understanding vital to any conservation measures that can be taken to safeguard it. More and more field workers have carried out painstaking studies of many species, analysing their intricate behaviour, relationships and the part they play in the general ecology of their habitats. To the time-honoured techniques of field observations and experimentation has been added the sophistication of radio-telemetry whereby individual animals can be followed, even in the dark and over long periods, and their activities recorded. Infra-red cameras and light-intensifying binoculars now add a new dimension to the study of nocturnal animals. Through such devices great advances have been made.

This series of volumes aims to bring this information together in an exciting and readable form so that all who are interested in wildlife may benefit from such a synthesis. Many of the titles in the series concern groups of related species such as otters, squirrels and rabbits so that readers from many parts of the world may learn about their own more familiar animals in a much wider context. Inevitably more emphasis will be given to particular species within a group as some have been more extensively studied than others. Authors too have their own special interests and experience and a text gains much in authority and vividness when there has been personal involvement.

Many natural history books have been published in recent years which have delighted the eye and fired the imagination. This is wholly good. But it is the intention of this series to take this a step further by exploring the subject in greater depth and by making available the results of recent research. In this way it is hoped to satisfy to some extent at least the curiosity and desire to know more which is such an encouraging characteristic of the keen naturalist of today.

Ernest Neal
Bedford

Preface

This book is about a group of small, northern hemisphere carnivores collectively known as weasels. Weasels are the smallest members of the family Mustelidae, which also includes the martens, badgers and otters. There are three species of weasels, all members of the genus *Mustela*. They are *Mustela erminea*, the stoat or short-tailed weasel; *Mustela frenata*, the longtailed weasel; and *Mustela nivalis*, which has two distinctly different subspecies, the common weasel *M. nivalis vulgaris* and the least weasel, *M. nivalis nivalis*.

The weasels are distinct and easily recognisable animals, but unfortunately the English or common name 'weasel' can be confusing unless it is carefully defined. It may be applied to the whole family Mustelidae, or to the smallest members of the genus, *Mustela nivalis*. The ordinary usage in England, which is 'weasel' for *M. nivalis* and 'stoat' for *M. erminea*, may be misunderstood both in America and in Ireland, where 'weasel' may mean either. Likewise, whereas it would be correct and acceptable to apply the American term 'ermine' to all European *erminea*, it would not be correct to apply their name 'least weasel' to European *nivalis* except in the far north.

In the technical literature this confusion can be forestalled by using only Latin names — that is, after all, their function. In this book the English names 'least weasel', 'common weasel', 'longtailed weasel' and 'stoat' or 'Irish stoat' are used for specific references to each form as defined in Table 2.1. The word 'weasel' is used alone to refer to all of the northern hemisphere forms collectively or to any unspecified member of the group. For the Latin names of other species mentioned, see the Index.

1 Introduction

In September 1967, I enrolled as a graduate student at the Bureau of Animal Population (later the Animal Ecology Research Group, part of the Department of Zoology) at Oxford. The Bureau occupied an old and idiosyncratic building, overshadowed by the magnificent tower of Magdalen College. It was bathed on that side by the roar of the High Street traffic, and on the other side by the tranquil beauty of the Botanic Gardens. Fortunately for his peace of mind, my supervisor's room was on the tranquil side. I shared a room with two other students and a weasel, on the noisy side. But traffic noise is constant and soon dismissed by the mind: instead we had the rose garden and the unfailing delight of the intricate Magdalen carvings in mellow Cotswold stone, and our days were punctuated at quarter-hour intervals by the chimes from the tower. There may be better-equipped or quieter laboratories for a course of study, but none that have the setting of the old BAP.

In British universities at that time, the usual period allowed for a student to produce a doctoral thesis was three years. At least, that's as long as one could obtain a grant for. For people in the laboratory sciences or the arts, whose work is not seasonal nor much influenced by the weather, and does not depend on the co-operation of wild animals, three well-organised years can usually suffice. But in field ecology, one cannot contrive things so well; one meets the animals on their own ground and on their own terms, and the student tends to feel rather like the junior partner in the arrangement. Animals which won't turn up where they are expected, or won't enter traps, or inconsiderately die at a critical moment, can upset the most carefully planned work schedule. The student who chooses to work on weasels finds out in due course that he has stacked the odds against himself even more than most.

Supervisors varied a good deal in how closely they watched their students. Some came round often and asked embarrassing questions and made suggestions unasked and even more or less rewrote the manuscript, so that the student felt it was no longer his own work. Others stayed too distant and unapproachable to be of any help at all. Mine did none of these things. Mick Southern was a tall, soft-spoken Lincolnshireman, usually dressed in a foxy-brown tweed jacket and puffing a pipe. He had the unflappable calm of one who had spent hours leaning over a gate just

1

watching the natural world, and he had a deep respect for all forms of life, including, even, that of students. He was always available, always patient, never interfered even when he thought I might be wrong, and he managed to convey the impression that he believed in me even when I didn't myself. Not many students are that lucky.

The University owned a wooded estate about four miles outside the city, in which most members of our research group had conducted their field studies since soon after the last war. It was a great advantage to work in such a place, except that, by the time I came along, most of the more obvious and easier projects had been done. But there was a resident gamekeeper at Wytham, who rejoiced in the wonderfully appropriate name of Mr Wood. I asked him what animals he knew lived on the estate, which I might conceivably study: as he reeled off a list, I ticked off each species as being either too difficult, too few, or too well-known already. Finally he mentioned that there were 'a few weasels'. The idea had instant appeal, although at that moment I had never seen one. I persuaded Mick to let me try. He was very reluctant; but, wisely deciding that I would work harder on a tricky job of my own choosing than on an easier one imposed by him, he agreed.

In the first year I very nearly lost the gamble. The so-called common weasels of Wytham were in fact very thin on the ground, and those that were there refused to come into my traps. Fearing total humiliation, I began establishing a second-string study, which involved collecting carcasses of dead weasels from gamekeepers. I learnt much from the local keepers, most of whom were willing to talk weasel-lore for hours. In the event both the live-trapping and the carcass analysis studies paid off. I ended up with more data on weasels than I had ever hoped for, and had to take a fourth year to compensate for my disastrous first.

After graduating in 1971, I travelled to New Zealand to take up a research job with DSIR Ecology Division at Lower Hutt. Stoats and common weasels had been introduced to New Zealand in the 1880s (see Chapter 13). Stoats were common in the contemporary forests, and obviously ate native birds. It was nearly universally believed that they should be controlled: all we needed to know was how. So in 1972 I embarked on what turned out to be a commitment of ten years of field, laboratory and desk work on the biology of stoats in New Zealand nature reserves, especially in the mainland National Parks. I had help from various sources for much of that time, and between us we collected over 2,000 carcasses of dead stoats, and undertook regular field observations to monitor the population changes of stoats and rodents. I have related the history of the predators introduced to New Zealand, and the consequences for the native fauna, elsewhere (King, 1984a), but some of the basic information about the biology of stoats that we worked out in New Zealand will be incorporated here whenever it is relevant. New Zealand has proved to be an exiting place to study evolutionary ecology — for example, the ways in which stoats and common weasels have adapted to a totally alien habitat.

Studying weasels can be difficult and unrewarding, as I know from my first year of trying and from letters I sometimes get from frustrated students. It is not so long ago that hardly anything was known about them. As an Honours student in November 1965 I was present when J.D. Lockie delivered his now well-known paper to the Zoological Society of

London, the published version of which (1966) begins with the words, 'The reviewer of territory and home range in small carnivores has a fairly easy task since the literature is meagre.' I was lucky, not once but twice, and not only in happening to choose workable projects but also in having the help of many people. It is a pleasure as well as a privilege to be able to share my admiration of weasels with others. Conversely, since I cannot imagine a time when I shall cease to be interested in weasels, I invite readers of this book to share with me their own stories, as well as any additions and corrections they can suggest.

2 Hair-trigger mousetraps with teeth

There is something enormously satisfactory about a weasel. It has the perfection, the grace and efficiency of a well-designed tool in the hands of an expert. Just as people love to watch and applaud a craftsman or artist at work, or a display of the skills of any top sportsman, so I have for years loved to study and applaud the life of the weasels. They are carnivores, among the purest of the type: they are perfectly adapted in every feature of their body and behaviour to live exclusively as hunters. The sum of these adaptations make up a design for an effective mouse-harvesting machine that we can only envy. In the past, farmers and foresters have tried to make use of the powers of weasels for their own ends, particularly to control various 'pest' species such as voles and rabbits. But the philosophies of weasels and of man toward such situations are quite different: what for us is a problem, requiring elimination, is for weasels an opportunity, to be exploited. Chapter 13 explores the reasons why biological control by weasels seldom works: for now, it is enough to note that one of the characteristics of a perfect tool is that it cannot be made to do a job other than the one for which it was designed.

All weasels have the sinuous physique common to most of the Mustelidae, the family of carnivores of which they are the smallest members. They have long, slender bodies, long necks and short legs: their heads are rather flattish and smoothly pointed, exactly suitable instruments for poking into every possible small hole. Indeed, their Latin name is said to be derived from their small stature and long, pointed shape; *Mustela* means a *mus* (mouse) as long as a *telum* (spear). They have no apparent shoulders or hips, so the general impression is of a furry tube ending in an excitable bottlebrush tail. They have large rounded ears lying almost flat among the fur; bright beady black eyes; very long sensitive whiskers on their faces, and, like a cat, short ones on their elbows. Their paws are furred between the pads (five on each foot); the claws are sharp, and not retractable. They swim well, climb trees easily, and run like small bolts of brown lightning.

Unfortunately, few animals are as misunderstood as weasels. An early description, phrased with all the vivid imagery that was still allowed in scientific writing in the last century, gives an idea of their reputation

A glance at the physiognomy of the weasels would suffice to betray their character. The teeth are almost of the highest known raptorial character; the jaws are worked by enormous masses of muscles covering all the side of the skull. The forehead is low and the nose is sharp; the eyes are small, penetrating, cunning, and glitter with an angry green light. There is something peculiar, moreover, in the way that this fierce face surmounts a body extraordinarily wirey, lithe and muscular. It ends in a remarkably long and slender neck in such a way that it may be held at a right angle with the axis of the latter. When the creature is glancing around, with the neck stretched up, and the flat triangular head bent forward, swaying from one side to the other, we catch the likeness in a moment — it is the image of a serpent (Coues, 1877).

At least since the beginning of the last century, weasels have had a bad press image. They appear only very rarely in animal fiction stories for children, and then always as thieves, robbers or other bad characters. Any kind of weasel is always seen as

the villain of any nature story . . . Most of us have an instinctive hatred of weasels. There is something decidedly sinister about their looks; something serpentine that makes us shudder . . . Weasels look like killers and they are killers, and many of us get a self-righteous feeling when we shoot one (Wood, 1946).

The character assassination of weasels extends even to their common name. In traditional railway slang, 'weaselling' meant extracting tips; Dickens used the phrase 'cunning as a weasel' in *The Old Curiosity Shop*; 'weasel pee' is a derogatory description of weak beer (hence the sign on our local pub door '100% weaselless'!). 'Weasel words' are those whose meaning is bent, neutralised, contradicted or sucked out for political purposes, as in, for example, the phrases 'authentic replica', meaning a genuine fake, or 'popularly priced' — popular with whom? and so on (Howard, 1988). The derivation seems to be from the idea, quoted by Shakespeare, that weasels suck eggs.

In addition to this moralising and emotional reaction to the physical appearance of a weasel, the rise of the game preservation industry in Europe and North America ensured that weasels generally were labelled as 'vermin' and systematically persecuted for a hundred years. The observations of early naturalists were liberally mixed with prejudice, fiction and misinterpretation, and led to uncritical conclusions. Accounts of weasels in the older natural history books — and even in some modern ones — tell us more about the writers and the attitudes of their times than about their subjects. Yet, in earlier times, the weasels were much appreciated by country folk for their willowy elegance and for their services in killing rodents. Many of the traditional vernacular names for the common weasel in Italy and Spain are complimentary, such as 'donina' (little lady or little graceful one), 'bonuca-mona-muca (pretty little one), 'comadreja' (little godmother). The ancient Egyptians apparently used to keep tame weasels (species unknown) in the period before the domestication of the cat, and the modern Egyptian *Mustela nivalis* is still so often found in houses that it is described as 'almost completely commensal' (Osborn and Helmy, 1980). The native Americans regarded the capture of a least weasel as a piece of great good fortune, and they told F.L.Osgood that, since he had caught one, he must be destined to have great wealth and power (Hall, 1951).

Weasels certainly do kill to live, but they are not vicious nor insatiable, and in nature death is not a tragedy, it is part of life. However, the old attitudes have filtered down the generations so subtly that the average person's knowledge of weasels is influenced, more than they may realise, by old folk-stories of dubious accuracy.

People who have been fortunate enough to have got to know a tame weasel at close quarters never fail to develop a quite different view. Drabble (1977) described his common weasel as 'a sprite . . . a golden leaf on the tongue of a whirlwind'; and Stephen (1969) had two which were an 'intriguing, entrancing, entertaining pair of will o'the wisps . . . doing a wall-of-death act round my sittingroom' . Weasels are difficult to observe in the wild, and though with luck one may witness some fascinating glimpses of their activities, seldom can one get so good a view as Drabble had of his tame Teasy. His description (Drabble, 1977) conveys a vivid impression of the delightful character and restless energy of weasels:

From whichever retreat hid him for the moment, a wedge-shaped head and wicked pair of eyes would appear. Then out he'd roll, turning cartwheel after cartwheel like an acrobat going round the circus ring. He moved so fast that it was impossible to distinguish where his head began and his tail finished. He was like a tiny inflated rubber tyre bowling round the room. Sometimes we thought this game was purely for exercise, since we could distinguish no pattern . . . Sometimes the weasel used his dance as a cloak for attack . . . He usually chose me for his victim, and his cartwheeling twisted this way and that, over the carpet and up on to the settee beside me. The fabric . . . was cut and ragged. . . It made a perfect foothold for the weasel, who could run up and down the perpendicular arms of the furniture with the ease of a squirrel . . . When his gyrations fetched him up on the seat beside me, I always knew what the next act would be. . . The tiny scratching of the pen and the movements of my fingers were irresistible. From the cover of his dynamic camouflage, he could dive on to my hand, grasp my first finger in his forepaws with the strength of a tiny bear, and bite the fingertip with mock ferocity but, in reality, as gently as a kitten . . . If I tickled his belly he'd roll on his back and attack as if his very life depended on it. Then he'd gradually relax, until he was licking the tips of my fingers, and croon his high-pitched little purring love-song . . . .

The larger weasels are just the same. One fur trapper who accidentally caught a live longtailed weasel took it home and kept it for a week. 'If lightning is any quicker than a weasel, the margin is of microscopic breadth,' he concluded, after watching it rocketing around its cage and eagerly fronting up to a terrier through the bars. When he released it, it hopped off in a leisurely way, so sure of itself that 'its calm . . . movements gave no suggestion of the electric potentialities embodied within the elongated anatomy of this testy little carnivore' (Edson, 1933).

Modern research has rapidly increased our knowledge of the lives of weasels, especially since the 1960s. Rigorous, systematic observations have replaced the more casual, subjective accounts, and experiments have replaced the descriptive anecdotes, which used to be all we had to go on. Something will be lost if the objective approach is taken too far, but it does help to interpret the old field observations and anecdotes collected by lucky chance, and to eliminate longstanding fallacies. The modern weasel-watcher needs to move in both worlds — the systematic, critical analysis of data in a computer, and the hours of patient field work, waiting for the occasional exciting glimpse of undisturbed weasels behaving naturally in the wild. I have tried to integrate both in this book.

SPECIES DIAGNOSES

The Mustelidae is a large family (67 species) and all its members have, to varying degrees, the long thin body and short legs so characteristic of weasels in general, which is perhaps why the whole group is also called the weasel family.

The genus *Mustela* is the largest in the family, and contains between 13 and 16 species, depending on who you ask. The three that are common throughout the north temperate and boreal zones — *M. nivalis*, *M. erminea*, and *M. frenata* (the latter also extends into Central and South America) — are by far the best known of all the species of *Mustela*, and they are the subject of this book. This is not because the tropical weasels are less important: only that they are less well known and probably rather different from the three northern temperate ones.

The general weasel appearance is common to all three species (Figures 2.1, 2.2, Plate 1). The differences between them hinge mainly on size, colour and reproduction. Size and colour are obvious to the eye, so one might think that they would be easily defined and reliable guides. Most of the early taxonomists based their species descriptions on size and colour, often using the standard practice of describing whole species — or at any rate, whole populations — from one or a few 'type' specimens. But the three weasel species between them occupy an enormous geographical range (Figure 2.3), across which there are immense differences in climate, habitat and distribution of prey. In these different conditions each has developed considerable variation in external appearance — especially in size (see Chapter 4), the details of the summer pelage, the length and colour of the tail (Table 2.1), and whether or not they turn white in winter (Plate 5 and Chapter 3). The 'type-specimen' method of the nineteenth century taxonomists led in time to glorious confusion, and dozens of named species and subspecies, which have still not been sorted out. In this book I recognise only two subspecies of *nivalis* (though there is a good case for a third) and one distinct subspecies in *erminea*. I treat all the other races of *erminea*, and all those of *frenata*, together (Table 2.1).

The colour patterns of weasels are very variable. In summer coat, the head, back, upper tail, and outer legs of all species of weasels are usually a rich chestnut colour, though some may be nearer a sandy tan and some may darken almost to chocolate; and the throat, chest and belly range from a pure white, through yellowish undertones almost to apricot in some longtails. The feet often have white markings, and the outer edge of the ear is often fringed with white in stoats. The boundary line between

Figure 2.1. The distinguishing characters of weasels in summer coat.

Common Weasel

Stoat

Longtailed weasel

Least weasel

Figure 2.2. The distinguishing characters of weasels in winter coat. The longtailed weasel is illustrating the 'pied' condition, which may also be seen in stoats.

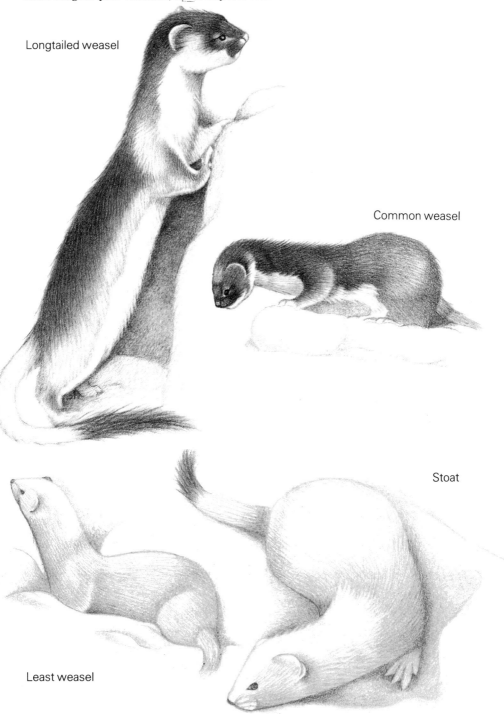

Longtailed weasel

Common weasel

Stoat

Least weasel

Table 2.1 Distinctions between the species of weasels

| Latin name | *M. nivalis* | | *M. erminea* | | *M. frenata* |
	n. nivalis	*n.vulgaris*	*e.hibernica*	others	
Authority & date	Linnaeus 1766	Erxleben 1777	Thomas & Barrett Hamilton 1895	Linnaeus 1758	Lichtenstein 1832
English name used here	least weasel	common weasel	Irish stoat[1]	stoat	longtailed weasel
Other names	grass weasel miniver		Irish weasel	ermine short-tailed weasel	
Summer coat demarcation line[2] tail tip	straight brown	wavy brown	most wavy black	straight black	straight or wavy black
White in winter	usually	no	no	maybe	maybe
Tail length[3]	<25%	<25%	30–45%	30–45%	40–70%
Delayed implantation	no	no	yes	yes	yes
Rank order of size	5	4	3	2	1

For species ranges, see Figure 2.3; for sizes, Chapter 4

[1] This form is also present on the Isle of Man and on Islay and Jura
[2] Demarcation line: the line separating the brown from the white summer fur
[3] Tail length expressed as a percentage of head-and-body length

Figure 2.3. The natural distribution of the three species of weasels in (A) Europe, (B) Asia and (C) North America. Distributions from Corbet (1978) and Ralls and Harvey (1985). The boundary between the two recognised subspecies of nivalis *(the common and least weasels) cannot be mapped from present data (see Figure 2.5). (D) shows the average yearly number of days with snow lying on low ground in the mornings.* Nivalis *and* erminea *have also been introduced into New Zealand.*

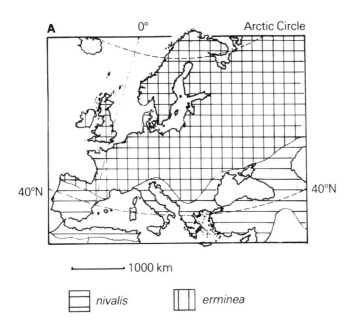

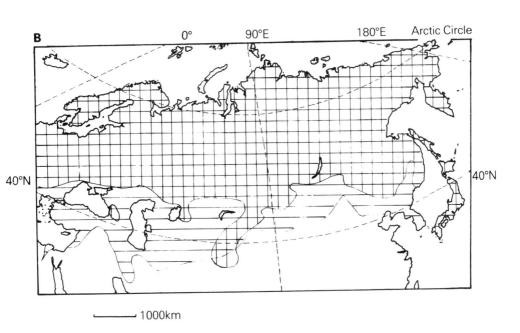

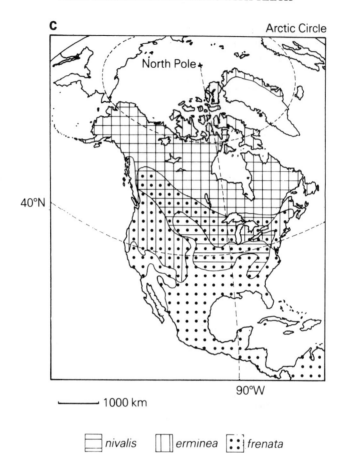

C

Arctic Circle

North Pole

40°N

90°W

⎯⎯ 1000 km

⊟ nivalis   ⊞ erminea   [∵] frenata

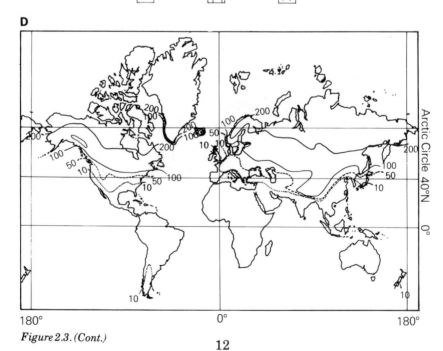

D

180°   0°   180°

Figure 2.3. (Cont.)

12

the brown and white fur is irregular in common weasels, and there are often odd spots or large patches of brown among the white (Figure 2.4, Plate 4). This pattern is also found in many longtails, in more than 80 per cent of Irish stoats (Plate 3), and in some stoats from coastal Washington and Oregon and on Vancouver Island (Sleeman, 1987). Common weasels usually have a brown spot, called the gular spot, behind the angle of the mouth (sometimes it is joined by an isthmus to the rest of the brown area), though least weasels do not. In common weasels the details of the belly pattern are individually unique and constant through successive moults (Linn and Day, 1966). In the least weasels of northern Eurasia and North America, in some of the large common weasels of the Mediterranean, and in under 20 per cent of Irish, most North American and all other stoats, the boundary between brown and white fur is straight.

Stoats and longtailed weasels also have a distinct bushy pencil of long black hairs on the tip of the tail. This is normally the most reliable distinguishing mark separating these species from the common and least weasels, though individual common weasels may have a few dark hairs at the tail tip, especially among the larger races. Longtails also have various degrees and combinations of white and dark markings on the face, which, for reasons so far unexplained, are more pronounced in areas with high humidity.

Until 1890, the names of European weasels were applied to their American cousins. Then, and for the next 50 years, all the local

Figure 2.4. The irregular, individually distinct patterns of brown and white blotches on the bellies of three English common weasels, redrawn from sketches made of anaesthetised live animals in the field. The male on the right was captured 54 times between September 1968 and March 1969; the pattern was retained unchanged through two moults (King, 1979)

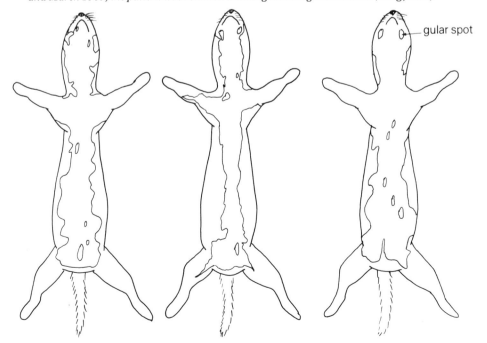

gular spot

variations of American weasels were regarded as separate species, and hosts of new names were published as each separate race was described. They make the older literature very confusing. Later, however, as more and more specimens were collected, taxonomists realised that *erminea* and *nivalis* were truly circumboreal species, and should be given the same specific name in both the Old and the New Worlds. The former separate species were then reduced to subspecies, of which Hall (1951) listed four in *nivalis* (he still called it *rixosa*), 21 in *erminea*, and 25 in *frenata* (not counting those south of the Mexican border).

The two European subspecies of *nivalis* are very different in appearance, and *nivalis nivalis*, with its much smaller size, straight belly pattern and regular winter whitening, is still considered by some authors to be a separate species. There are other differences too, in reproductive cycles and consequently in population dynamics (see Chapter 9), so there is certainly something to be said for the idea. Unfortunately, there are two arguments against it. First, there is no reliable connection between size and colour pattern in *nivalis*. The Mediterranean races of *nivalis* are all very large in body size, but some populations have the straight belly pattern, some have the irregular pattern, and some have both (Figure 2.5). In Sweden the two types are quite distinct, and meet at a definable boundary (Stolt, 1979), but that does not necessarily mean they are separate species. Second, their chromosomes are the same; and Fritz Frank's breeding experiments have shown that they are fully inter-fertile, and that their size and colour patterns are inherited independently (Frank, 1974; Mandahl and Fredga, 1980).

Therefore, differences in size and summer colour pattern between local populations on the European mainland cannot be recognised at the species level. The two indisputably distinct forms, the least weasel of the far north and east of Eurasia and the common weasel of Britain and western Europe, can reasonably be recognised as subspecies. There is some reason to consider five isolated populations, in Sardinia, North Africa, Egypt, Japan and North America, as separate subspecies too (Corbet, 1978), but there is not enough information to decide. So for the moment, I have taken the conservative view and included the first three with *nivalis vulgaris* and the opther two with *nivalis nivalis*. The result is unsatisfactory, but there is no alternative until a new taxonomic revision of *nivalis* is done.

In parts of England, country folk will swear that there are two species of common weasels, the smaller one known as a 'grassweasel', 'finger weasel', 'mousehunter' or 'miniver'. Museums have tried to obtain specimens, but without success. The only plausible explanation so far has been that the smaller individuals may be late-born young that were overtaken by the winter before they were full grown, but there is no proof that growth in weasels depends upon season rather than food supply. But perhaps this is just an example of the confusion created by imprecise use of names. One experienced head keeper, when asked: 'When you use the word "weasel", do you apply that term in the generic sense, including both the larger Stoat and the smaller Weasel?', replied 'Yes . . .the smaller animal goes under the name of *mousehunter*' (Harting, 1894). So far as is known *nivalis vulgaris* is the only common weasel in Britain.

Figure 2.5. Among the large collection of skins of European nivalis *in the British Museum of Natural History, some have the irregular belly pattern and brown winter coat typical of the common weasel (*nivalis vulgaris*), and some have the straight belly pattern and white winter coat typical of the least weasel (*nivalis nivalis*). This map shows the approximate distribution of the two types (King, unpublished).*

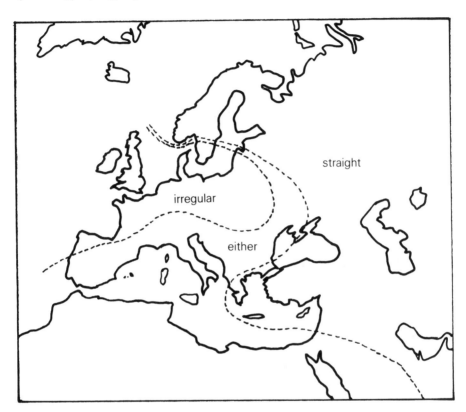

THE EVOLUTIONARY ORIGINS OF WEASELS

The weasels are among nature's more recent inventions. The stoat is probably nearest to the ancestral type, but the earliest fossil stoats, not the modern species but an earlier one classified as *Mustela plioerminea*, appeared in Eurasia only in the late Pliocene, about 4 million years ago (Kurtén, 1968). During the long transition between the end of the Pliocene era and the beginning of the Pleistocene, through the first of the four great glacial epochs conventionally recognised and into the first (Cromerian) interglacial starting about 0.7 million years ago, an intermediate form called *M. palerminea* was very common. Definite specimens of the modern species, *Mustela erminea*, date only from before or during the third major glaciation, which started about 0.5 million years ago. Stoats have been living in Britain, at least intermittently, since the last glaciation or before; remains dating from 33,500 years BP have been found at Castlepook Cave in Ireland (Stuart, 1982).

During glacial periods when sea levels were low, stoats were able to cross the Bering land bridge from north-east Russia into Alaska, and so they colonised North America roughly half a million years ago. At Conard Fissure, in Arkansas, there are fossils of both stoats and longtails of glacial age. In the succeeding interglacial period, stoats would have moved north with the returning vegetation, and now none may be found closer than 600 km from Conard Fissure.

The earliest form of the common weasel was probably *Mustela praenivalis*, which appeared in Eurasia shortly after *M. plioerminea*, and survived for nearly two million years alongside *M. palerminea*, until the Cromerian Interglacial. Then it was replaced by the modern form of *M. nivalis* from the time of the second major glaciation (about 0.6 million years ago) onwards. The modern form is found among a forest fauna of that age at West Runton, Norfolk, and is common in European cave deposits dating from the last glaciation. In the late Pleistocene, during the last glaciation (perhaps only 200,000 years ago), *nivalis* crossed the Bering Bridge too, and followed *erminea* into North America.

M. frenata appeared quite abruptly in North America more than two million years ago, that is, even before the first glaciation. It has therefore survived in its present form much longer than either of the other two modern species. Its ancestor is unknown: the only suggested candidate so far is *M. rexroadensis*, a medium-sized weasel, known only from two fossil sites containing mammal faunas dating from around three million years ago (Kurtén and Anderson, 1980).

The interesting implication of these family histories is that, although the stoat and the longtail look and behave alike, they cannot be closely related: the one evolved in Eurasia, and the other in North America.

Both the relatively recent origin and the small size of weasels generally are due to their evolutionary profession, or 'niche', as specialised hunters of small mammals, especially rodents. In the Miocene period, beginning about 26 million years ago, the ancestors of the weasels were forest-dwelling hunters, probably somewhat like martens. Several marten-like carnivores are known to have lived in the Miocene, and by the early Pliocene there were at least three separate lines of true *Martes* already well established, as well as some other forms intermediate between *Martes* and *Mustela*. Throughout the Pliocene, extensive open savannahs began to develop, as the climate cooled towards the approaching glacial periods, and the grasses evolved and progressively replaced the forests. The grasslands were soon populated by the early kinds of field voles and mice, and then by the ancestors of the weasels. I have suggested (1983b; 1984b) that these early weasels descended from the larger, marten-like mustelids already existing, which became small so that they could exploit the new niche for predators able to get into the burrows and runways of voles, mice and lemmings. Later, during the cold phases of the Pleistocene, the weasels found themselves already adapted to live under snow, finding there both food and shelter from the killing cold above (Figure 2.6, Plate 2). They were already the right shape to burrow through soft powder snow on the surface, dive through the deeper layers and follow the tunnels made by rodents on the ground underneath, just as they do today (Formosov, 1946). Most of the huge ranges of the stoat and least weasel, and the northern edge of that of the longtail, still lie within climatic zones having a severe winter with prolonged snow cover (Figure 2.3). Weasels live all the year round at altitudes of 2000–3000 m or more in the snows of the high mountain ranges of, for example, the Sierra Nevada of California, and the Caucasus, Altai and Tien Shan of Asia.

Figure 2.6. Weasels are quite at home in snow.

To me, the origin of the northern weasels as Pleistocene rodent specialists is the key to understanding everything about them. All the details of their ecology and behaviour can be explained by the idea that they have evolved to exploit a particular kind of high-risk, high-reward resource — the boom-or-bust, unstable populations of small rodents — in a simple and savagely inhospitable environment. They are outstandingly successful in this profession, and their natural distributions are among the largest of any mammals in the world. Not only that, but they have also spread south to milder climates. There, the greatest problems are likely to arise, not from fierce cold and unpredictable food supplies, but from the more constant dangers of competition and predation from other species. Nevertheless, their primary home is the far north, and that is where they display their marvellous adaptations to best advantage.

For these reasons and others, the weasels as a group are among nature's most interesting example of the co-evolution between predators and prey. They are much less conspicuous than the better-known big cats and wolves, and their predatory exploits are conducted on a less dramatic scale; but in their own way they are equally spectacular. They are also vastly more common and easier to handle than bigger carnivores, and so are much more available and amenable as subjects for teaching and research.

THE GENERAL ANATOMY OF WEASELS

In general body plans the weasels are pretty much like the standard mammal type. They have the same stock pattern, the five-toed limbs and usual arrangement of internal organs, that many other small mammals have. Their specialisations are mainly in the elongation and extraordinary flexibility of the spine, and in the strength and shape of the skull and teeth.

The Skeleton

Everything about a weasel is attuned to the profession of hunting for small prey in dark, confined spaces. In motion, weasels appear almost boneless; I have seen one leap into a hole and then look out again in a single fluid action so fast that the tail was not in before the nose came out again. It could do this because its vertebrae are articulated in such a way that it can turn round in a tight corner by rolling over and then walking back over its own hindquarters. Living and working in tunnels are normal and natural activities; the short legs (only half the length of the body) swing through their normal arc in a space only about twice the depth of the animal's head (Figure 2.7). (In the 'average-shaped' carnivore the legs and the body are about the same length, and in a confined space the legs are cramped, folded, and hampered in movement). The neck is so long that prey can be carried in the mouth without tripping the front feet. No part of the skeleton of a weasel is wider than the skull, so that anywhere the head can go, the rest of the body can follow. The head can certainly get into some small places, but the old story that a common weasel can pass through a hole the size of a wedding ring is probably an exaggeration; a skull can do it, but the live animal cannot. The limb girdles at the shoulders and hips do not have to bear any great weight, so they are small; they fit in with the sinuous lines of the spine, and allow great freedom of movement to the limbs.

By contrast, the skull is relatively rather heavy, as it has to anchor the powerful neck and jaw muscles. To hold up this extra weight, the vertebrae of the neck are strong and provide plenty of anchorage for the large muscles of the neck (Figure 2.8A). The joint between the skull and the first vertebra (the atlas) is relatively wide, and they move together across smoothly curved surfaces. On each side of the atlas there are large flat wings, which receive muscles from the skull and move the head up and down. The second vertebra in the neck, the axis, is a completely different shape, compressed sideways instead of flat, and it receives a different set of muscles from the skull which allow the head to move from side to side. The rest of the vertebrae are much smaller than these two, and usually number five more in the neck (total seven cervical vertebrae), 14–15 in the chest (the thoracics), 5–6 in the abdomen (the lumbars), 2–4 in the hips (sacrals) and 11–16 in the tail (caudals). In least and common weasels, the tail is short, partly because its normal function, that of maintaining balance in jumping and turning (as in tree-dwelling animals) is not needed in burrows, and partly because it

Figure 2.7. *The short legs and long neck of a weasel enable it to move normally and carry prey in confined spaces.*

could be a source of serious loss of heat, especially in very cold climates. The longtail has 19–33 caudal vertebrae and certainly lives up to its name, and the stoat's tail is intermediate (Table 2.1).

The Skull and Teeth

The skull is strongly built, long and narrow with sturdy bony crests along the top and at the back to anchor the large temporal muscles that are responsible for the weasel's powerful bite. The zygomatic arches (cheekbones) are widely separated so as to leave room for those muscles to pass through to the coronoid process at the back of the jawbone (Figure 2.8B). The jaws are short and the teeth specialised for a diet of flesh to a degree second only to that of the cats. The most important teeth are the four carnassials — the two first lower molars and the two fourth upper premolars. They are strategically placed at the back of the jaw so as to take the utmost advantage of the leverage of the jawbone and the strength of the huge temporal muscles. This arrangement is why weasels, like dogs, chew bones at the corner of the mouth (Figure 2.9).

Figure 2.8A. *The skeleton of a weasel.*

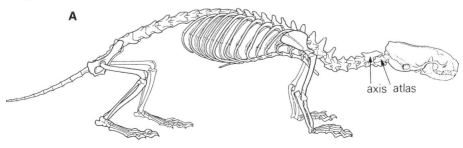

A

axis atlas

19

Figure 2.8B. The skull of a weasel.

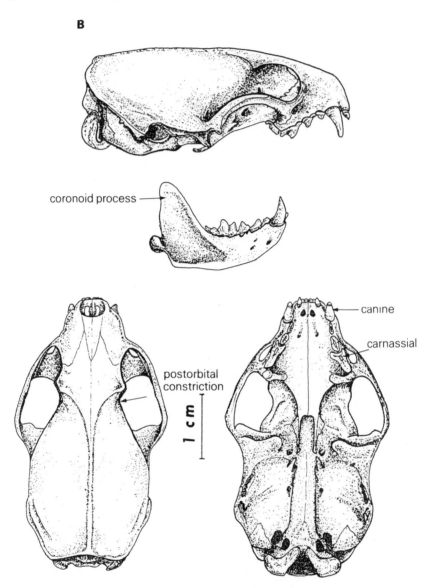

The upper and lower carnassials on each side are parallel and slightly offset, and they shear closely past each other. In the upper jaw the first molar is set a little behind and crosswise, with a deep recess in its centre; the rearmost blade of the lower carnassial slots exactly into it to form a crushing guillotine of devastating effectiveness. The joint between the lower jaw and the skull is a narrow hinge, so that the only movement possible is up and down: sideways movement would make the carnassials less effective, like scissors held together with a loose screw. The carnassial teeth are used for slicing flesh and bones off a carcass into swallowable lumps. Weasels do not grind up their food finely, partly

Figure 2.9. Because the carnassial teeth are at the back of the jaw, bones are always chewed at the corner of the mouth.

because meat is digestible in chunks without grinding, and partly perhaps to save time.

The next most highly specialised teeth are the long, slim canines, whose function is not to slice food but to catch it. The canines act together as a trap and humane killer, grabbing hold of a fleeing mouse and dispatching it with a piercing bite through the bones of the neck and skull. The crunch can quite clearly be heard several feet away.

The rest of the teeth of a weasel have little to do, and most of them are small or have been permanently lost. The incisors are jammed into such a short space at the narrow front of the mouth that, in the lower jaw, two of the six have been squeezed out into a second row behind. Between the incisors and canines in the upper jaw is a large gap on each side, which, when the mouth is closed, is filled by the canines of the lower jaw. The first premolars are absent in both jaws, and so are the second molars in the upper jaw.

This reduction in the number and size of the non-essential teeth has permitted the front part of the face to become shorter, forming the characteristic wedge-shaped head. The dental formula is:

$$\frac{\text{I3 C1 P3 M1}}{\text{I3 C1 P3 M2}} = 34.$$

This means that weasels have three incisors, one canine, three premolars and one molar on each side of the upper jaw, and the same in the lower jaw except for an extra molar on each side. Most of the work is done by only ten of the 34 teeth. With this equipment a weasel can kill a mouse or bird in seconds. The big cats of Africa are usually regarded as the ultimate in predatory power; but in relation to their size, the weasels are equally formidable and efficient predators.

The Senses

In order to find and catch its prey, a predator is absolutely dependent upon its acute senses. Prey must often be located from a distance, and the actual attack requires accurate orientation and judgement of distance. Weasels, especially the smaller ones, hunt often in burrows or dense cover, or in the dark, humid silence under the snow, so it is likely that hearing and smell are important in finding prey; but they also have the sharp eyes, with binocular vision, needed to make a clean kill.

Ears The ears of weasels are well adapted for the profession of hunting rodents in confined spaces. The outer ear is flat to the head, since a direction-finding flap or pinna, like that of a horse, would collect soil and get in the way underground. Instead, as in many burrowing animals, the sensitivity of the ear is magnified by the greatly enlarged tympanic cavity, or bulla, of the middle ear, which is braced inside with bony struts or trabeculae. One would expect all weasels to be very sensitive to the high-pitched squeaks of mice, which range up through the ultrasonic to 92 KHz. In fact, the range of hearing in the least weasel runs from <1 to at least 61 KHz, best at 1–16 KHz. Its sensitivity to low threshold sounds is one of the best known among mammals (Heffner and Heffner, 1985).

Eyes The short, pointed face of a weasel allows both binocular vision forward and a wide arc of monocular vision on each side. Weasels as predators need to be able to judge distances using both eyes together, but they are also often themselves prey of other predators, and need to keep a sharp lookout all round.

Many animals are active either by day or by night, but weasels are not confined to a schedule: they hunt at any time, presumably whenever they are hungry. The eye of the weasel, like that of the cat, is constructed so that it can see well in both bright and dim light. Since the requirements for good vision by day and by night are not the same, the eye of an animal active at any time has to be something of a compromise.

In the retina, there are two kinds of receptor cells, called (from their appearance in histological sections) cones and rods. The cones are used for perception of bright light and colours, and are found only in diurnal species. The rods are particularly sensitive to low-intensity light, and are most numerous in the eyes of nocturnal animals. The balance of rods and cones gives a fair idea of how sensitive and acute the eye is, and whether or not it can see in colour. For example, the eyes of both the common weasel and the stoat have the mixed retinas of diurnal animals, and this suggests the possibility of some degree of colour vision. Unfortunately, although Herter (1939) and Gewalt (1959) set out to test the colour discrimination abilities of common weasels, neither got past the preliminary training before their animals died. But the structure of the retina in common weasels is histologically very similar to that in the stoat, which has been shown by behavioural tests to be able to see at least red, and perhaps also yellow, green and blue. On the other hand, the presence of cones need only show that the eye is adapted for use in bright light. Since all weasels and most of their prey are shades of brown, white or grey, and important markings on them are usually black or white, weasels may not need colour perception for identification of food, potential rivals or mates; even if they can see it, colour may not mean much to a weasel anyway.

In most carnivores, the sensitivity of the eye in dim light is increased by the tapetum lucidum, a reflective layer behind the retina. The eyes of animals which have a tapetum, such as the cat, have very obvious 'eyeshine' when caught in a flashlight, compared with the dull red glow of human eyes. Weasels have a vivid green eyeshine, a fact well known to naturalists: Wood (1946) wrote that 'their eyes are fearsome things, glowing with a strange green fire'.

Animals which have very sensitive eyes for night hunting also have to be able to protect them well if they are about during the day. The brown iris of the eye, which automatically closes in bright light, protects the retina from damage: the more sensitive the retina, the more protection it needs. A slit pupil can close more tightly than a round pupil, so that even very sensitive eyes are not blinded in sunshine. Weasels have slit pupils, but the slit is horizontal, not vertical as in the cat.

Eyes which are good at seeing in dim light often achieve this ability at the expense of sharp acuity in bright light. As every photographer knows, prints of pictures taken on film of 400 ASA should not be too greatly enlarged. Most carnivores see movements rather than pictures, but that does not mean they cannot be sharp-eyed when it suits them. A long series of patient form-discrimination tests with one common weasel in Germany showed that this individual at least was able to distinguish quite minor variations in shapes presented as cues for food-rewards (Herter, 1939). In fact, this animal eventually learnt to distinguish seven letters, offered in various combinations. The letters were attached to a pair of boxes, in one of which was the reward (a mealworm). By the end of the series, it could 'read' the label on the box containing the reward, which was *WURM* (worm), and consistently prefer this box to the other one, which was labelled *LEER* (empty). The location of a reward, and detours to it, are easy learning tasks for any weasel; and their memory for pathways and places is excellent.

Voice

All the weasels are capable of making a range of sounds, which no doubt mean much more to other weasels than to us; but some of the messages they convey are quite unmistakeable even to our ears (Huff and Price, 1968; Svendsen, 1976). A weasel that feels slightly uneasy will make a low hissing sound, often whilst retreating into a safe place, which indicates low-intensity fear or threat. If the danger is more pressing, the weasel will probably turn and stand its ground, making a series of sharp, explosive barks or chirps, loud enough and aggressive enough to deter all but the most steely-nerved attacker. Taken unawares, nine out of ten people will jump out of their skins at the sudden noise. If the danger is really acute and all retreat cut off, such as when a weasel is cornered or trapped, the chirp escalates into a prolonged defensive squeal, a really pitiful wail often accompanied by a 'stink-bomb' (see Chapter 8). At the other end of the scale is a low-intensity trilling sound, often heard during friendly encounters between mates, or when a mother is calling to her young. Occasionally it may be heard from exceptionally tame hand-reared weasels playing with a trusted human companion. This trill is the only friendly sound in the weasel's vocabulary.

Figure 2.10. The advantages (circled) and disadvantages (boxed) of small size to the weasels as a group (from King, 1989).

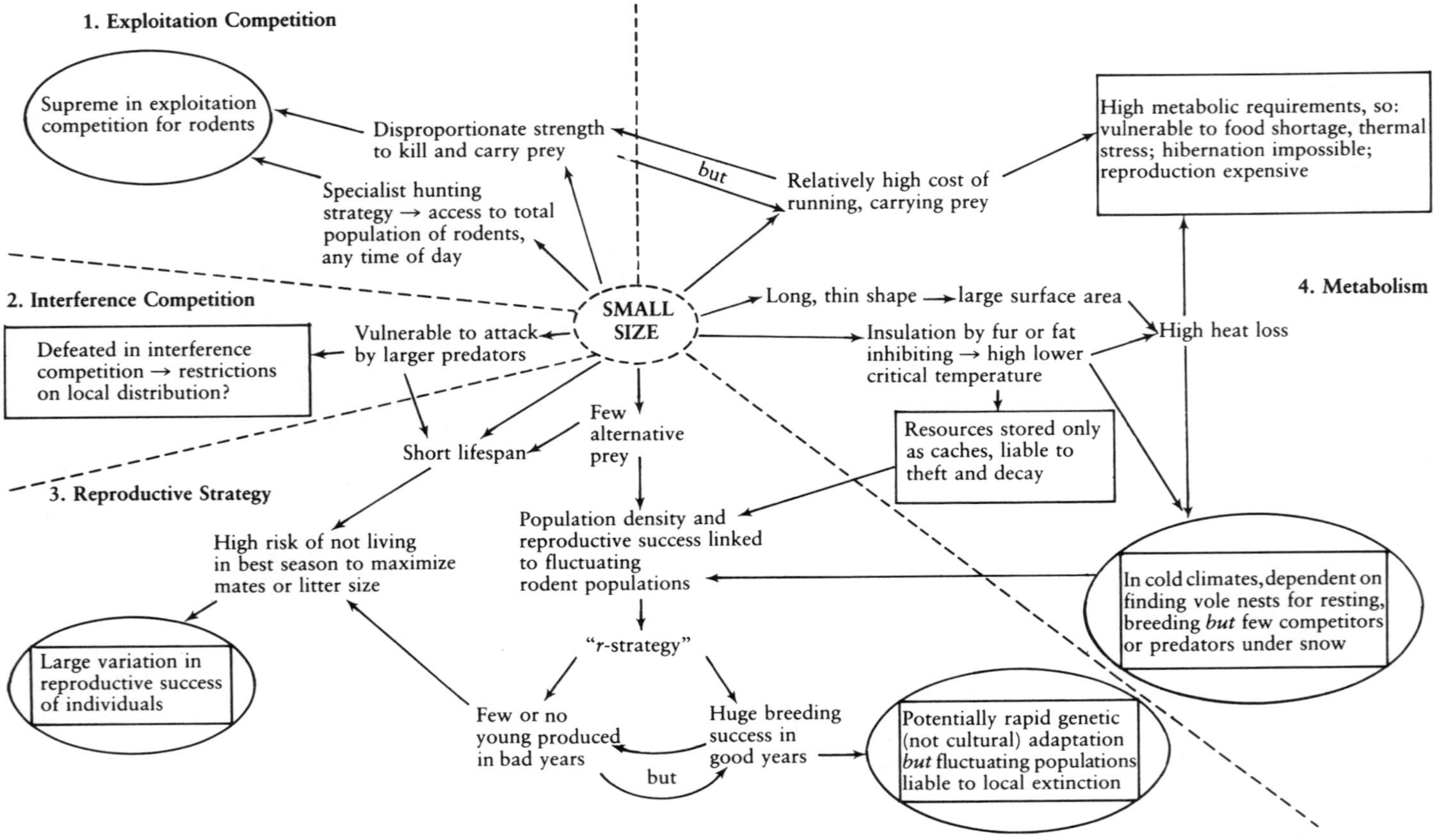

1. Exploitation Competition

Supreme in exploitation competition for rodents

Disproportionate strength to kill and carry prey

Specialist hunting strategy → access to total population of rodents, any time of day

SMALL SIZE

but Relatively high cost of running, carrying prey

High metabolic requirements, so: vulnerable to food shortage, thermal stress; hibernation impossible; reproduction expensive

4. Metabolism

Long, thin shape → large surface area → High heat loss

Insulation by fur or fat inhibiting → high lower critical temperature

Resources stored only as caches, liable to theft and decay

In cold climates, dependent on finding vole nests for resting, breeding *but* few competitors or predators under snow

2. Interference Competition

Vulnerable to attack by larger predators

Defeated in interference competition → restrictions on local distribution?

Short lifespan

Few alternative prey

Population density and reproductive success linked to fluctuating rodent populations

"*r*-strategy"

Huge breeding success in good years

Few or no young produced in bad years

but

Potentially rapid genetic (not cultural) adaptation *but* fluctuating populations liable to local extinction

3. Reproductive Strategy

High risk of not living in best season to maximize mates or litter size

Large variation in reproductive success of individuals

THE CONSEQUENCES OF BEING WEASEL-SHAPED

The small size and thin shape of the weasels, so essential to the profession of burrow-hunting rodent predator and so advantageous in competition with other predators, have both advantages and disadvantages (Figure 2.10). The size and shape of a weasel's body affect the whole of the rest of its life, and exploring these relationships is one of the recurring themes of this book.

Some of the consequences of being weasel-shaped enter the discussion in later chapters. For example, the short legs, large home ranges and tight energy budgets of weasels make regular direct communication between neighbouring residents — friendly or unfriendly — too difficult; hence, they have developed an advanced scent communication system (see Chapter 8). Small size makes weasels almost as vulnerable to larger predators — especially raptors — as voles and lemmings are; the white winter coat of all species, and the black tail tip of the two larger, can be seen as defences against the hunter being hunted (see Chapter 11). Small size, short lifespan and the capacity to make a large reproductive effort early in life tend to go together, especially in species which stand to gain a huge advantage from a rapid response to a sudden increase in food supplies (see Chapters 9–12). The consequences of the weasel body plan relevant here concern metabolism and physical strength.

Metabolism: the Cost of being Long and Thin

The lists of advantages and disadvantages illustrated in Figure 2.10 more or less cancel each other out except with respect to metabolism. The advantage in hunting efficiency is countered by the risk of attack from larger predators, and the advantage of being able to increase production rapidly in good years is countered by the risk of starvation in bad years. But the metabolic penalties incurred by a small animal in a cold climate are all serious, and the advantage of being able to shelter under the snow does not entirely compensate for them. The size and shape of a weasel is hugely inefficient in physiological terms, and this imposes a real addition to the cost of living the weasel way of life.

Vulnerability to Cold   One of the principal problems of life for any animal is in keeping a balance, every day, between the energy gained from food and the energy spent in getting it. Small mammals have to spend relatively more energy in maintaining a constant body temperature than large ones, because they have a large surface area, relative to their mass, from which heat may radiate. For weasels, this problem is even greater than for other small mammals. Their long, thin shape is ideal for hunting through small spaces and burrows, but it has the huge disadvantage of giving them a larger surface area than 'normally' shaped animals of the same weight (Brown and Lasiewski, 1972), even when they are asleep (Plate 6).

The result is that weasels feel the cold badly. Their body temperature is 39–40°C (102–104°F), and their body heat escapes easily, not only because of their shape, but also because they cannot afford to insulate themselves too much. Layers of fur or fat would get in the way and

25

perhaps prevent them from entering vole runways and burrows. Their winter fur is hardly warmer than their summer fur, and any fat is confined to dips in the body outline. Few weasels get the chance to accumulate much fat anyway, but even those that do retain their sleek figures. The cold northern winters that weasels endure over much of their range are therefore periods of great energetic stress: just the simple maintenance of body heat at rest requires twice as much energy as in summer, at three times the cost incurred by a lemming of similar size resting at the same temperature (Casey and Casey, 1979). Arctic and alpine weasels at rest absolutely depend upon having a thickly insulated nest, which they take over from recent prey and improve by lining with fur (Plate 11). The thickness of the lining indicates how long the weasel has been in residence.

However safe and attractive a warm nest may be, a weasel cannot stay in it indefinitely. Hunger will eventually drive it out into the cold again, and that means using up yet more energy for running. Curiously, researchers who have studied the energy metabolism of weasels disagree as to whether weasels are restricted in their movements by subzero temperatures. In Alaska, Casey and Casey (1979) estimated that arctic weasels outside their nests may have to generate up to six times the basic metabolic rate just to keep warm, and they may have little capacity left in reserve to provide energy for active hunting. If so, weasels should stay under the snow when the air temperature drops too far; and Kraft's (1966) tracking studies in Western Siberia confirmed that stoats did not emerge onto the snow surface after the air temperature got below −13°C. On the other hand, Sandell (1985) in Sweden concluded that weasels do not need to generate more than three times basic metabolic rate in any conditions, and that, since 75 per cent of the energy expended during activity is released as heat, a running animal does not need to spend any extra on keeping warm whatever the temperature. If the second interpretation is correct, an active weasel is virtually independent of air temperature, and is safe even in severely freezing conditions so long as it keeps moving. It is not clear whether the difference between these two interpretations is real or merely technical (the authors used different methods and materials), but the general conclusion stands: weasels balance their energy budgets with little to spare, and in the far north they probably survive at the limit of their metabolic capacity.

Huge Appetites   To supply the massive amounts of energy they need, weasels have large appetites. Captive animals eat between a quarter and a third of their body weight each day, and more active wild ones probably more (Table 2.2). They are tied to a life of frequent meals, 5–10 a day, and to the necessity of finding food at frequent intervals (Gillingham, 1984). They cannot endure going without food for long, which is one of the difficulties of live-trapping them. Nearly all this enormous intake of food is burnt up merely to keep warm.

Rapid Metabolism   The alert, rapid movements of weasels well reflect their constant hunger, geared-up metabolism and galloping pulse — measured at rest at about 360–390 beats per minute in stoats, 400–500 beats per minute in common weasels (Tumanov and Levin, 1974; Segal, 1975). If you put your ear to the chest of an anaesthetised weasel, you

Table 2.2 Food consumption by captive weasels

Species	MALES			NON-BREEDING FEMALES			REFERENCE
	Wt food/day	Body wt weasel	% body wt eaten/day	Wt food/day	Body wt weasel	% body wt eaten/day	
erminea	57	—	23	33	—	14	Day 1963
	—	—	19–32	—	—	23–27	Müller 1970
nivalis vulgaris	41	133	33	28	81	36	Moors 1977
nivalis nivalis	32	81	40	—	—	—	Gillingham, 1984
frenata	—	—	c. 33	—	—	—	Hamilton 1933

cannot count the heartbeats. This frantic pace of life is also reflected in the anatomy of organs that have to do with metabolic processes. The load on the heart and lungs is great, so the heart is large relative to the weight of the body, especially in the smaller species. A weasel's food comes in large, infrequent packages, so the digestive system is adapted to deal with alternate feast and famine. The gut is short and meals pass through quickly. Dyed bait fed to a least weasel reappears in 2–4 hours, and the defecation rate is high, averaging 19 scats per 24 hours (Short, 1961). Weasels often nap after a meal, but not for long.

Strength and Loading

Hunters small and thin enough to enter rodent burrows must still not be too small to execute a kill, so weasels make up extra size in length rather than in girth. They use it by wrapping their long bodies around a catch, which helps to hold it down (Figure 6.5). But they do not have to sacrifice muscular strength for size. On the contrary, weasels appear to be relatively stronger than larger carnivores; no lion can run at speed carrying a carcase of even half its own weight. A stoat can easily kill a rabbit of twice or more its own weight, and then carry it away, looking like a terrier bounding off with a sheep.

The difference is a simple result of scaling. The apparently disproportionate strength of a weasel is one of the mechanical advantages of being small, arising from the curious fact that the force that can be exerted by an individual muscle is the same, per unit of cross-sectional area, in mammals of any size (Schmidt-Nielsen, 1984). With decreasing size, the mass of an animal decreases in proportion to the third power of its length, whereas the cross-sectional area of its muscles, which determines the force they can exert, decreases only as the square of their length. Hence the force exerted by the muscles, relative to mass, increases in proportion to the decrease in body size.

The economics of hunting have some peculiar costs and benefits for a small predator (King, 1989). For example, the energy cost of running is relatively high in short-legged animals, because they have to take many small steps or jumps to move one unit of body mass over one unit of distance, each step requiring work in proportion to mass. Weasels never merely walk anywhere: they either glide along with a straight-backed scuttle or bound at speed with a hump-backed gallop — either method takes a lot of energy. Bounding is especially energetic, because the supple back is used as an extension of the legs, so the whole body is involved in every step. On the other hand, when a weasel climbs a tree or a steep slope, the additional energy required to work against gravity is negligible. Running is always an expensive activity to a weasel, but it makes hardly any difference whether it is going along the ground, straight up or straight down. Small predators also have the problem of carrying prey that may be as big as themselves or bigger. The energy cost of carrying a load increases in direct proportion to its weight. If the load is 100 per cent of the weasel's own mass, its oxygen consumption (a measure of energy expended) increases by 100 per cent. Weasels routinely carry prey that heavy. Even the smallest of them have the strength, but the cost is high.

3 Moult and winter whitening

All weasels moult twice a year, in spring and autumn. In mild climates the incoming fur is always about the same colour as the old, so it is usually impossible to tell from the outside, on cased musum skins or on living animals, whether a particular individual is moulting or not. But in the autumn in cold climates, the incoming fur is white, and then the patterns and timing of the moult process become easily observed. For example, van Soest and van Bree (1969) took 300 skins of stoats from the collections of the Amsterdam Museum, ranging from full brown through all the intermediate pied stages to full white, and arranged them in order on a table. They showed that the autumn moult starts on the belly, and the new white hair with its thicker underfur appears there first. Then new fur grows on the flanks and back, and finally on the head. In spring the pattern is reversed; the old white coat is replaced first on the head, then across the body, and finally underneath. The very same pattern can be seen in northern longtails (Glover, 1942). It means that the belly is the last part of the body to lose its extra insulation in spring, and the first to acquire it in autumn, which seems a practical arrangement for a shortlegged animal living in a cool climate.

The process of winter whitening in the stoat is really a compound of two other processes, which quite independently control the growth of the new hair, and the colour it shall be. Growth of new hair is stimulated when the lengthening days of spring, or the shortening days of autumn, reach a certain critical number of hours of daylight, which acts like a trigger. But winter whitening is controlled by temperature and heredity. It is better to think about moult and winter whitening separately if possible — although of course they are not entirely separate. Cold temperatures also affect a third process, the shedding of the old hair, the final stage in the replacement of the old coat. So in the Arctic, where the shortening days of autumn always herald the rapid onset of a severe winter, the old coats are replaced quickly, within a few days. In mild climates, the shortening days of autumn set off the moult process just as predictably, but it is slower, spread over a month or six weeks. In spring, cold temperatures delay the shedding of the old fur, so that in changeable temperate climates, stoats do not lose their winter coats too early if the spring is particularly cold or late. So there is quite a lot of variation possible in the moulting patterns shown by individual animals in different places and years.

THE MOULT CYCLE

The Skin Follicles

Each of the two moults in a year involves a series of changes in the shape and activity of the hair follicles in the skin (Figure 3.1). First, the follicles enlarge and extend themselves deeper into the skin. There they produce the new hair, which grows out alongside the old. If the growing hair is to be brown, the follicles contain a dark pigment, melanin. So in spring, the active growth of new brown hair can be detected from the small dark flecks on the inside of the skin, which represent the enlarged, active melanin-containing follicles. By the time the new hair is fully formed and anchored in the follicle, the melanin is used up, and the follicle retreats back to its smaller resting state, nearer the surface of the skin. The inside of a dried skin now appears a clear, almost translucent honey-colour. The old hair is shed a few days, or even weeks, later.

Figure 3.1. The cycle of activity in the hair follicles of the skin during the moult and regrowth of brown hair. (a) normal condition; (b) preparation stage; (c) growth of follicle and accumulation of melanin; (d) formation of root; (e) shedding of old hair; (f) process complete.

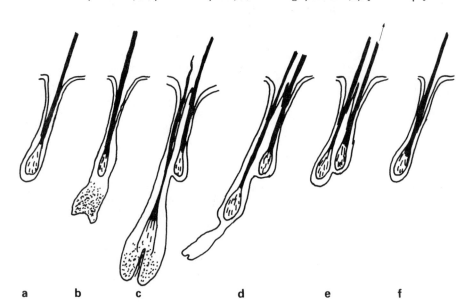

a   b   c   d   e   f

The Timing of the Moult

A complete moult cycle lasts from the beginning of the active phase of the follicles through to the end of the shedding of the old fur. Since these are quite separate processes, even in one follicle, the cycles of growth and shedding can overlap. To work out the length of the whole cycle, it is necessary to observe both sides of the skin. Most studies of moult and colour change in weasels have been done only from the outside, in climates where all or most individuals turn white every year. But these studies really only observe the last stage, shedding, and the vital early stages of preparation by the follicles and most of the phase of growth of new hair are not detected this way. Also, observing moult only by colour change compounds the effects of two quite independent processes, and is not a suitable method to use in places with mild climates, where most weasels do not turn white.

Fortunately, the moult process can be studied quite easily, even in places where both summer and winter coats are brown, from the inside of the skin. On a flat weasel skin, which has been scraped clean of fat and dried in air without preservative, the distribution of the dark active follicles, the small black flecks along the inside of the summer-brown area, show what phase of moult that animal was in when it died. In the belly fur, the follicles do not accumulate pigment because they are growing white hairs, so the onset of the moult there cannot be detected by this method — nor, of course, by the colour-change method, as the underside is white all the year round. But since the active follicles appear on the back and sides just before the new brown hairs grow, and fade as their melanin is used up, it is possible to plot the progress of the moult by following the migration of the active follicles across the summer-brown area and estimating the period at which moult activity might have reached the underparts (Figure 3.2).

I used this method (1979) to show that the pattern of moult in the common weasel in England is the same as in Dutch stoats. The spring moult begins in March on the head, then spreads along the spine and down across the flanks, ending in May or June on the underside. The autumn moult follows the same route in the opposite direction, beginning in about September or October and ending in about November. The spring moult ends, and the autumn moult begins, in the white fur, so the period during which the summer coat is worn is not exactly known. A few animals were still completing their winter coat in December and January: these were all young ones born late in the season, which were probably late in starting.

Later I applied the same technique to a large collection of stoat skins from New Zealand. There the spring moult begins in August and ends in October (although in the cooler parts of the country the old hair might still be hanging on into December); and the autumn moult begins in March and ends in June. Because the skins came from 14 study areas representing a wide range of habitats, altitudes and latitudes, my colleagues and I were able to confirm from wild animals that the moult is controlled by day length rather than temperature. On average, stoats in the far south of New Zealand (44–45°S), which is cooler and reaches a given day length later than the north (39–40°S) in spring and earlier in autumn, were always the last to start moulting in spring and the first to start in autumn. Stoats from high and low altitudes at the same latitude, whose homes differed in temperature but not in day length, moulted at the same time (King and Moody, 1982). In fact, the control over moulting by day length is so powerful that stoats in captivity can be induced to moult into their summer coats in midwinter and vice versa, merely by manipulation of the lighting over their cages. For example, five Wisconsin stoats kept on 18-hour 'days' moulted into their summer coats at a temperature of −6°C (Rust, 1962). They took longer to get started

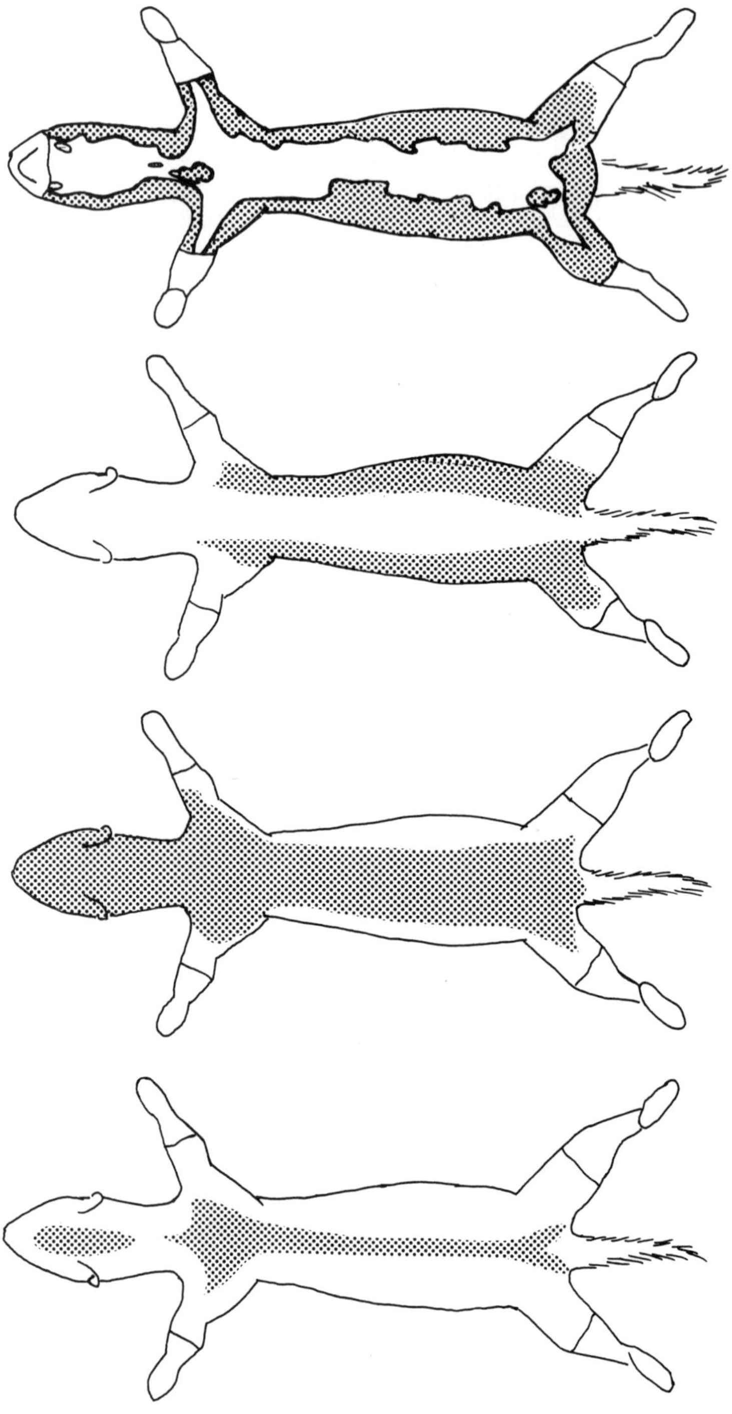

Figure 3.2. Four common weasels killed at successive stages in the spring moult. Active follicles first appear on the back and then migrate down each side to the belly (from King, 1979).

than a control group kept at 21°C, but they could not postpone the change for more than three weeks when their eyes were insisting that spring had arrived.

The difference between day length in summer and in winter increases towards the poles, and so the rate of daily change in day length from one solstice to the other speeds up in the same direction. Therefore, the higher the latitude of a stoat's home, the more rapid the transition from winter to summer coats: also, the longer the part of the year during which the day length is too short to maintain the summer coat, so the longer the winter coat is worn. The lower the latitude, the slower the transition from one coat to the other. This explains why the moult of the stoats of New Zealand is slower and more diffuse than that of the common weasels of England studied by the same method. New Zealand is generally nearer the equator than England: the Antipodes Islands, at 49° 41'S, are 850 km south-east of New Zealand and are classified as subantarctic islands, whereas almost the whole of England lies north of 50°N.

The winter fur is thicker and, even in animals which stay brown all winter, it often appears to be slightly paler in shade. The difference is best appreciated during the spring moult. Among my common weasels were several which showed quite a marked change in colour as the incoming new fur, noticeably darker, contrasted with the old, paler fur. This was obvious only on animals caught at just the right moment, when the new fur had extended along the middle of the spine as a dark dorsal stripe, but before it had widened and spread across the curve of the flanks. On the best specimens, the dark moult patches on the inside of the skin could be seen spreading along in front of the new fur, while the area of new fur itself was clean again. Once I knew what to look for I found this colour change on over a quarter of the 122 skins. The actual colour of the fur is found mainly in the long guard hairs, whereas the underwool is a nondescript grey at all seasons. Winter fur contains more underwool, and this may be the reason for its paler appearance.

Moult and Reproduction

The seasonal cycles of moult and reproduction are closely related, and are co-ordinated by the neuroendocrine system. The nerves receive stimuli from the outside world (Is it day or night? Is it warm or cold?); the brain then instructs the endocrine organs to secrete the appropriate hormones. Hormonal messages travel, via the bloodstream, more slowly than the electrical messages that flash along the nerves, but they reach every cell of every limb, organ and tissue in the body. Cells for which the message is not intended will ignore it; cells sensitive to it will swing into co-ordinated action, even if they are spread from one end of the body to the other — as the skin follicles are.

The pivot of this system is the pituitary, a small gland under the base of the brain (Figure 9.5), constructed so as to maximise the contact between brain and circulation. When the eyes perceive the lengthening of the days after the winter solstice, the brain orders the pituitary to release gonadotropins which stimulate the gonads to prepare for the approaching breeding season. The same message is also received and understood by the hair follicles. So in males in early spring the testes and the hair follicles enlarge together, and the testes begin to manufacture testosterone and sperm, while the hair follicles accumulate melanin and manufacture hair. The connection between the two systems can be demonstrated experimentally by showing that it fails in stoats in which the pituitary has been removed (Rust, 1965). In intact wild stoats we found a significant correlation between the spring rises in testis weight and in readiness to moult (King and Moody, 1982). The autumn moult takes place in the opposite conditions, with shortening days and falling levels of plasma testosterone.

In females the pituitary gonadotropins also have a stimulating effect on both the hair follicles and the ovaries, at least to start with. But when the ovaries begin to manufacture large quantities of the female sex hormone, oestrogen, things suddenly change. Among the common weasels I examined, I found several that had obviously started their spring moult, because they had a dark dorsal stripe, but there were no moult patches on the inside at all. These females were all in breeding condition, and it appeared that, when they came on heat, moulting had stopped. In the ferret, moulting is inhibited when the blood contains high quantities of oestrogen; possibly the same thing happens in common weasels. However, when the heat period subsides, moulting is resumed, and several female common weasels were found to be still moulting late into spring.

Moult and reproduction are both active processes for which the small female must find energy, in addition to the already considerable energy required just for daily living. Van Soest and van Bree (1969) suggested that female stoats complete their spring moult earlier than males, before their embryos implant, because they could not provide the energy for moult and gestation simultaneously. But female common weasels are able to do this, because they resume moulting after they have been fertilised; and if they can do it, there is no obvious reason why stoats could not. If there is any difference between the two species, it is probably less to do with energy conservation than with their different reproductive cycles. Female stoats are on heat in summer, so their spring moult is not interrupted by oestrogen, and there is time for them to finish growing their summer coats before their embryos implant. The winter coat is a different matter, since it is thicker and no doubt more expensive in energy to grow, but by that time both stoats and common weasels are in their winter (anoestrous) period, and no energy need be diverted from the serious business of preparing for the winter.

WINTER WHITENING

The Southern Limit of Winter Whitening

Hall (1951) pointed out that in North America the southern limit of regular whitening in longtails is not a sharp line, with white animals on one side and brown ones on the other, but a broad zone about 350 km wide in which white, brown and pied animals could be found in various combinations. He mapped the position of this zone as running for most of its length along one side or other of the 40th parallel but extending north on the west coast (Figure 3.3). From Figure 2.3D it is possible to work out that this zone corresponds very roughly to the southern limit of regular snow cover at least 2.5 cm thick and lying for at least 40–50 days a year.

Figure 3.3. North of the chequered zone, all longtailed weasels turn white every winter; south of it, all stay brown; in the zone itself, all gradations can be found from white through pied to brown (after Hall, 1951).

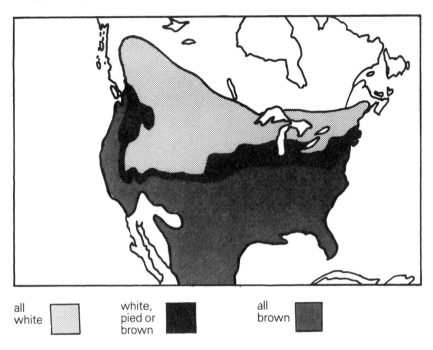

all white | white, pied or brown | all brown

The transition zone for stoats snakes through Britain at between 52° and 56°N, in a reverse S-shaped curve (Figure 3.4): white coats are common in Wales and Scotland, brown is the rule in England. Coastal Holland straddles the transition zone at 51°N. Going eastwards on the Continent, however, the moderating influence of the Gulf Stream is left behind, and the southern limit of whitening probably follows the snowline southeastwards.

The weather conditions required to set off winter whitening are apparently not the same for all species of weasels, or even for the same species in all places. British stoats seem to whiten in relatively mild winters: the hilliest parts of Britain where white stoats may be seen are much less snowy than the country occupied by white longtails in the USA, even though they are 1800 km further north. The same is true of the stoats of British stock introduced into New Zealand. By contrast, Russian stoats behave just like longtails; in Byelorussia (50–55°N), just over the USSR border from Warsaw, the transition zone for stoats again coincides with the southern limit of stable snow cover lasting at least 40 days a year (Gaiduk, 1977).

The southernmost limit of regularly white *nivalis* in western Europe lies at a much higher latitude than for stoats. All-white *nivalis* are a great rarity in Britain, even in the north where stoats regularly achieve full ermine. Salomonsen (1939) calculated, from the geographical distribution of white and brown winter skins from Greenland, Scandinavia and Britain, that the critical minimum temperature associated with whitening in *nivalis* is a full 5°C lower than that for *erminea*. He

Figure 3.4. In Britain, the boundary between white and brown winter fashions for stoats in the winter of 1983–4 was calculated from observations sent in by viewers of the BBC wildlife programme Wildtrack.

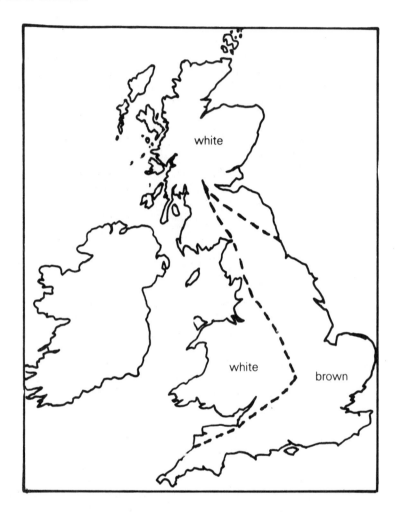

concluded that, even though *nivalis* were much smaller than *erminea*, they were much more resistant to the cold. But from what we know about the metabolic stress endured by small mammals in the Arctic, this seems an unlikely explanation; and besides, there is a better one.

In southern Sweden, *nivalis* stay brown all winter as far as about 59–60°N (the latitude of Lewis and the Orkneys); then there is a narrow boundary zone, about 100 km across, roughly from Norrkoping through Stockholm to Uppsala, beyond which all *nivalis* turn white (Figure 2.5). But this boundary does not, as in *erminea* and *frenata*, mark a transition zone where individuals of one species turn white or not according to the climate. It marks the meeting of the two distinct subspecies of *nivalis* (see Chapter 2), which may well have different histories and genetic make-up, and which are distinctly different in their summer coats as well as in winter. Only the northern one is the true winter-white 'snow-weasel' described and aptly named as *Mustela nivalis* by Linnaeus in 1766; evidently he did not distinguish the southern one, so that was named *Mustela vulgaris* by Erxleben in 1777. The two are now regarded as sibling subspecies of *Mustela nivalis*: the intriguing implication is that *M.n. vulgaris* evolved at a more southerly latitude than *M.n. nivalis*, and so the *vulgaris* group may not be so well endowed with genes for winter-whitening as the *nivalis* group. British common weasels all belong to the *vulgaris* group; hence the fact that they do not turn white in Britain may have more to do with evolutionary history than with climate.

The Mechanism of Winter Whitening

In the autumn in a warm climate, the moult process is the same as in spring. The difference in a cold climate is that the manufacture of melanin is inhibited by cold temperatures. If there is no melanin in the follicles, the hairs grow out white.

The temperature inside the body of the stoat is, of course, constant, but the outside temperature is monitored by the animal's brain, through the nerves to the skin. It seems that there is, as it were, a switch in the brain, which may be in either one of two positions. When warm autumn temperatures put it in one position, it directs the pituitary to produce MSH (melanocyte-stimulating hormone), and the melanocytes (small cellular factories in the skin) make melanin. Cold autumn temperatures turn the switch to the other position, and then an inhibitor is produced, which turns off the supply of MSH and of melanin (Rust and Meyer, 1969).

The lowest critical temperature below which new fur grows only white is different for different parts of the body. Gaiduk (1977) calculated that in Byelorussia, where he worked, the fur of the hindquarters and lower flanks of stoats would grow white if the temperature at the time was 2°C, but it had to be below −1°C before the head and back would turn white. In cold climates the autumn temperatures plunge quickly down to well past −1°C, so all stoats always turn entirely white. But in milder regions the critical temperatures required for whitening may be different, probably higher, and the autumn weather may be more variable, so that the threshold may be exceeded for one part of the body but not for another. The 'switch' may turn off the supply of melanin while the new fur grows on the tail and sides; but by the time the new dorsal fur is growing, it may be 'on' again. The result is that the animal appears to be 'pied', and in places where the weather conditions in autumn are very variable, there may be a mixture of white, brown and pied individuals in different proportions each winter. These animals look as if they were caught in the middle of moulting (Figure 2.2); but they are more often wearing a full-grown winter coat which has, as it were, changed its mind about turning white.

Because there is, in the broad view, a very general relationship between minimum temperature and snow cover, there is also a general connection between whitening in the landscape and in weasels. Locally of course, the connection is less reliable, especially in the transition zones, but minor local discrepancies do not destroy the general statistical connection between whitening and climate. Neither does the fact that, at the individual level, the relationship is also often less than perfect, and in variable climates white stoats can be seen long before any snow has fallen, and later into the spring than the last of the snow.

On the other hand, the winter climate alone does not provide a complete explanation of the control of winter whitening, and the best evidence for why it does not comes from transplant experiments across the transition zone between all-white and all-brown winter fashions. If temperature or some other purely environmental condition were the sole controlling agent, then weasels born on one side of the dividing zone and transferred to the other side should change to white or not according to the custom in their new home; but they do not. In the summers of 1936 and 1937 a male and two female longtailed weasels, captured on the warm, snowfree coast of California, were transported east along the latitude lines to Lake Tahoe, high up in the cold and snowy Sierra Nevada; in the other direction, a female from Lake Tahoe and a male from Salt Lake City, Utah, were moved from snowy environments to the mild Mediterranean climate of Berkeley, California (Hall, 1951). All the animals were kept in outdoor cages with wire mesh sides open to the elements; all were exposed to about the same day length as at home; all moulted at the usual time — but into the 'wrong' winter coat. Those from east of the line turned white even in California where all weasels wear brown in winter; and those from west of the line stayed brown even in the mountains, where all the residents turn white. In 1953 a rather similar experiment was carried out in England, after Rothschild and Lane (1957) caught a young stoat in the Swiss Alps and brought it home. In September the transplanted animal turned pure white, despite the mild autumn and the established custom of locally resident stoats to stay brown. Yet another case is that of the longtail which stayed in its native country, in New York, but in heated quarters; kept at a constant temperature of 18–24°C since June, it still turned snowy white in October-November and back to brown in March–April (Noback, 1935).

These results suggest that heredity, as well as temperature, must somehow be involved in the control of winter whitening. The animals of a local population must be adapted to the expected conditions of their homeland. Where it is always very snowy or always very mild it is easy to predict whether a white coat will be needed or not: only in that 'zone of indecision' is it an advantage to have a temperature switch, enabling the animal to make an adjustment one way or the other. A second argument for some degree of genetic control is the fact that, in all temperate countries where not all individuals turn white automatically, those that do are significantly more often females. This is the observation that gives us the clue to the whole problem.

Hutchinson and Parker (1978) have pointed out that a correlation between sex and tendency to turn white would necessarily follow if the gene controlling winter-whitening is sex-linked — that is, dominant in one sex and recessive in the other. The advantage of this arrangement is that it is an efficient way of maintaining a genetic polymorphism, a constant readiness to meet sudden changes in the characters favoured by natural selection in present conditions. With respect to winter-whitening, those animals which stay brown in a mild winter are best adapted, whereas those that turn white in the occasional exceptionally long snowy winter are the lucky ones. A stable, sex-linked genetic polymorphism ensures that there are always a few individuals with every combination, every winter, so there are always some who will benefit whatever happens.

New Zealand is one of the temperate countries where conditions are variable enough to operate the switch. Most of the country has a mild climate, and fewer stoats were caught in winter than in summer anyway, so the great majority of skins we collected were brown: 81 per cent of 375 adult females and 82 per cent of 562 adult and subadult males showed no white fur at all. A total of 173 stoats showed some white in the summer-brown area of fur, but among these only 36 stoats of both sexes showed more than half the summer-brown fur as white, and only 8 of these were in almost full ermine; and even these still had a few brown hairs remaining around the eyes. All the rest were pied at best, and many had only a few white hairs just in front of the black tail tip.

The few white or pied stoats we did find were caught between June and November, and in them we could demonstrate that the 'switch' is controlled by temperature, rather than day length, by comparing the proportion of white and pied stoats in a sample with the local weather records. The proportion of pied males was significantly correlated both with the mean daily minimum temperature in July (the coldest month) and with the number of days of ground frost per year. (The proportion of white females varied in the same direction as in males, but not significantly; even though relatively more females whiten than males, females are very difficult to catch in winter and samples of them at that time were small.) Further, white and pied stoats were more common at higher altitudes and more southerly latitudes, although even there, the vast majority of stoats stayed entirely or mostly brown.

Britain is much nearer to the North Pole than New Zealand is to the South, so it is not surprising to find that stoats from the cold end of Britain turn white more consistently than those from the cold end of New Zealand. In north-east Scotland at 57°N, over 90 per cent of stoats of both sexes seen by Hewson and Watson (1979) in each January from 1969 to 1974 had changed colour, of which most were in full ermine; in Otago and Fiordland at 44–45°S, fewer than 80 per cent of the females, and just over 40 per cent of the males, collected in July and August from 1972 to 1976 had any white hairs at all, and hardly any of these were in full ermine. But when we look more closely at the weather records for the particular areas from where these animals came, we find that the Scottish animals were not exposed to a much colder or snowier climate than the New Zealand ones; in both study areas, the minimum temperature for the coldest month is usually within 5°C either way from zero, and in both, snow seldom lies more than 10–20 days in any winter. Perhaps the stoats that have lived in north-east Scotland since soon after the ice ages still have some kind of genetic memory of colder periods in the past, a greater proportion of genes for whitening than for not whitening. By contrast, stoats have lived in New Zealand for only a hundred generations, and most are probably descended from English (non-whitening) stock. Those that have spread into the coolest parts of their new homeland might still be in the process of retrieving latent genes for whitening.

In England, most stoats stay brown, even in the north-east. An enquiry conducted by questionnaire in 1931–2 in Yorkshire found that, of 2,930 stoats killed, only 21 were in full ermine (all females) and another 175

(85 females, 90 males) were pied. Ninety per cent of the informants had never seen a fully white stoat, and 40 per cent had never seen a pied one (Flintoff, 1933, 1935).

THE ADVANTAGE OF WINTER WHITENING

Why do weasels turn white at all? The mechanism must be maintained by natural selection — that is, it would disappear if it did not confer an advantage more often than a disadvantage. In the far north the penalty for staying brown in winter must be substantial, since no Arctic weasels ever try it — or those that do never live long enough to be observed. At least three explanations have been suggested.

The first is that white fur is supposed to conserve heat. According to the laws of physics, a black body is a perfect radiator of heat; biologists have therefore assumed that a white body would be a less perfect one. But this idea is mistaken, because the radiation of heat from an animal's body is in the far infra-red regardless of the colour of its coat, so all animals are 'black bodies' with respect to heat loss by radiation. It is the length and thickness of the fur, not its colour, that determines whether or not it conserves heat well.

The second suggestion is that white fur is a camouflage which helps a weasel catch its prey. Predators which lie in wait for their prey to pass by unawares, or which sneak up on them quietly from some distance away, rely on camouflage and appropriately stealthy behaviour to conceal themselves from their intended victim for as long as possible. This might explain the white coat of the polar bear; but weasels, brown or white, do not hunt by stealth and cunning, but by constant, active searching in every possible runway and hiding place. Even if the match of a white weasel's coat against snow were perfect, which it is not, its movements would give it away — a weasel is hardly ever still except when asleep. The trick of melting into the background works only for animals prepared to move very slowly or to sit immobile for long periods, and that is too much to ask of a weasel.

The third suggestion is that white fur is a camouflage which helps a weasel avoid larger predators. All weasels are small enough to be in danger of attack from hawks, owls and foxes (Figure 11.7). Predation by raptors can be a serious hazard for individual weasels, which explains several things about them including the old question of why stoats and longtails have black tips on their tails and common and least weasels do not (see Chapter 11). It seems most likely that the northern weasels try to match their snowy backgrounds, not to catch a meal, but to avoid becoming one.

ROBES OF STATE

Northern members of the weasel family wear fine, lustrous furs which are not only beautiful in themselves, but have also become symbols of luxury and status. The ancient American Indians used ermine skins to trim the ceremonial bonnets and costumes of their chiefs; in medieval Europe, the furs of ermine, marten and sable were reserved for the upper ranks of the nobility, whilst lesser folk had to make do with rabbit and cat. Ermine is traditionally worn by British justices and peers; in 1937, 50,000 ermine skins were sent from Canada to make robes for the coronation of George VI (Haley, 1975).

Ermine skins were once very important in the international fur trade, and still do have some value, though much less than before. In the late 1920s and early 1930s in New York State alone, Hamilton (1933) reckoned that 100,000 ermine skins were traded each year, at an average price conservatively estimated at $US 0.50 each. These figures imply that, during an economic depression, stoats and longtails between them were generating an income of $50,000 a year for the rural community in that state alone. But by the 1970s, the annual harvest of weasel pelts for the whole of the United States and Canada together was considerably less than that (Table 3.1), and those that were collected comprised only a tiny proportion (under 2 per cent) of the millions of carnivore pelts traded in those years.

Table 3.1 Recent figures for weasel skins traded in USA and Canada (from Svendsen, 1982).

SEASON	LONGTAILS		STOATS	
	Number	Total value (US$)	Number	Total value (US$)
1970–71	47,693	28,616	8,949	5,369
1971–72	22,717	11,358	21,159	10,579
1972–73	61,819	30,909	29,907	14,953
1973–74	38,002	19,001	30,316	15,158
1974–75	50,616	25,308	51,474	25,737
1975–76	38,521	34,669	42,895	38,605

The lack of interest in weasel furs nowadays was brought home to me when I visited the huge fur warehouse of what used to be the Hudson's Bay Company in London. Among their stock of thousands upon thousands of pelts, they could find only one small string of old and unsaleable weasel skins to show me. The reason for the decline is probably that the small ermine skins are so fiddly to prepare, and so many are required to make even a collar for an earl's cape. Cheaper kinds of fine white fur can now be obtained from elsewhere. It is certainly not that fur trapping has had any influence on weasel populations (see Chapter 13). Nevertheless, the fur trade did in its time stimulate some important research on the biology of weasels, especially in the USSR and the USA.

The ironical contrast between the villainous reputation of living weasels (pointed out in Chapter 2) and the use of their pelts to adorn the robes of the highest-ranking justices has inspired this piece of anonymous doggerel:

> Me you'll quickly determine,
> My name rhymes with vermin,
> A bloodthirsty, vicious, detestable crook.
> I'm a slippery sneak
> Seven days of the week,

And believe me, I've pulled every trick in the book.
And if that's not enough to damn me to hell,
Twice a year I'm a cowardly turncoat as well.

Strange metamorphosis! Sublime translation!
With snowy death begins my transformation.
The wheel of fate revolves. Behold the crook
Adorn the judge, the dowager, the duke.

4 Body size

The Importance of Being the Right Size

Animals are not the size they are just by chance. One of the most important facts of life for any animal is its own body size. Size governs, among other things, what foods it can reach or catch; what refuges it can get into; what other animals are its enemies or competitors; how successful it will be in obtaining a home range, one or several mates, and in leaving young; and, for mammals and birds, how much it costs in energy to keep warm.

Because size is so important to the lives and family prospects of individuals, it is a powerful agent of evolution. In any generation there will be individuals of various sizes, but the ones which happen to have developed the best size (and other qualities) for the conditions of the time will be the ones that leave the most offspring, which will also presumably be more or less that size. If the conditions change, the best size will be different, and natural selection will quickly favour some other genetic lineage for preferential survival. Evolution is the result of a conversation between the environment and the lives, particularly the reproductive processes, of the animals.

We may therefore expect to find that the average body size of each kind of weasel living in a given place is the one that gives individual breeding adults the best chance of success in producing young in the local conditions. The best size to be in a particular environment need not be the same as in any other environment; hence, there is enormous local variation in size across the huge geographic range occupied by weasels (Table 4.1). Moreover, the best size to be is not the same for both male and female weasels, for reasons explained in Chapter 12. Males are always substantially larger, but not by a constant amount.

Problems of Measuring Size

Study of the geographical variation in body size of animals is a hazardous business, especially when weasels are the subject. The first problem is to decide which measure of body size to use. The two most obvious are head-and-body length and total body weight, but records of these are scarce. However, properly cleaned and dried skulls are small, inoffensive,

43

Table 4.1 Some representative examples of local variation in mean body size of weasels (− species absent in that area: ? data missing). For geographical variation in skull length, see Figures 4.2 to 4.4.

		n. nivalis	M. nivalis n.vulgaris	others	M. erminea e.hibernica	M. frenata
British Isles (Corbet & Harris, 1990; Fairley, 1981)						
HBL[1]	Male	−	202–214	297	252–278	−
	Female	−	173–181	264	208–230	−
BWT[2]	Male	−	106–131	321	233–334[3]	−
	Female	−	55–69	213	123–165	−
Sweden (Stolt, 1979; Erlinge, 1987)						
HBL	Male	166	189	?	−	−
	Female	148	154	?	−	−
BWT	Male	54	73	184–230	−	−
	Female	35	36	98–137	−	−
Egypt (Osborn & Helmy, 1980)						
HBL	Male	−	278	−	−	−
	Female	−	242	−	−	−
BWT	Male	−	?	−	−	−
	Female	−	200	−	−	−
New York State (Hamilton, 1933)						
HBL	Male	−	−	201	−	270
	Female	−	−	181	−	218
BWT	Male	−	−	81	−	225
	Female	−	−	54	−	102
Sierra Nevada (Fitzgerald, 1977)						
BWT	Male	−	−	59	−	256
	Female	−	−	45	−	122
Siberia (Heptner et al, 1967)						
HBL	Male	160	−	260	−	−
	Female	?	−	212	−	−
BWT	Male	53	−	166	−	−
	Female	41	−	?	−	−
New Zealand (King, 1990)						
HBL	Male	−	217	285	−	−
	Female	−	183	256	−	−
BWT	Male	−	127	324	−	−
	Female	−	58	207	−	−

[1] Head and body length, mm. N.B. Sexual dimorphism is more pronounced in weight than in length. Measurement ranges are of local means, not of individuals.
[2] Body weight, g.
[3] N.B. Substantial N–S variation in Irish stoats and Swedish (larger in south) and in British common weasels (larger in north)

and can be stored indefinitely in air, and large numbers of skulls of weasels can be kept in a few drawers: some natural history museums have collections going back for a hundred years. The condylobasal length of the skull (defined in Figure 4.2A) is easily measured from existing material, so is therefore the most readily available measure of size. The simpler phrase 'skull length' used here refers to this, not to any other measure of skull length. Skull length has the slight disadvantage that it gives a less immediately obvious picture of body size than body weight or length, but it is easy to measure accurately, and in the adult is immune to temporary variations in environmental conditions.

A second problem is that, since variation in size of a species as a whole must be studied from adult animals, it is important to reduce the amount of error due to the accidental inclusion of young animals, not yet full-grown. Fortunately, this too can readily be done from the skull. The skulls of all young animals have open sutures between the growing skull bones, whereas in the skulls of older animals these suture lines are closed or even invisible (Figure 4.1). The skulls also change in shape with age; the fully adult form is quite distinct from the juvenile form, especially in the larger species in which the sequence of changes continues through most of the first year of life. The single feature that best expresses these changes is the development of the postorbital constriction. The ratio between interorbital and postorbital widths (the postorbital ratio of King, 1980e) is a reliable method of identifying young animals and, unlike the best alternative method, tooth sectioning, it can be used on museum material which must not be damaged.

A third problem is that of comparing measurements taken by different people at different times and perhaps in different ways. This is less troublesome with skulls of small animals, which can be measured with a micrometer between easily definable points. Even so, the data on variation in body size of North American weasels, all available from a single source (Ralls and Harvey, 1985) are much more reliable than the data from Eurasia, gathered from the scattered literature of the past 50 years.

Yet a fourth problem arises particularly acutely in weasels, in which pronounced sexual dimorphism in body size is very marked and variable both with locality and in time. Males are nearly always better represented in samples of weasels than females, but fortunately, there is a general co-variation in size of the males and females of one species (Ralls and Harvey, 1985). If the objective is only to map the variation on the small scale required to make comparisons across whole continents, it is fair to take the males as representing the species as a whole.

SIZE VARIATION IN THE WEASELS OF THE NORTHERN HEMISPHERE CONTINENTS

Of the two species, *erminea* and *nivalis*, which live together over almost the whole of Eurasia, *erminea* is always the larger. Both are smallest in the far east and north, and become larger towards the west and south (Figures 4.2, 4.3). There are local populations of stoats living at high altitude in the Alps, Caucasus, Altai and Tien Shan Mountains, which are particularly small; otherwise the largest Continental stoats are found at the south-western edge of their range (from Holland across the North European Plain), and the largest *nivalis* are found south of the southern limit for stoats, particularly in Egypt, where they are much larger than are stoats in eastern Siberia. The general patterns are very obvious from skins (Figures 4.5 and 4.6).

45

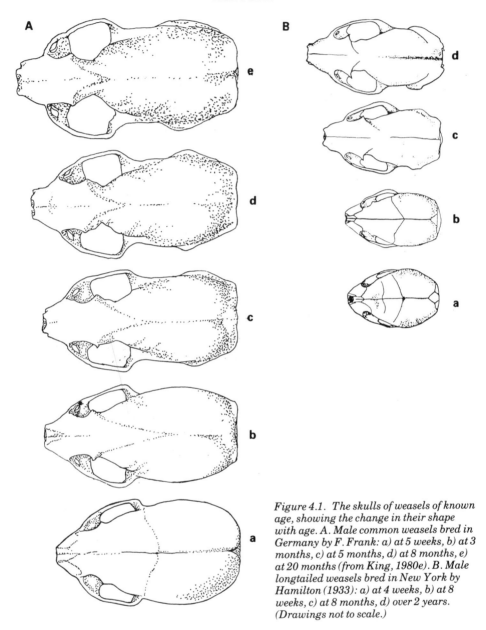

Figure 4.1. The skulls of weasels of known age, showing the change in their shape with age. A. Male common weasels bred in Germany by F. Frank: a) at 5 weeks, b) at 3 months, c) at 5 months, d) at 8 months, e) at 20 months (from King, 1980e). B. Male longtailed weasels bred in New York by Hamilton (1933): a) at 4 weeks, b) at 8 weeks, c) at 8 months, d) over 2 years. (Drawings not to scale.)

All three species, *erminea*, *frenata* and *nivalis*, are found in North America, although only two of them are represented in most places. The most widespread combinations are *nivalis* and *erminea* in the north, and *erminea* and *frenata* in New England and the west. All three are found together in a broad stretch of country from Minnesota across to Pennsylvania (Plate 7). If *frenata* is present, it is always the largest species in the set, and if *nivalis* is, it is always the smallest. In the southern United States and south into Mexico and beyond, *frenata* holds the stage alone.

In North America, stoats become larger in the north-west, where they are about the same size or a little smaller than the north-eastern Eurasian stoats just across the Bering Strait. The smallest American stoats, in the south and especially in the south-west, are considerably smaller than European common weasels (Figure 4.3, Table 4.1). By contrast, least weasels and longtails are no larger or smaller in any particular direction (Figures 4.2, 4.4); one can find longtails of roughly the same size from Canada right down into South America (Figure 4.7). Almost all North American *nivalis* are smaller than even the smallest *nivalis* in the Old World, those inhabiting Siberia; and longtails range in size from much smaller to much larger than Eurasian stoats. In parts of the south-western USA, there are places where there are longtails that are smaller than west European stoats, and stoats that are smaller than west European common weasels. For various practical reasons the size classes plotted on the Eurasian and North American maps in Figures 4.2 to 4.4 are not exactly comparable, but the general trend is unmistakeable.

The patterns of variation in the individual weasel species are confusing and contradictory. There is no obvious reason why the smallest stoats should be found in the north and east of Eurasia but in the south and west of North America. Even more difficult to explain are the smaller-scale trends which contradict the general regional pattern; for example, although *nivalis* in Europe generally tends to become larger southwards, in Britain the largest *nivalis* are in the north (Table 4.1). Stoats vary over a much smaller range of sizes in the Old World than in the New, while *nivalis* varies much more in Europe than in North America.

However, if we view all the weasels as a single group, the continental-scale pattern is the same in both the Old and the New Worlds. Weasels in general are relatively small in the far north, both in Eurasia and in North America. The mean skull length in *erminea*, always the largest species in the north, seldom exceeds 46 mm right around the Pole, and *nivalis nivalis* measures 30–32 mm in Alaska and Canada and 33–35 mm in Russia. The largest weasels are always found in the south: *frenata* in the USA, and *nivalis vulgaris* in Egypt, reach 50–53 mm in skull length or more.

Geographical variation in the body size of animals is common, and many explanations have been offered since the last century. At that time, many zoologists still believed that it should be possible to explain much of the riotous variety of life in terms of simple, formal 'rules', comparable with those of physics and chemistry and based on the same properties of energy and matter that govern inanimate things. For example, warm-blooded animals living in cold climates have to expend a huge proportion of their total energy budget on keeping warm, and the smaller they are the greater the relative expenditure and the greater the danger of irreversible chilling. Some species of mammals living in colder climates have larger bodies than their relatives in the south, and shorter ears and tails. In 1847, Bergmann suggested that the larger size of northern mammals is a matter of energy conservation, since larger mammals have relatively less surface area exposed to the cold air in relation to the mass of the body in which heat is generated. Bergmann's Rule therefore predicts a steady increase in body size northwards in related mammals and birds living in habitats equally exposed to increasingly severe

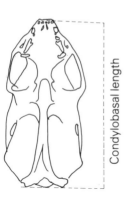

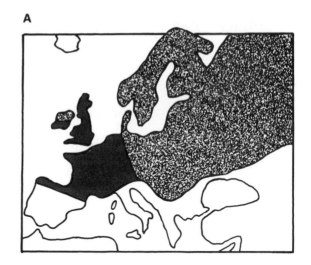

A

B

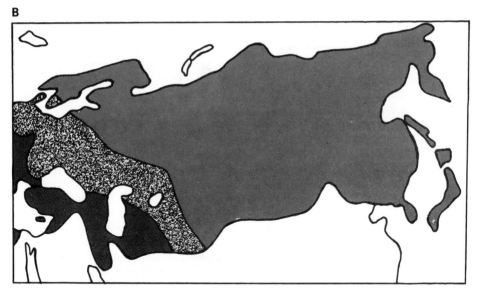

environmental conditions. The same logic underlies Allen's Rule, which explains the relatively shorter ears and tails of northern mammals as a means of reducing the area of vulnerable appendages from which heat may escape.

Weasels generally are particularly sensitive to thermal stress at low temperatures (see Chapter 2). Metabolic inefficiency costs them very dear in the vast, cold northern parts of their ranges, so one might expect them to be prime examples of Bergmann's Rule. However, a simple comparison between skull size and latitude does not confirm this expectation. Only stoats in North America are substantially larger in the north of their range; common weasels in Eurasia are just as substantially larger in the south, and all the rest are more or less indifferent (Table 4.2). Moreover,

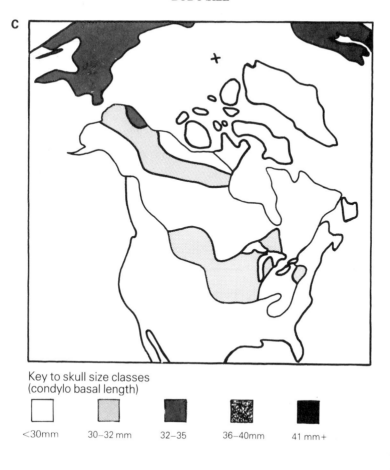

C

Key to skull size classes
(condylo basal length)

<30mm   30–32 mm   32–35   36–40mm   41 mm+

Figure 4.2. Geographical variation in skull size (condylobasal length) of male Mustela
nivalis *in (A) Europe, (B) Asia and (C) North America. The females generally vary in the
same way, although the degree of difference between them is locally variable. Data from
Reichstein (1957), Kratochvil (1977a), Stolt (1979), Morozova-Turova (1965), and Ralls and
Harvey (1985). The distribution of size classes is schematic only, because few data are
available for Eurasia and the precise data for North America have been simplified. Inset:
definition of condylobasal length.*

the American stoats that are larger in the north can be said to be so only
by comparison with their exceptionally small relatives further south in
North America; they are not larger than their relatives at the same
latitudes in Eurasia. Within single regions spanning a range of climates,
Bergmann's Rule does not explain the local variation of stoats in Russia,
Europe or New Zealand (Petrov, 1962; Erlinge, 1987; King and Moody,
1982).

Bergmann was of course assuming that temperature is directly
correlated with latitude. At low altitude this is generally correct, and the
skull lengths of weasels in North America are about as well correlated
with temperature as with latitude. But temperature is also correlated
with altitude. The high mountains that cross Eurasia from east to west at

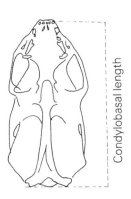

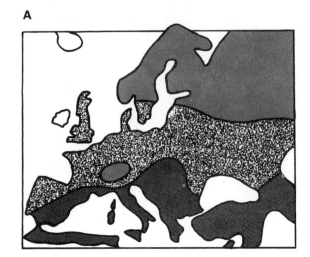

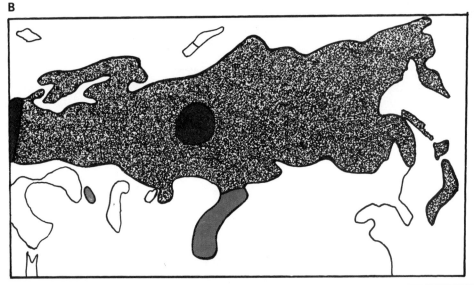

low latitudes (e.g. the Alps, Caucasus and Tien Shan) therefore confuse the simple size-latitude correlation for that part of the world. This problem can be removed by comparing size directly with mean annual temperature; the result (Table 4.2) shows clearly that both sexes of both species of weasels in Eurasia are significantly smaller in colder environments — the very opposite of what Bergman's Rule predicts.

This result is puzzling only until we remember that weasels evolved their long, thin shape in order to be able to hunt small rodents in their own burrows and under snow. This means that, for much of the time that the northern weasels are hunting, they are not exposed to the full rigours of the winter air temperatures as their southern relatives are, so comparing the sizes of northern and southern weasels in terms of Bergmann's Rule is logically invalid anyway. Besides, the relationship

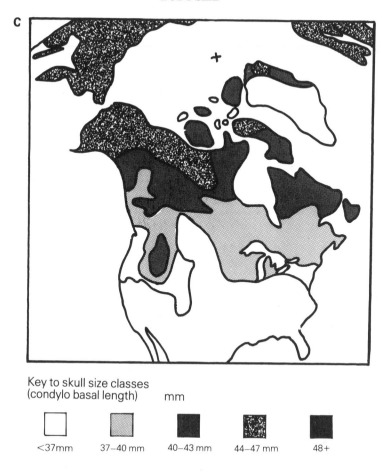

Key to skull size classes
(condylo basal length)   mm

| <37mm | 37–40 mm | 40–43 mm | 44–47 mm | 48+ |

Figure 4.3. Geographical variation in condylobasal length of male Mustela erminea *in (A) Europe, (B) Asia and (C) North America. Data from Reichstein (1957), Heptner et al (1967), Kratochvil (1977b), and Ralls and Harvey (1985). See comments on Figure 4.2.*

between size and temperature cannot be crucial for weasels, since there is often at least as great a difference between the males and females living in one place as there is between the northern and southern members of either sex. We need, then, to find another explanation for the general north-south variation in size of the weasels as a group.

Because the size of a body affects many of its functions, and the best size for one function is not necessarily the best for any of the rest, the actual size of the whole animal is usually a compromise. Sandell (1985) has proposed a model predicting the best possible size that male and female stoats could be, which takes into account the differences in the reproductive roles and in the seasonal energy requirements of each. He started from the assumption that the total amount of energy available to any animal in any one day, expressed as a multiple of the basal metabolic

Figure 4.4. Geographical variation in condylobasal length of male Mustela frenata. *Data simplified from Ralls and Harvey (1985). See comments on Figure 4.2.*

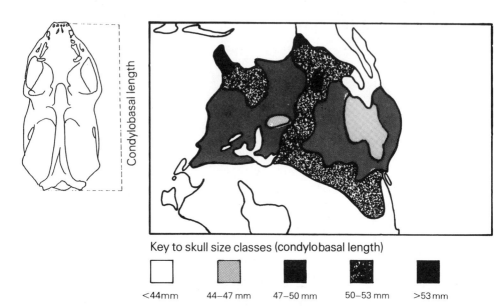

Key to skull size classes (condylobasal length)

<44mm	44–47 mm	47–50 mm	50–53 mm	>53mm

rate, is limited. This certainly seems reasonable for weasels (see Chapter 2). Then he allowed for the important fact that a weasel's priorities for energy expenditure are not the same all the year round, and they are not the same in the two sexes.

In winter, when the huge costs of keeping a small thin body warm in a cold climate load the loss columns of a weasel's budget with high 'overheads', the most important thing for weasels of both sexes is to economise on their daily expenditure of energy as much as possible. The best way to do this is to be extremely efficient at hunting, so as to be able to spend the least possible time each day out of the nest searching for food. For any combination of values measuring foraging efficiency and air temperature, there will be a theoretically 'optimum' body size, which will be the same for both sexes. In the breeding season, however, the equations must be different. In the intense competition for mates, larger males tend to be more successful, so at that season the optimum size for males is larger than in winter. Conversely, even in the breeding season, foraging efficiency is still the most important consideration for females, since it determines the number of young they can rear. The optimum size for a female in summer is therefore controlled by the same variables as in winter. Real animals, of course, vary in size individually; but the most successful in the range, Sandell suggests, should be the ones that have chanced on a compromise between the best sizes to be at different seasons. Sandell's idea seems very reasonable, and I suggest that it is possible to extend it to explain the general, continental-scale variation in body size of the weasels as a group.

The advantages and disadvantages to weasels of being small, summarised in Figure 2.10, tend to outweigh each other in all respects except that of metabolism. The physiological consequences of the small size and

Figure 4.5. Skins from the collection of the British Museum of Natural History, arranged to represent the range of variation in body size of adult male Eurasian weasels with latitude. Above, Mustela erminea; *below,* Mustela nivalis. *Origin of specimens, left to right:* erminea; *Switzerland, Norway, France, Hungary:* nivalis; *Switzerland, Norway, France, Hungary, Italy, Egypt. Scale is approximately ⅕ of actual body size.*

elongate shape of weasels are nearly all unfavourable. Their constant need for shelter is a handicap, especially in years when rodents are scarce, hunting expeditions must be long and ready-made dens few. They can store surplus food only as caches, liable to theft and decay, not as body fat. They are extremely vulnerable to temporary food shortages, yet hibernation and long-distance migration are impossible. The huge additional energy needed for breeding must be hard to find except when

Figure 4.6. Skins from the collection of the British Museum of Natural History, arranged to represent the range of variation in body size of adult male Eurasian weasels with longitude. Above, Mustela erminea; *below,* Mustela nivalis. *Origin of specimens, left to right, both species: England, Germany, European USSR, Asian USSR. Scale is approximately ⅕ of actual body size.*

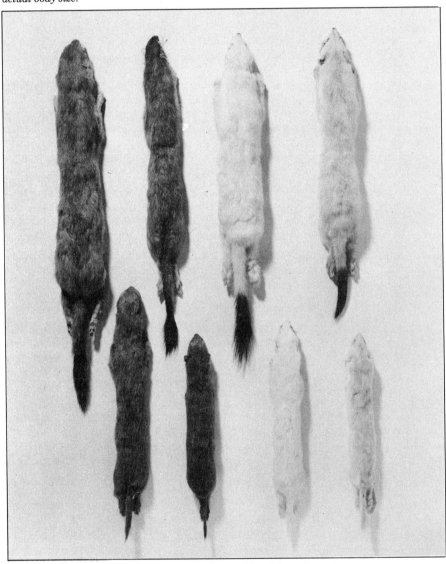

rodents are abundant. These are all serious problems for small, short-lived warm-blooded mammals living in cold climates. Of course, the list of considerations in Figure 2.10 is not exhaustive, and none of them can be assigned to a scale of relative values, but on the whole it confirms Sandell's assumption that body size is probably most strongly influenced by whatever is the most workable balance between hunting efficiency and energy balance in the local conditions.

In very cold climates, the metabolic toll imposed on weasels by being long and thin must be outweighed by the advantages of being able to live

Figure 4.7. Skins from the collection of the British Museum of Natural History, arranged to represent the range of variation in body size of adult male and female frenata *with latitude. Origin of specimens, left to right: Colombia (female right, male left), north-eastern USA, Canadian Northwest Territories. Scale is approximately ⅕ of actual body size.*

and hunt under the insulating blanket provided by the snow. The snow pack plays a crucial role in the life of northern animals and plants, and conditions within it and under it are well studied (Formosov, 1946; Chernov, 1985). Like their small mammal prey, the small northern weasels can pass the entire winter under the snow; in fact, the ability to escape from the infinite heat sink of the clear night sky is the condition of existence for all small mammals in the far north (Pruitt, 1978), including weasels. Under the snow there is both food and shelter — two pressing reasons why northern weasels must not be too large to live for many months of the year in the subnivean runways and nests of voles and lemmings (Figure 6.1). Small weasels are still deadly hunters, because for them small size does not reduce killing power as fast as it increases searching efficiency. In the far north for much of the year, that means being efficient at searching under snow. When the air temperature is

Table 4.2 The relationship between geographical variation in body size and climate (from King, 1989).

| | | Direction of environmental change associated with increased size: | | |
		nivalis	*erminea*	*frenata*
Males				
Eurasia	Latitude	southwards	not significant	–
	Temperature	warmer	warmer	–
	Snowlie (days)	fewer	fewer	–
North America	Latitude	not significant	northwards	not significant
	Temperature	not significant	colder	not significant
Females				
Eurasia	Latitude	southwards	not significant	–
	Temperature	warmer	warmer	–
	Snowlie	fewer	fewer	–
North America	Latitude	southwards	northwards	northwards
	Temperature	not significant	colder	not significant

mild and the wind-chill factor low, weasels can emerge onto the surface, and their tracks are often seen (Plate 8), but they are still absolutely dependent on sub-nivean nests and prey. For example, Teplov (1948) tracked male stoats chasing gamebirds and squirrels across the snow in the Pechorsk state game reserve, but subnivean species (rodents and shrews) still comprised 88 per cent of their stomach contents, and 98 per cent in females. Therefore, the need to retain access to undersnow tunnels and nests imposes a distinct limit to the size of northern weasels, which overrides all other considerations (King, 1989).

By contrast, in the milder climates of western Europe, there is less need to avoid exposure to the winter weather, and this relaxes the restrictions opposing larger size in males. Larger males probably enjoy greater breeding success, and this is a powerful reason why genes for larger size in males will be favoured wherever larger size is permitted by energy economy. This process, called sexual selection, acts only on males, but it affects females too since both sexes share the same gene pool. Both sexes would also respond to the opportunities presented by the presence in the south of various larger prey, such as rabbits and squirrels, that could more easily be caught by larger weasels and offer a better economic return than smaller prey. The net energy value of small prey is low, because a weasel has to invest energy into finding and killing each one separately and has to eat it whole, including the bones and the fur. Larger prey are more risky to attack, but once secured they provide more than one meal, and the second and later meals are all free. There will be local variations of course, but all in all, larger-sized weasels are better off in the south.

This interpretation predicts that, even in the south, females will tend to remain nearer the 'right' size for rodent hunting than males, because in most places in the northern hemisphere efficient rodent hunting is still the key to their breeding success even where other prey are available (see Chapter 10). It would be interesting to know more about the relationship between body size and breeding success in females. One might expect that, in rodent peak years when hunting is easy, females of any size might be successful, but in poor years a small female might be more likely to be able to feed a litter than a female the size of a male.

If this idea is correct, then the size of weasels, taken as a group, should be inversely correlated with the mean number of days of snow cover per year. This is true in Eurasia (Table 4.2). In North America, the niche for a large weasel is occupied by longtails, and they were already established in it by the time the ancestors of the present American stoats trekked across the Bering Bridge from Siberia (see Chapter 2).

It is one thing to demonstrate (1) a southwards increase in body size among the weasels as a group, (2) the penalties of getting too large in the north, and (3) the advantages of getting larger in the south, eg the presence of larger prey. It is quite another thing to suggest that (1) is caused by (2) and (3). All three could be unrelated consequences of something else altogether. As both Erlinge (1987) and I (1984b) have pointed out, in different contexts, it is very difficult to distinguish between a causal relationship and coincident side effects of some other process of adaptation. But it is possible to suggest falsifiable explanations for observed patterns that future students of weasels can think about. My suggestion is that it is the combination of energy balance, size of available prey and sexual selection, in unknown proportions, that explains why the niche for a weasel-shaped carnivore allows for only smaller individuals in snowy northern and high mountain climates, but larger ones in the milder lowlands.

It is important to emphasise that the idea put forward here, that it is advantageous to weasels to be relatively small in the coldest and snowiest climates, is very general and applies only to the weasels as a group, or rather, to the largest or only local species. Other considerations govern the sizes of the separate species and of the two sexes of weasels relative to each other (see Chapter 12). The general idea is derived from the size distribution of contemporary populations of living weasels; but it is also consistent with other evidence that small size really is advantageous to cold-climate weasels, both in the past and now.

First, Kurtén (1960) has shown that fossil stoats belonging to *M. palerminea*, the direct ancestor of modern stoats, were smaller during the cold phases of the middle Pleistocene, and larger during the warm ones. Wojcik (1974) pointed out that the fossil *nivalis* found in Polish caves and dated to the Eemian, the last interglacial period (about 120,000 years ago) resemble modern Polish common weasels, but those from the Weichselian, the last glacial period, are smaller, like the modern boreal least weasels which no longer live so far south. Less numerous fossil stoats from the same caves and dated to the last glacial period are within the range for modern stoats but smaller than average. Second, among more than 4,000 skulls of stoats collected over five years from Tjumen, at 57°N in the northern USSR, there was a progressive decrease with age in mean skull length in every annual cohort, which to Kopein (1969) meant that the smaller individuals were better adapted, and lived longer, in that severe climate than the larger ones.

SIZE VARIATION IN WEASELS ON THE NORTHERN HEMISPHERE ISLANDS

There are thousands of islands off the mainland coasts of Eurasia and North America, ranging in size from Britain and Newfoundland down to scattered rocks. All those now separated from the mainland by water less than 100m deep must have been joined to it during the last glaciation, so all those that were not glaciated, or were freed from the ice before the rising sea level cut them off, could presumably have been colonised across dry land by animals from the range of the continental fauna living at that time. Some islands were no doubt colonised by weasels then and have been continuously inhabited by weasels ever since. Other islands have been colonised since their isolation, once or many times, by weasels swimming across, from the nearest point on the mainland, or, occasionally, deliberately or accidentally carried in boats by farmers or traders, not necessarily from the nearest mainland port. Only the largest islands provide enough space and enough prey for a permanent population of weasels (among the offshore islands of Britain the lower limit is around 60 km^2: King and Moors, 1979b) and, except on mainland Britain, only one kind of weasel lives on each island.

Weasels on islands are often at least slightly different in size from those on the nearest mainland. Even though the published data on island weasels are sparse and inadequate, and the origin, route and date of colonisation of the immigrant weasels are seldom known, many people have offered explanations for the differences they could see. Unfortunately, so far none of these explanations has been very convincing, and some have been quite misleading.

For example, the stoats of Ireland have provided endless puzzles. For many years the only measurements of Irish stoats available were those of Fairley (1971), whose material came from the northern part of the island. The stoats there are intermediate in size between the stoats and the common weasels of mainland Britain, and they were assumed to represent all Irish stoats. One early theory, quoted with approval by Kratochvil (1977b), was that Ireland and mainland Britain were occupied by different colonising stocks — one larger in body size than the other. It is true that some physical characters remain stable over many generations, but size is not one of them. Size is too important to be determined merely by ancestry: it is acutely sensitive to contemporary conditions. The mean body size that we observe in a population of weasels is the one that best suits the present environment. To understand how that best size is determined, it is interesting and important to know the history of the colonising stock, and the size the colonists were when they arrived; but these things do not determine the outcome.

Another theory, put forward in a famous paper by Hutchinson (1959), linked the small size of northern Irish stoats with the absence from Ireland of common weasels. There was at that time a lot of interest in a theoretical idea called character displacement, which proposed that if two similar species have to be different in size so as to be able to concentrate on different resources (see Chapter 12), then when one is alone it could be intermediate in size and free to exploit everything available. Hutchinson noted that Irish stoats seemed to fulfil these predictions very well. In fact, so also do the very large common weasels in the Mediterranean, especially on islands such as Sardinia, where there are no stoats (Figure 4.2A and 4.3A). Unfortunately, both examples are completely invalid. The common weasels in the Mediterranean are large because common weasels consistently become larger towards the south of Europe (Figure 4.2A); in Sardinia and Sicily they are merely continuing the trend. More recent data from Ireland show that, although the stoats in the north are indeed very small, only 250 km away in the south they are as large or larger than in Britain (Table 4.1: Fairley, 1981). Since there is also a southwards increase in the proportion of Irish stoats that have the straight-line belly pattern typical of British stoats, Sleeman (1987) suggests that both trends might have been influenced by an unrecorded introduction of British stock into southern Ireland at some time in the past. Whether or not this is true, the small size of the northern Irish stoats remains to be explained.

Could the development of small island stoats be stunted in some way? The stoats on Terschelling Island suffer badly from skrjabingylosis, an unpleasant condition caused by a parasitic nematode in the nasal sinuses, and van Soest et al (1972) have suggested that this could be the cause of the distinctly small size of the Terschelling males. But there is much less evidence for this suggestion than against it (see Chapter 11), even as an explanation specific to Terschelling. Another possible cause of stunting is that young stoats cannot reach their full potential size if they are not well fed in the first few months of their lives, and Sleeman (1987) suggests that the limited choice of prey and short growing season in northern Ireland might restrict the growth of young stoats there.

The real explanation for the body size of the weasels of Ireland, Terschelling, and most other islands is still unknown. My guess is that the average size of the weasels on any island will drift towards whatever gives them, in the local conditions, the best year-round compromise between the advantages of smallness (Figure 2.10) and the upward pull exerted by sexual selection. The point of balance may be determined, in ways we do not yet understand, both by the climate and by the size distribution of available prey. For example, the range of potential prey available on islands is usually relatively smaller than on continents, and weasels colonising an island may find that the staple prey items they are used to are missing and the alternative supplies are different in various ways. On islands supporting abundant small prey and no large ones, small weasels would have some advantages and suffer few penalties; on islands with fewer small prey than large ones, larger weasels would be favoured.

Unfortunately, we have no information on the size ranges and relative abundance of the prey eaten by weasels on any of the northern hemisphere islands, or even any certainty as to what characters of the prey to measure. We do not know how long we might expect any local adaptation to take, or how far it might go. If the size of the weasels on each island is a unique local compromise, no general theory will explain the whole pattern unless it includes detailed information on the weasels living in all the island habitats, how long they have been there and where they came from. But there is one group of islands in the South Pacific where some at least of this information is known, and any attempt to construct a general theory about what determines body size in weasels must take account of what is happening there.

ADAPTATION IN BODY SIZE OF STOATS TRANSPORTED TO NEW ZEALAND

The stoats and common weasels that were introduced into New Zealand over the 20–30 years after 1884 were already relatively large, because they almost certainly all came from the large British stock. They found an environment quite different from the one they left, with a generally milder climate (ranging from warmer in the north to colder in the high mountains), and a prey fauna completely different in size distribution. The newly established pastures where stoats were first released were teeming with rabbits, which were familiar prey from England; and in the neighbouring forests there were ship rats and birds (Chapter 5). But the staple prey of stoats almost everywhere else in the world, the various kinds of voles, were completely missing. The only small rodent was the house mouse, widely distributed but not nearly abundant enough (except during occasional, shortlived outbursts) to compensate for the loss. Insects, especially large ground-dwelling forms, were common, but generally, the new environment offered more large and fewer small prey for the 'average' stoat than did Britain.

Of course, the 'average' stoat does not exist, for two reasons. First, the factors determining the body sizes of male and female stoats are not exactly the same, so the two sexes might not respond in the same way to the same change in conditions. Secondly, the new environment offered by New Zealand to the immigrant stoats is not the same everywhere. Forests of southern beech (*Nothofagus* sp.) are quite different from those dominated by native conifers (the podocarps) and broad-leaved trees; and both are totally different from anything in the northern hemisphere, as well as from the alpine grasslands, open gravel riverbeds, pastures and second-growth scrub elsewhere in New Zealand. Different habitats often have different prey species: for example, rabbits are common on grasslands and rare in damp podocarp/broad-leaved forests, while brush-tailed possums (introduced from Australia for their fur) are distributed the other way round. Mice are more common than ship rats in beech forests, vice versa in podocarp forests. So the way in which the immigrant stoats responded to the shift in the theoretically optimum size need not be the same in both sexes or in all habitats. And indeed, it was not.

Within New Zealand, adult male stoats collected in the 1970s from podocarp or mixed forest habitats, mostly at lower altitudes, were smaller than those from higher-altitude southern beech forests and grasslands, by about 3 per cent in skull length and about 4 per cent in head and body length. The same difference appeared, less clearly, in adult females and in young of both sexes. It even appeared in samples from the two kinds of forests taken within a short distance of each other; adult male stoats from podocarp forests on the west side of the Main Divide of the Southern Alps were smaller than their neighbours less than 20 km away in the beech forests on the east side, in two quite separate pairs of samples. Compared with contemporary British stoats, the male colonists have become larger in the beech forest/grassland habitats, and unchanged, or possibly smaller, in the podocarp and mixed forests (Figure 4.8). That means that the males living in the foothills of the Southern Alps are probably the largest stoats in the world; in fact, they are near the top of the range of

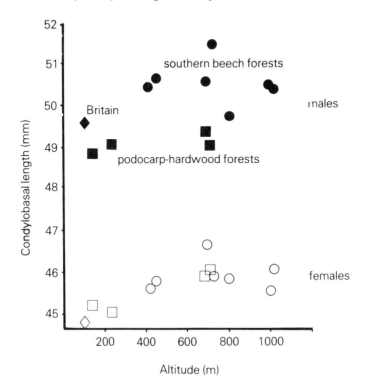

Figure 4.8. Local adaptation in size of the stoats transported to New Zealand. Filled symbols, males; open symbols, females. Circles, southern beech forests and grasslands; squares, podocarp-hardwood forests; diamonds, mean of contemporary samples from Britain. Females have become larger than their British ancestors in all habitats, males only in the higher-altitude beech forests (from King and Moody, 1982).

sizes of male longtailed weasels in North America. Female stoats in New Zealand have become larger in both habitat types; they are larger than any Eurasian females, and near the middle of the range of sizes of female longtails.

To make such comparisons we have to assume that the rather modest sample of British stoats we have is representative; that the ones we measured in BMNH are still much the same size as their ancestors that were transported to New Zealand in the last century; and that the local variation in size of the New Zealand animals is real and has arisen since they arrived (i.e. is not due to sampling error or to variation in body size of the original colonising stock). If all these things are true, then we can say that, in less than a hundred years, stoats in New Zealand have developed a range of variation in body size between local populations no less than than exists on the whole of continental Europe (King and Moody, 1982).

In evolutionary terms, this is an extremely rapid step, though not unique. Such remarkable shifts of mean body size in colonising populations have been observed before. Moreover, we do not know if the variation is genetic (due to long-term genetic changes in nature) or phenetic (due to short-term changes in nurture). Only if observed changes are genetic can we speak of evolutionary adaptation, and for New Zealand stoats this remains to be tested. On the other hand, the New Zealand example is one of rather few in the world where such substantial shifts in mean body size can be clearly correlated with sex and habitat, and precisely dated. Besides, even simple phenetic changes, if as consistent as that, tell us that to a stoat, there is something different about New Zealand, and the most obvious explanation is that it is the kind and size of prey available (Chapter 5).

The increase in body size of stoats in New Zealand is quite consistent with my interpretation of the geographical variation in body size of the northern-hemisphere weasels as a group. Since the climate of New Zealand is generally milder and the prey available larger rather than smaller compared with Britain, there are more advantages than disadvantages for the colonising stock in an increase in size. The effect is most substantial in females, and this too is just as expected. The cardinal advantage of small size for a female stoat, the ability to hunt rodents into their last refuges, is irrelevent in New Zealand, whereas larger size would be a help in dealing with rats, rabbits and possums.

Common weasels were introduced to New Zealand in greater numbers than stoats, but are now much scarcer. Their body size (Table 4.1) lies towards the upper end of the range for their British ancestors.

5 Food

Analyses of the diet of weasels can be made from scats (droppings), gut contents or food remains at nests, although each method gives a slightly different kind of information. The procedure is straightforward, and the quantities involved are small and relatively painless to the nose, but interpretation of the results is often hazardous.

IDENTIFYING AND INTERPRETING WEASEL DIETS

Scats are dry and inoffensive, and many samples can be obtained from known individuals, but scats can usually be collected only in conjunction with a successful live-trapping programme. The stomachs of dead weasels can be collected from gamekeepers or wildlife rangers, but they give only one sample per individual, and are less pleasant to work with. Teeth and large pieces of bone discarded in the nest can often be identified, but nests are usually hard to find unless their owners are radio-tracked. Only in alpine and arctic grasslands can weasel nests be found quite easily, by systematic searching immediately after the thaw. There, weasels often take over the large and conspicuous overwintering nests made by voles (Plate 11). Those which have been used during the winter by weasels are strewn with easily identifiable remains, and often the actual number of voles eaten can be calculated (Fitzgerald, 1977).

Scats and gut contents contain remains of hairs or feathers, with a few crunched-up bone fragments. Because metabolism in weasels is rapid, stomachs contain undigested meat only from very recent meals. Usually, only hairs and feathers remain, and these can be identified from a combination of minute differences in their fine structure (Day, 1966). The differences are fine enough to distinguish between genera, and therefore to species if only one representative of a genus is present on the collection area: for example, in Britain bank voles (genus *Clethrionomys)* can be distinguished from field voles (genus *Microtus*). On the other hand, species of *Sorex* (the shrews) cannot be separated, nor can hares from rabbits even though they are of different genera. Rabbits and hares therefore have to be grouped together as 'lagomorphs'. Carrion taken from a large carcass, especially the inner parts without hair, often cannot be detected at all.

The list of potential food items to be identified in a weasel gut is relatively short, since they are specialist predators of small mammals and birds and almost never take vegetable foods on purpose. Moreover, since it is fair to assume that weasels never eat hair or feathers except in the course of eating the animal to which they were attached, it is also relatively simple to make a rough estimate of the total number of items even though the number of individual prey eaten cannot be counted from their hairs. The stomach capacity of most weasels is only about 10–20 g, whereas the average weight of a small rodent would be about 20–30 g. Hence, a weasel usually cannot eat more than one small rodent at a sitting, so a single stomach, intestine or scat usually contains only one item. Conversely, one item can appear in more than one scat, so a group of scats collected at a single time and place is usually treated as a single sample.

The nutritional value of each kind of prey is partly related to its average weight. We can see which are the most profitable to eat by calculating the diet in terms of the weight of each kind of prey eaten rather than the number. The imbalance between large and small items is then corrected, because, for example, 7 birds' eggs at 3 g each count the same as 2 mice at 10 g, or one meal of 20 g taken off a dead rabbit. In a sample from which 10 birds' eggs, 8 mice and 6 rabbits were identified, the total weight of prey eaten would be 30 + 18 + 120 = 230 g, of which eggs contributed 13 per cent, mice 35 per cent and rabbits 52 per cent. That looks quite different from the same data expressed as percentage frequency of occurrence, i.e., eggs 42 per cent; mice 33 per cent; and rabbits 25 per cent. On the other hand, the results of weighting the prey in this way have to be treated with caution, for two reasons. First, the proportion of any one item is by definition relative to the total, so the items are not independent; hence we cannot say from these kinds of figures that weasels from one area rely more on a given kind of prey than those from another area. Secondly, the results are greatly influenced by how much one assumes a weasel eats off a single large carcase. Even so, the calculations are worth making in order to point out that, in general, smaller prey are much less profitable than larger ones.

Identifying a weasel's menu is the easy part of the job. It is far more difficult to decide what the figures mean. To begin with, simple lists of prey eaten by weasels from different sample areas are interesting but not very useful, because they will be biased towards the season, sex and habitat most fequently represented. Likewise, samples of different composition cannot be compared with each other, because weasels of different sexes or ages, or at different seasons, may eat different things. For example, some foods, such as birds' eggs, are available only in spring: it would not be valid to compare the proportion of birds' eggs in samples from two areas unless both had been collected in spring. And, of course, samples give more and more reliable information as they get larger. Any analysis has to reach some compromise between splitting, to avoid compounding different effects in one sample, and lumping, to increase the sizes of the samples.

The large and scattered scientific literature on weasels contains many descriptions of what they eat. Figures 5.1–5.3 summarise some of them.

Much can be learnt about the feeding habits of these little carnivores by setting out the available information systematically in this way, but there are problems. In the original papers the data were presented in different ways. Some counted the number of, say, mice that were identified and expressed it as a percentage of all the food items identified; others counted the number of samples containing mice and expressed it as a percentage of all the samples examined; some included empty stomachs in the figure for total samples, some excluded them. Wherever possible I have standardised the data by recalculating all the results as the number of each item counted as a percentage of all items. This is not, in fact, the best way to compare the diets of weasels in different places, for the same reason that weighting the numbers according to the size of prey introduces difficulties; the proportion of each item is not independent because it depends, by definition, on its relationship to all the other items. However, pie charts calculated in this way do give a quick and vivid impression of the differences in diets of weasels in different environments, and within broad limits these patterns probably do reflect real variations in how weasels get their living in different kinds of places.

FOODS OF THE COMMON WEASEL IN BRITAIN AND EUROPE

The first general study of the foods of common weasels in Britain was that of Day (1968) (Figure 5.1e). Day's work has been widely quoted for many years, and it is still the only British study to include animals collected (mostly from gamekeepers) from all over the country. His identification key to the hairs of the small mammals of Britain opened the door to many later studies, including my own (the keys to the hairs of North American species, available long before, could not be used in Britain). Later studies have been much more localised, and some have included estimates of the prey as well.

Young plantations are probably the ideal habitat for weasels, because the ground between the young trees quickly becomes overgrown with rank grass, neither mown nor grazed, which provides absolutely ideal living conditions for the favourite prey of all weasels, voles of the genus *Microtus*. In such a place, common weasels feed almost entirely upon voles (Lockie, 1966). Two of the four habitats observed in southern Sweden by Erlinge (1975) were young plantations, one recently established and the other seven years old. Both areas had the same combination of small trees and thick grass, and in both, voles were the most important single item (Figure 5.1c). In spring when voles were scarce, male weasels turned to the newly available young rabbits. The scats also contained bank voles, wood mice, water voles and shrews and, in one of the plantations, also birds and even lizards. Weasels avoided an older spruce plantation and a deciduous alder woodland, because the trees were tall enough to shade out the grass and the density of prey there was lower than in the young plantations.

On my study area at Wytham Woods, near Oxford, I collected 250 scats from marked individual common weasels caught in wooden box-traps. I used a simple trick to make sure I got a sample from each captured weasel: I supplied a dead white mouse in each trap, and the weasels

Figure 5.1. Some representative examples of the food habits of local populations of Mustela
nivalis. *n = the number of food items identified, if stated, excluding plants and debris. (a)
North America generally (Hall, 1951); (b) North European USSR, tundra and taiga
(Parovshchikov, 1963); (c) Sweden, young spruce plantations (Erlinge, 1975); (d) Holland,
mostly marshes (n=161, Brugge, 1977); (e) Britain generally (n=152, Day, 1968); (f)
England, farmland (n=445, Tapper, 1979); (g) England, woodland (n=285, King, 1980b);
(h) Scotland, farmland (n=206, Moors, 1975). The mean body size of the animals sampled
increases through the series.*

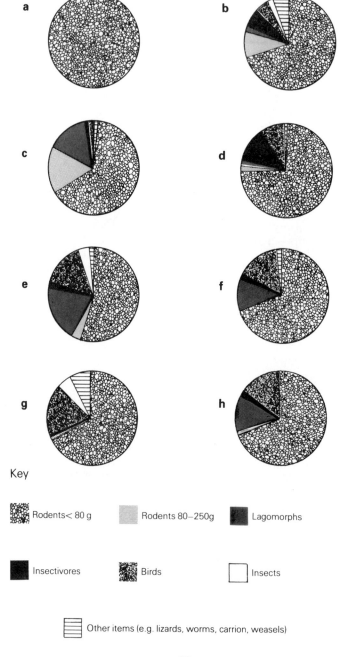

(wnich, judging from their lean condition and the known, rather low, food supplies) were usually hungry enough to eat it even after it had got distinctly 'high'. Eating one thing shoves everything else previously eaten along in the gut, and the result was usually at least one sample for me of the weasel's last wild-caught meal. The white mice I provided were easily distinguished from the brown wild ones. The Wytham weasels ate mostly bank voles, wood mice, field voles and birds, more or less the order of their abundance. Bank voles were by far the most common of the small rodents in the wood, followed by wood mice. Few field voles lived in the wood, but some were picked up by the weasels which had parts of their home ranges in a neighbouring young plantation (Figure 5.1g). There were very few rabbits about, and no rats. There were plenty of shrews and moles, although I found no shrews and only one mole in the scats.

Interesting and important as it is to know what weasels eat in woodlands of different types, these habitats are in the minority. In Britain at that time, woodland comprised under a tenth of the total land area, whereas arable and pasture land comprised two-thirds of England and Wales, and almost a quarter of Scotland. The majority of British weasels live on farmland. Studies in, for example, Sussex and Aberdeen-shire (Figure 5.1f, h) show that small rodents are still the most important fare; but in open country the commonest small rodents eaten are usually field voles, which are at home in any kind of grassland, and wood mice, which often live in hedges and are not afraid to venture out into the fields, especially before harvest. Bank voles stick to thick cover, so they are less often caught in open country than in woodland.

In general, then, common weasels depend on small rodents and small birds, and where these are scarce, these tiny hunters do not thrive. In every sample shown in Figure 5.1, as well as in other samples not shown, the proportion of small rodents is never less than half of the total number of prey items identified, and is usually nearer three-quarters.

FOODS OF THE LEAST WEASEL IN NORTHERN EURASIA AND NORTH AMERICA

Much less is known about the least weasels of the far north than about their larger brethren living in milder climates further south. In part this is because there are fewer students to study them; working conditions in the tundra are daunting at any time, especially during the long Arctic winter. Still, it is clear that in the places where least weasel foods have been sampled, such as at Barrow, on the north coast of Alaska, and in the extreme north of European USSR (Figure 5.1a, b), least weasels live almost entirely on lemmings and voles in the years when these rodents are abundant. But in the years when the lemmings disappear, life for the least weasels becomes extremely precarious. In the summers of lemming crash years, the tundra is still occupied by vast flocks of migratory birds which feed and nest on the ground, and these become unwilling providers of eggs and young for the hungry least weasels. In the lemming crash year of 1969 at Barrow, the nests of sandpipers and Lapland longspurs suffered unusually heavily. In such straitened circumstances least weasels are probably also more prepared to tackle alternative prey, such as water voles or shrews, or make use of the carrion of large animals they could not kill themselves or left-overs from kills made by larger predators (Nasimovich, 1949). Averaged over many years, as in the long collection from the Arkhangelsk region in the far north of European Russia, these various subsidiary resources give a false impression of variety in the least weasel diet (Figure 5.1b). But when the migratory birds have returned south, the seasonally active mammals have gone into hibernation, and subzero air temperatures freeze carrion solid and prevent all small mammals from venturing out for long, the least weasels have no choice but to stay under the protection of the snow and continue to search for the last few live lemmings or voles.

In central North America the range of the least weasel extends past the Canadian border, into the northern prairie states and along the Appalachian chain. Here the least weasel, still virtually confined to small rodents, has to share its only resource with many other more generalist predators. Perhaps this is the reason that, in relation to them, it is seldom common except after a plague of voles, just as in the Arctic.

FOODS OF THE STOAT IN EURASIA AND NORTH AMERICA

Far more has been published about the eating habits of stoats than of common weasels. Ermine has long been an important but unreliable item of trade in the far north, and Soviet studies on the biology of stoats date back to the 1930s. The Russian literature on stoats, and on their larger fur-bearing relatives such as sable and marten, is therefore exceptionally rich, and some of it is now available in English (King, 1975c, 1980a). In North America, too, both the stoat and the longtailed weasel have been trapped, skinned and traded for many years, and scientific interest in them goes back at least as far.

There are huge differences in body size, habitat and choice of prey available to stoats living at opposite ends of their enormous geographic range. Figure 5.2 shows the results of a dozen studies selected to illustrate some of the ways in which these adaptable little animals have responded to such variable living conditions. The pie charts are arranged in order of increasing body size downwards; the smallest (North American) stoats may be as little as a quarter the size of the largest (southern Irish and New Zealand) animals of the same sex, and have a totally different way of life.

On the tundra-covered island of Igloolik, at 69°N off the coast of northern Canada, lemmings were at low density in the summer of 1977 when Simms (1978) collected a pile of scats and prey remains from an active stoat den. Nevertheless, the stoat was still able to catch lemmings, since they made up more than three-quarters of the 142 remains tallied; birds and one insect accounted for the rest. Clearly this stoat, like the Alaskan least weasels, took birds when it could in summer. As Simms pointed out, not much else was available.

Further south, the stoats living in the farmlands and forests of Canada and the northern USA are smaller even than British and European common weasels (see Chapter 4). So, although they have a much wider choice of prey, including various kinds of voles, mice, shrews, lagomorphs and squirrels as well as birds, those sampled in New York and in Quebec

Figure 5.2. Some representative examples of the food habits of local populations of Mustela
erminea. *(a) New York generally (Hamilton, 1933); (b) Quebec, farmland (n=384, Raymond,
Bergeron and Plante, 1984); (c) Ontario, grassland (n=305, Simms, 1979a); (d) Central
European USSR, grassland (n=1,055, Aspisov and Popov, 1940); (e) Southern Sweden,
grassland (Erlinge, 1981); (f) Switzerland, farmland (n=690, Debrot, 1981); (g) Holland,
marshes (n=61, Brugge, 1977): (h) Britain generally (n=168, Day, 1968); (i) England,
farmland (n=31, Potts and Vickerman, 1974); (j) Northern Ireland generally (n=27, Fairley,
1971); (k) New Zealand, forests, and (l) New Zealand, alpine grassland (n=1,484 and
n=232, both King and Moody, 1982). The mean body size of the animals sampled increases
through the series.*

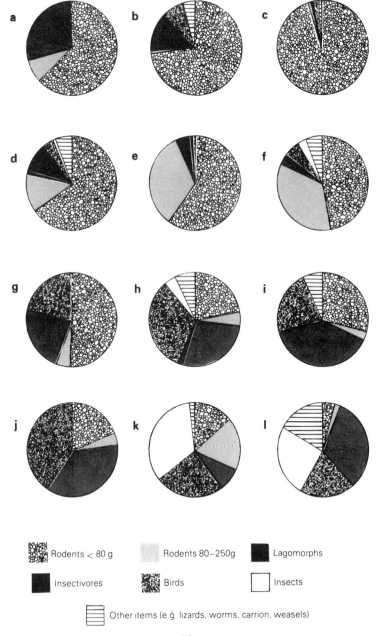

were still concentrating on small rodents (Figure 5.2a, b). In Ontario, *Microtus pennsylvanicus* was almost the sole item on the menu (Figure 5.2c) even though *Peromyscus* was also abundant; and in the alpine meadows of the Californian Sierra Nevada, remains of *Microtus montanus* were practically all there was to show for an entire winter's feasting by the tiny stoats observed by Fitzgerald (1977).

The larger Eurasian stoats still rely on small rodents, especially *Microtus*, for half or more of their kills, but the other half includes a substantial proportion of bigger prey. A particular favourite is the water vole, *Arvicola terrestris*, the familiar 'Water Rat' of the *Wind in the Willows* stories. Both the pioneering studies in the Volga-Kama River flood plains of the central European USSR (Figure 5.2d), and the more recent work in southern Sweden (Figure 5.2e) and Switzerland (Figure 5.2f) have shown how important water voles are to the feeding economy and, as a direct consequence, to the population dynamics of stoats in those areas (see Chapter 10). By contrast, no water voles turned up in a small sample of stoats collected from osier beds and along the riverbanks of low-lying Holland — only the occasional muskrat, a large water-loving rodent introduced from North America (Figure 5.2g).

In Britain the stoats are larger again, and the proportion of small rodents in the diet is down to a third or less. Mainland stoats eat small rodents, lagomorphs (mostly rabbits) and birds (Figure 5.2h, i) in almost equal proportions. Even in the aftermath of myxomatosis, rabbits supplied by far the most nutritive value, and British stoats have come to depend so strongly on this source of supply that the near-total destruction of rabbits by myxomatosis in the mid-1950s almost wiped out the stoats as well (see Chapter 10).

In Northern Ireland there are no field voles or bank voles, so the only small rodents available in the north are wood mice and house mice. Even though the northern stoats are much smaller than the British ones, they must rely on rabbits, birds and rats at least as much as their bigger brethren, *faute de mieux* (Figure 5.2j). In the south-west of Ireland there now are bank voles (since at least 1964; Fairley, 1984); but ironically, the southern Irish stoats are about as large as British ones (Table 4.1). Sleeman (1987) collected road-killed stoats mainly from the south, and found only three bank voles among the 91 prey items identified, but, unexpectedly, 24 shrews. (The full data, received too late to include in Figure 5.2, also included 29 rabbits, 13 rats, 17 birds, and 5 wood mice.)

FOODS OF THE LONGTAILED WEASEL IN NORTH AMERICA

Longtailed weasels range from the southern Canadian snows south through the USA, Mexico and into South America. They encounter a great variety of habitats and climates, and they range in size from much smaller to much larger than Eurasian (except British) stoats. It is a fair expectation that the smaller ones will concentrate on small rodents and the larger ones will take bigger prey when they can, just as stoats do, but the data are rather sparse. In some samples, such as the one from Iowa (Figure 5.3a) and another (not included in Figure 5.3) from Michigan (Quick, 1944), the pattern is the typical small weasel type — more than three-quarters of the prey are small rodents. In other samples, the diet is more variable and more often includes medium-sized rodents such as ground squirrels, chipmunks and rats, and also cottontails and shrews (Figure 5.3b–f). Longtails also eat insects occasionally, though not as a staple food, nor even necessarily in emergency, since insects are usually common only in summer when other kinds of food are abundant. About the most unusual longtail on record is the one which entered an Indiana barn in broad daylight and climbed into the rafters, where there was a nursery colony of bats. It ignored the farmer, and had killed three nursing female bats and their five young by the time he shot it (Mumford, 1969).

Figure 5.3. Some representative examples of the food habits of local populations of Mustela frenata. *(a) Iowa, farmland (n=166, Polderboer et al 1941); (b) Colorado, alpine (n=84, Quick, 1951); (c) New York generally (Hamilton, 1933); (d) Pennsylvania, farmland (n=112, Glover, 1942); (e) Ontario, grassland (n=34, Simms, 1979b); (f) Manitoba generally (n=200, Gamble and Riewe. 1982).*

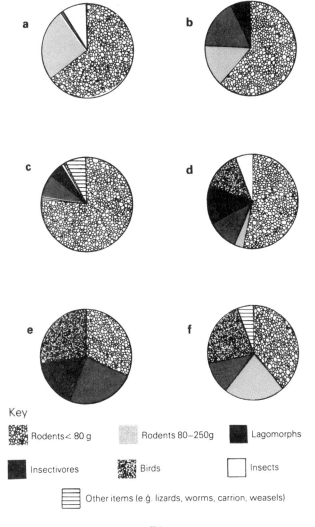

FOODS OF STOATS AND COMMON WEASELS INTRODUCED INTO NEW ZEALAND

One of the constant themes of this book is the close relationship between weasels generally and the various species of northern hemisphere voles with which they evolved. So close is this relationship that one might predict that weasels would not be able to survive anywhere where there are no voles. In New Zealand, history has provided a test of this idea.

The stoats and common weasels transported from Britain to New Zealand in the last century were liberated on pastures literally teeming with rabbits. The stoats were certainly well enough skilled at killing rabbits to stay on the sheep-runs indefinitely. On the other hand, the neighbouring forests contained house mice, the only small rodents afforded by this strange new country, together with native birds (despite a hundred years' attention from Norway rats and cats, there were still some which fed and nested on the ground and did not know how to protect themselves from predators) and the enormous native wetas, cricket-like insects some of which were as good as an invertebrate mouse. Ship rats, the flying birds and some of the wetas often nest in trees, but that did not put them out of reach of the agile stoat; and, of course, the rabbits came right up to the edge of the forest, and at the peak of their invasion, right through it to the alpine grasses above. The largest and most common mammals in the forests were Australian brushtailed possums, introduced for their fur and often left lying around in winter as trapper's carrion. So the stoats moved into the forests at once, and even though their new home contained a radically different array of potential meals, compared with what they were used to, it did not take stoats long to adjust, and they certainly thrived on what they found. Common weasels, on the other hand, find hunting rabbits more difficult, and the various possible substitutes of smaller size (native lizards and wetas) insufficient. As expected, the absence of voles makes New Zealand an inhospitable place for common weasels, and, in contrast with stoats, they have definitely not thrived. They are not extinct, but they are certainly very scarce compared with stoats.

It would be interesting to know what the first colonising stoats ate, but it is, of course, not possible now to find out. Fortunately, it is just as interesting to find out what contemporary stoats eat, because this could give us an unusual insight into how a predator adjusts to a totally unfamiliar prey fauna. In the course of a survey of the biology of stoats in all the national parks of New Zealand during the 1970s, King and Moody (1982) found that the most important single class of food in the total sample was birds (in 43 per cent of the 1,513 guts examined), although this figure includes all kinds of birds, as all feathers look the same after they have been through a stoat's gut. The remaining categories of food were found less often, partly because each contains fewer kinds: feral house mice, lagomorphs, possums, rats (mainly ship rats, but maybe including a few Norway rats or the very occasional Polynesian rat), geckos and skinks (small lizards), and freshwater crayfish. In forests, birds and insects between them made up more than half the items eaten, and rats, mice and possums were also very important (Figure 5.2k); in open tussock grasslands, lizards and lagomorphs substituted for possums and rats (Figure 5.2l).

Some of the larger mammals found must have been eaten as carrion, for example deer or sheep (found in 1 per cent of guts), plus some unknown proportion of rabbits, hares and possums. Many of these are killed on the road, and travellers often report seeing stoats eating road-kills or attempting to drag them under cover.

Insects, mostly wetas, were found in an astonishing 41 per cent of the total guts. New Zealand stoats eat insects all year round, and much more often than in Britain. This is understandable; even though a weta supplies only a small parcel of food for a stoat, it is still large enough to be worth snapping up in passing, and much better value than any insects a British stoat might find. In the colder parts of their enormous range, in Canada and Russia, stoats and longtails eat insects only occasionally, and then only in summer. On the other hand, very few of the 1,127 individual insects and spiders we found were species that inhabit carrion, which suggests that stoats are quick to find dead animals while they are still fresh, or else are seldom desperate enough to eat carrion after the maggots and carrion beetles have moved in. All in all, it seems that New Zealand stoats eat just about anything there is going: the only animal within the range of sizes that a stoat could tackle, that they normally avoid (found only twice) was the hedgehog, which hardly needs any explanation.

When the figures are loaded so as to show the relative importance of items of different sizes, it is clear that large prey (possums, lagomorphs and rats) supply about half the total food value; birds and mice together only a third; insects only about a tenth. Presumably the nutritional value of the only small prey available to stoats in New Zealand is no substitute for the voles which are their mainstay in Britain and elsewhere in the northern hemisphere. This probably explains why most New Zealand stoats have found it advantageous to become larger than their British ancestors (see Chapter 4), and why they do not scorn the carrion provided for them by road traffic and possum hunters.

6 Hunting behaviour

The hunting behaviour of wild weasels is very difficult to observe. You can go every day to an area you know to be inhabited by weasels, and never see one. But weasels are so small, as carnivores go, that it is possible to set up fairly natural conditions for them in captivity. By providing them with wild-caught prey in a large enclosure furnished with grass and trees, and watching — or better still filming — through a window, one can learn much about their hunting and killing behaviour. In cold climates, a lot can be deduced about the hunting tactics of weasels from reading trails and signs left in snow. Chance encounters with wild weasels are important as they can give fascinating glimpses of natural behaviour, although they have also spawned a whole literature of unlikely stories impossible to interpret.

Being a predator is a risky profession. Some kinds of prey are easy to find but dangerous to attack. For example, an enraged doe rabbit with young to protect may chase and kick a stoat halfway across a paddock; and of course, the spines of the hedgehog are a completely effective defence, at least while their owner is alive. Predators dealing with well-defended prey have to choose the weak and the disadvantaged, or band together in a pack. Other kinds of prey are easy to kill but very widely dispersed and well hidden. For example, although most voles offer little physical resistance once found by a weasel, the weasel runs a high risk of failing to find enough voles each day to fulfil its needs. If that happens often enough, the weasel dies. Death is the ultimate penalty for predators that misjudge the hazards of hunting — not merely the death of their own bodies, for that is inevitable sooner or later, but the worse failure of dying before having raised any young.

There are three main kinds of predators, which balance the risks of hunting in different ways. All weasels are solitary searchers, which specialise in the ability to explore every likely place for small prey, especially rodents, that are more easily killed than found. They are not like the sociable African lions, that depend on and live within sight of formidable prey that are more easily found than killed, and they are too impatient to be ambushers, like the leopards that quietly lie in wait up a tree for a suitable prey to pass by. Weasels hunt with all the restless energy and fierce concentration typical of their kind. They are adaptable and efficient, and tailor their methods according to their targets and their opportunities.

SMALL MAMMALS

A weasel on the hunt runs from one patch of cover to the next, investigating every small hole, and occasionally looking around from a vantage point, listening and testing the wind. Its habit of standing up on its hind legs (Plate 4) is an obvious way of overcoming the disadvantages of having such short legs, and the Germans have coined an expressive phrase describing it: they say *er macht Mannchen* ('it is making a little man'). In snow, the track of a hunting weasel is very irregular, turning this way and that, missing nothing of interest (Powell, 1978). In woods it often goes down under the snow into the hollows at the roots of trees, usually by pushing down into natural fissures in the snow cover beside logs, or by burrowing through the looser snow on the leeside of a trunk (Figure 6.1). A thick stable covering of snow protects small rodents from most other predators, but not from weasels. Sometimes it dives straight through the snow blanket; if there is a snow crust buried underneath it can get no further down, but moves along it, pushing up the new snow with its back and making characteristic bulges, like those of the surface passages of moles. A captive weasel can be seen burrowing in peat or leaves in the same way. Both stoats and common weasels are capable of travelling up to 1.5–2 km in a single hunting expedition of a few hours, more if food is scarce, but less (only a few hundred metres) in times of plenty. They concentrate on the habitats where they know, perhaps from experience, that they are most likely to find prey (Nams, 1981). The favourite hunting grounds where a resident weasel will spend almost all its time often comprise less than half the area of its home range.

Voles make extensive tunnels through the grass and moss under the snow, and weasels are the supreme experts at tunnel hunting. The smaller ones tend to be exactly the right size for getting into the tunnels of the local voles. In Ontario, Simms (1979b) calculated that the small female stoats could get into over 90 per cent of subnivean vole tunnels (22–28 mm diameter), and male stoats and female longtails could get into over 70 per cent. The small Canadian stoats whose stomachs were examined by Northcott (1971) had apparently made a speciality of digging fat jumping mice (*Zapus*) out of their winter hibernation nests. Female common weasels in Scotland can run easily through all but the very smallest vole burrows (averaging 23 mm diameter) and males can get through the largest with a squeeze (Pounds, 1981). Mole runs (Figure 8.4) are easily accessible and much used. The larger weasels are excluded from vole tunnels (Simms' male longtails could get into only 10 per cent of them) but freely enter the wider tunnels of rabbits, water voles and ground squirrels. For example, at dusk one evening Florine (1942) set two traps at the entrance of a pocket gopher burrow, so that only animals coming from within would be caught. By 9 pm one of them held a pocket gopher, and the other a longtailed weasel.

Weasels may not actually make their kills in such confined spaces. Erlinge *et al* (1974) describe captive common weasels attempting to bolt small rodents out of their holes:

Figure 6.1. The northern races of nivalis *and* erminea *are small enough to hunt a vole through its under-snow tunnels, and to follow it into its last refuge.*

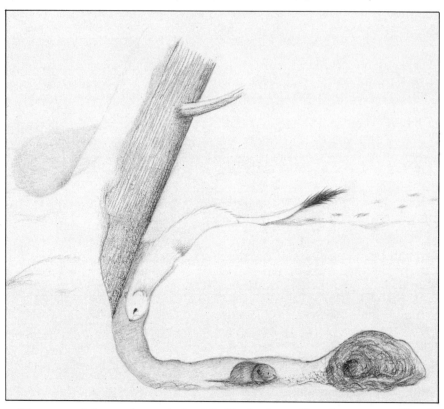

The weasel hopped around with lively bounding jumps ... clearly trying in different ways to frighten or drive out the prey animals. In narrow holes it seems to find it difficult to catch and kill full-grown voles. Sooner or later, however, some prey animals left their retreats and ... as a rule they had little chance of escape when they were outside their holes.

From snow-tracking in Finland, Nyholm (1959) deduced exactly similar behaviour, regularly in stoats and occasionally also in least weasels. On the other hand, my tame female common weasel was easily able to kill house mice in artificial tunnels about 5 cm square.

LARGER MAMMALS

In theory, larger predators should tend to tackle larger prey, because larger predators have more killing power, and also larger food requirements. Smaller predators should avoid the risk of injury by sticking to smaller items, which are often more numerous than large ones, and which take refuge in places more easily searched by smaller predators than larger ones. Weasels are small predators, and small prey certainly are their bread and butter, so to speak. However, weasels are also bold and confident out of all proportion to their size, and they do not seem to know the rules. Their extraordinary courage, strength and tenacity puts them among the few solitary predators able to attack prey larger than themselves. It may not happen every day, but eyewitness accounts of weasels attacking large prey are too common to be ignored, and full of vivid details such as the lightning thrusts with the teeth, the legs propped on widely straddled paws, and the tail furiously bristling with excitement. There seems to be no doubt that such things really do happen; the question remains, however, as to why weasels should run the risk of injury that they must involve.

J.L. Cooke of Kent described one such incident in a letter to me. He was standing by a hay-rick when he heard much squealing and rushing about in the bottom of it. Out dashed a common weasel with a half-grown rat, which it carried up a nearby earthen bank, deposited there, and returned to the rick. The rushing and squealing started again, and then out came the weasel with another rat, which it placed on top of the first. In the space of about 20 minutes the weasel collected together 17 rats. Cooke was quite certain, when I questioned him, that it was a common weasel he had seen, not a stoat.

Most predators tackling large prey have to find some way to reduce the odds against them. One way is for two or more to co-operate. Although weasels are normally solitary, related individuals may stay together for a while. Bullock and Pickering (1982) described in detail an incident involving two common weasels, which persisted in attacking an adult brown hare, even though the hare defended itself with its forepaws. They suggested that the two weasels were helping each other. More frequent are accounts of families of weasels hunting together before the young disperse. A family of weasels can be large after a good breeding season, and when on the move in a bunch would give the impression of great energy and alarming predatory power. There are even persistent stories that such large groups of weasels are actually dangerous to man. Take, for example, a perfectly serious letter (reproduced verbatim below) which I received in my first year as a student of weasels, from J.A. Torr of Cheshire:

One morning in November 1968 as I walked along the road [about 6.30 am] I saw a weasel come out into the road, then it ran back into the grass, it did this a second time, and as I got near to where it went into the grass there was such an awful noise and out came a number of weasels they came straight at me so I run away as fast as I could and the weasels after me, as I was running my hat came of and looking back I noticed the weasels had stopped with it, I managed to count eleven of them, I mentioned this to a Gamekeeper a short time after, and he said weasels will attack when in large numbers, I hope this will help you in your research, and please be carefull.

When I questioned him on the details of the story, he replied:

(1) they were definitely weasels, not stoats (2) there was no one with me at the time when the weasels chased me, but the story is perfectly true so do not be afraid to quote it.

Figure 6.2. Weasels are among the few predators that regularly kill prey larger than themselves without having the advantage of hunting in a pack, but the risks are considerable.

Accounts of such behaviour are not confined to the weasels of Europe. Oehler (1945) reported an incident in New York in which two men tried to catch a longtailed weasel which they had seen run under a log. It attacked the first, and then the second who went to rescue him. It took both of them half an hour to subdue it, and then it would not run off when they tried to let it go. Oehler commented that he had 'never witnessed . . . a more remarkable exhibition of ferocious aggressiveness and stamina'. Stories such as these, told in all earnestness and often in remarkable detail, can hardly be made up, but I am not at all sure how to interpret them.

Another way to reduce the risk of injury when attacking large prey is to use what might be called psychological pressure. Stoats are commonly believed to be able to mesmerise rabbits, often a particular one out of a group, and reduce it to dithering helplessness while the others go on as if nothing had happened. To countryfolk the sight of a 'stoated rabbit'(Forsyth, 1967) used to be nothing unusual, and they thought that the rabbit's paralysis of terror and pitiful squealing was induced by the musky scent of a stoat excited by the chase. 'Och aye,' said a Scottish keeper to Mortimer Batten (1936), 'a rabbit will nae run after he gets a whiff of the wash.' There could be something in this idea, first because a stoat which is not hunting may be seen to pass through a field of rabbits without causing any of them to do more than hop out of its way, and secondly because the teeth and jaws of a stoat are rather small for getting through the well-muscled neck and strong vertebrae of an adult rabbit. In fact, Hewson and Healing (1971) carefully examined several rabbits killed by stoats and concluded that, as the injuries inflicted did not seem to be severe, the rabbits must have died of fright. 'Stoated' rabbits rescued from their relentless pursuers without a mark on them may recover from their paralysis and totter away, only to sink down and die later, apparently from heart failure. This form of 'shock tactics' might reduce somewhat the chances of injury to a stoat attacking a large rabbit or hare (Figure 6.2, Plate 9). All the same, this sort of encounter is still risky and energy-consuming for the weasel, and small rodents are more profitable targets when available.

BIRDS

Weasels climb trees easily and well (Figure 6.3), even to great heights, visiting the nests of birds and squirrels, running fearlessly along the branches and down again head first. J.M.Smith of Sussex described to me his astonishment on seeing three pigeons come tumbling out of a fir tree and flounder about on the ground as though stupefied. Seconds later a brown streak came down the tree and a weasel leapt at the throat of one of them and began to drag it away. DeVos (1960) once caught a hare in a trap, left it lodged a metre up a small tree, and came back to find a longtailed weasel dragging it off. He retrieved it and put it into a larger tree, this time 3.5 metres up, and stood back to watch. The weasel searched around and eventually found it, climbed up and got it down again. When the hare was returned to the same place, the weasel found it again within one minute. Every time it climbed up and down with as much skill as any squirrel. The longtail watched by Pearce (1937) climbed spirally, hugging the trunk with its paws and wrapping its sinuous body around it. The animal appeared to be familiar with this method of climbing, and did not go up more directly even when in great haste.

Weasels can leap upwards at least their own standing height, and will reach up and grab prey well above their heads, often coiling the body up behind to hold on with all four sets of claws. In this way they will attack even quite large birds, always going for the neck, and will not let go even if carried high into the air. Barrow (1953) saw a waterhen flying overhead with a weasel clinging to its throat (Figure 6.4). Unfortunately for the weasel, the bird dived into deep water, taking the weasel with it. The same story is more commonly told of predatory birds which had made the mistake of attacking the weasel (see Chapter 11), but in this case it seems that the weasel had attacked the bird.

Weasels are sometimes seen to catch birds by what is claimed to be a psychological trick known as 'the weasels' dance of death'. Over the departmental tea table one morning J.H. Lawton related how, standing beside a flooded gravel pit near Oxford, he watched a stoat dancing for half an hour. It ran rapidly around in small circles, leaping and twisting, rolling over and turning somersaults, climbing up a wire fence and jumping down, and all the while flashing its white chest in the early morning sun. Throughout, the performance was watched intently by four waterhens, which slowly walked towards it from the water's edge. Occasionally the stoat stopped and definitely (Lawton emphasised this) looked directly at them. Three times it dashed at the nearest bird, but on each charge the waterhens scattered and the stoat missed. The stoat simply began its dance again, and the waterhens returned.

Figure 6.3. Weasels are nimble climbers, and can easily scale any rough surface (photo by A.Brandon).

This habit of common weasels and stoats is so well known, though I have not had the luck to see it, that there is (or was) a restaurant near Manchester called *The Waltzing Weasel.* Yet there is no evidence that they do it as a deliberate hunting technique. Weasels in general are intelligent and opportunistic hunters, and if they find themselves surrounded by a curious crowd of birds, for whatever reason, they will certainly take the chance to catch one if they can. They might well learn to take that chance without knowing how to make it happen again. If there is no purposeful connection between 'dancing' and hunting, there need be none between 'dancing' and the presence of potential prey. Michael Evans wrote to me from Cambridge to describe how he had watched two common weasels bounding, twisting and turning on a road, without a rabbit or a bird in sight. During months of radio-tracking stoats in Scotland, Pounds (1981) watched 13 'dances', of which some were performed without any audience at all. This rather supports the alternative explanation for it — that it is an involuntary response to the

Figure 6.4. A weasel that attacks a large bird runs the risk of being carried into the air, since it will not release its grip while its prey is still moving.

intense irritation caused by parasitic worms lodged inside the skull (see Chapter 11).

Like many predators, weasels sometimes have to put up with having the tables turned on them by flocks of aggressive birds. For example, Hunter (1969) traced a loud outburst of chattering to a group of sparrows mobbing a common weasel. It darted into the flowers, pursued by sparrows dive-bombing it from all directions. Twice it broke cover, and twice was driven back. It had to work its way under cover about nine metres, followed all the way by the mob, before it could finally escape. It seems unlikely that a weasel in such a position would retaliate, since birds in such an excited state would be virtually uncatchable, and neither could they do it much harm, except to alert every other possible quarry in the neighbourhood.

THE KILL

Whether the prey is found by vision, hearing or scent, the final kill is certainly done by eye, and stimulated by movement (Heidt, 1972). Voles usually respond to the presence of a weasel by running away, and these can be overtaken in a couple of bounds and dispatched with hardly time for a squeak (Plate 19). Some rodents, however, especially wood mice, may respond by climbing upwards or 'freezing', and both these tactics are often successful. A weasel does not seem immediately to recognise as prey a mouse which, though in plain view, is sitting motionless, and in the wild this must often give the mouse a chance to escape. Tests have shown that wood mice react less to the pungent musk of weasels or stoats than field voles do, so are less likely to give themselves away (Stoddart, 1976; Gorman, 1984). Even larger, more visible animals can get away with the same trick so long as they sit still. Murie (1935), perched up a tree, watched a longtailed weasel trying to catch a varying hare. There was about six inches of snow on the ground, and both were in their white winter coats. The hare came loping along, then criss-crossed its tracks in a small area just in front of the tree and sat down. The weasel followed, tracking the hare's prints through the maze exactly, at times passing quite close to the hare. When it had followed every turn of the trail to within a metre of its end, the hare skipped off. The same game was played twice more before the hare ran off in top gear, and the weasel gave up.

Weasels orientate their killing bite to the back of the neck by visual cues, particularly the position of the eyes and ears of the prey. The final strike is made with deadly accuracy. The long upper canines pierce the back of a rodent's skull and meet the lower canines entering below the ear or the throat. This neck-bite is very characteristic, and death is just about instantaneous. Skinned mice killed by weasels often show no injury beside the two pairs of needle-like punctures in the neck. In a more confined space the weasel may first grab the mouse almost anywhere, often wrapping its long slender body round its victim and using its feet to manipulate it and gain leverage to transfer its hold to the neck (Heidt, 1972; Figure 6.5). The whole process takes only 10–60 seconds, though the weasel often keeps its grip until the mouse stops kicking, perhaps shaking it about a bit in the meantime. Weasels attack larger prey by jumping on their backs, to get at the neck from above, or by darting in to reach unprotected parts from below. An animal which backs into a corner or makes cries of threat or fear only increases the weasel's excitment.

If there are more live prey in sight, a weasel will kill one after another, and even search around for more, until it is exhausted. This is not because it enjoys killing, but because the entire sequence of killing behaviour is instinctive and is set off by the sight of moving prey whether or not the weasel is hungry. A weasel in a pen full of chicks is psychologically unable to ignore the flutterings of the live ones in order to settle down and eat.

The weasel's favourite part of a mouse is the brain, and it nearly

Figure 6.5. Weasels can make up in agility what they lack in stature, by wrapping their long bodies around a prey to help contain its struggles (after Powell, 1978).

always begins its meal by eating the head, then proceeding backwards to the rest of the body. The point of the nose, the teeth, feet, tail and intestines are left until last, and if prey is very abundant, the weasel may simply eat the brain and abandon the rest, or eat the brains of all and the body of only one, or even alternate between several carcasses. A weasel presented with any of the small rodent species common in Europe (field voles, bank voles and wood mice) would eat any of them equally readily, that is, in the order they are caught: no one species is preferred, but voles are more easily caught than mice (Erlinge, 1975). If a drop of blood appears at the neck-bite, the weasel may first lick it up, but there is no truth in the old belief that weasels suck the blood of their prey. Very many observations made on weasels in captivity have never recorded this happening, and besides, weasels are physically incapable of it.

CACHEING

Weasels have a strong tendency to store surplus food. Where prey is very abundant, or unusually vulnerable, carcasses can be accumulated in astonishing numbers. For example, in the days when corn-ricks were common and always infested with huge numbers of rats and mice, weasel caches were often found inside when the ricks were dismantled for threshing. A typical cache would contain 40–50 freshly killed mice with the typical puncture marks of the weasel's teeth in the neck. Parovshchikov (1963) records the details of 15 common weasel caches found in Russia, which contained an average of 30 carcasses each. Besides various kinds of voles and mice, the weasels had stored water voles, common shrews, moles, frogs, lizards, garden dormice, and goldcrests. Parovshchikov mentions that the goldcrests were buried in the snow, with their brains eaten out. This happened in a forest after a heavy snowstorm, which forced the birds to come down and spend the night on young spruces, where they were vulnerable to weasels. Ten to 16 birds were counted in the cache.

Of course weasels prefer fresh meat, but if none can be had and the need is pressing, they will remember the location of their cache and return to it. Svendsen (1982) watched a female longtail hunting in an alpine meadow in Colorado. She found two nests of golden-mantled ground squirrels, killed all nine young and carried them to an old pocket gopher burrow. She visited the cache three times in the next few hours, and added new items to the same store during the following two weeks. She was lactating, and had young in another burrow about 175 metres away.

The weasel's tendency to kill everything in sight used to be regarded as evidence of 'blood lust' or of some dislocation of normally more reasonable hunting behaviour. In warm climates, the usefulness of this habit certainly appears rather short-term; surely it must be wasteful if the stored food spoils, and it could well increase the chances that later hunting expeditions will not be so lucky. But weasels need to eat frequently, although not much at a time, so almost all food is cached for a while. In cold climates, where energy demands are high and alternative prey few, the cache habit could have real survival value. Oksanen *et al* (1985) suggest that it should be regarded as a positive strategy, at least in winter and in the far north. This is a much more likely explanation: really damaging behaviour should be weeded out in the course of evolution, and after all, weasels evolved in cold climates, and are still completely at home in them.

ENERGY EQUATIONS AND A WEASEL'S CHOICE OF PREY

The food eaten by a hunting animal is determined largely by three things: what there is to hunt, what the hunter can catch, and whether the chase is worthwhile. The best kind of prey for a hunter is one that is easy to find, easy to kill, provides a much greater return in energy than the hunter spent in getting hold of it, and is always available. These are the reasons that, for weasels, the ideal prey are voles, mice and lemmings. They make clear runways and burrows leading straight to their nests, marked with scent when occupied; they are not usually dangerous to tackle; they contain a worthwhile amount of meat, minerals and most of the other things a weasel requires in its diet, conveniently wrapped in a waterproof package; and they may be so abundant that a weasel can supply all its needs for the day in only a few hours. All weasels therefore specialise on small rodents, of whatever species are present in the habitat they live in, because they can obtain the most energy for the least expenditure and risk by making a profession of hunting them.

Outside their specialisation, weasels will eat whatever makes a profitable catch, and this means that they are restricted to a certain range of sizes of prey. The common weasel might receive a good return for the investment of energy it has made in subduing a large animal, but the risks are high. At times when the chances are good that in the time it took to make that effort, it might find a more profitable small prey instead, common weasels avoid adult rats and rabbits. These larger prey are therefore tackled regularly only by the larger stoats and longtails. Young rabbits are different, of course, and common weasels feast on young rabbits whenever they can get them. At the other end of the scale are the items which, like insects and earthworms, are so small that the amount of energy gained from digesting them scarcely exceeds that spent in catching them. If a hungry weasel comes across an earthworm lying on the surface of the ground, it will certainly snatch it up in passing, and I often found earthworm setae in the scats of common weasels from Wytham. One stoat was observed apparently carrying worms to its young (Osgood, 1936). But I doubt if a weasel with a stomach full of vole would bother, and nor could I imagine even a hungry weasel actually digging for worms. In general, the food actually taken by wild weasels is much as theoreticians predict (Erlinge, 1981). The species present can be ranked in order according to the net return in energy gained by the weasel in relation to the time and effort it has to invest. The local weasels will start at the top of the list, and add the increasingly less profitable items one by one until their requirements are met.

But small rodents have one great disadvantage: they are not reliable. The population densities of rodents in the far north go up and down across a huge range, so that every few years weasels can catch far more than they need, while in other years they are hungry, or have to find other food. The least weasels and stoats of the northern forests and tundra have little else to turn to, except perhaps a few berries, or a bit of frozen carrion, when the voles and lemmings disappear (Nasimovich, 1949). Larger mammals such as rabbits and hares are absent or too big to tackle; pikas and ground squirrels hibernate, and birds migrate south, for more than half the year.

In milder climates, the choice is much better. Birds and rabbits are available all the year round, and normally vary less in numbers from year to year than do small rodents. The eggs of birds provide a glut of nutritious and defenceless prey in spring. In North America there is a range of medium-sized rodents, including pocket gophers, ground squirrels and chipmunks, which are important food for longtailed weasels. But a weasel's choice is still limited by seasonal and geographical variations in the density of prey. For instance, birds' eggs, young rabbits and hibernating rodents are not available in winter.

SHREWS

Weasels often seem positively to avoid one whole order of small mammals whose members are common everywhere, that of the insectivores (the hedgehogs, moles and shrews). Shrews are said to be distasteful to carnivores; captive weasels eat dead shrews provided as food only with the greatest reluctance, and when given live shrews as prey, most weasels ignore them. Shrews may be killed and cached with the rest, but are eaten only as a last resort, so tend to accumulate in the caches in a somewhat higher proportion than the live animals are available (Rubina, 1960). Several analyses have detected no shrews eaten at all, even when they were known to be present. For example, shrews were common in

Wytham throughout my 22-month live-trapping study, but I found none in any of the 344 weasel scats I analysed, even though I was looking out for them (see Chapter 11). Erlinge *et al* (1974) believed that shrews were caught less often because they gave off an offensive smell which deterred the weasel from making a serious attempt at a kill — 'The weasels seemed doubtful at the decisive moment', as they put it.

On the other hand, weasels living on small islands and in cold climates do seem to eat appreciable numbers of shrews. In both places, the choice of prey is very limited. On Terschelling Island and in Ireland, there are no voles, and shrews are eaten there much more often than on adjacent mainlands with voles (van Soest *et al*, 1972; Sleeman, 1987). In the far north, only voles, shrews and weasels are active under the snow all winter, and in vole crash years shrews may be the weasels' only possible alternative to starvation (Figures 5.2, 5.3). The density of shrews there tends to decline at the same time as the voles with which they live (Sonerud, 1988).

BODY SIZES OF PREDATOR AND PREY

The link between the sizes of a predator and its prey is well demonstrated in 'sets' of species of similar hunting habits and tastes but different sizes, such as the three species of *Mustela* in the northern hemisphere. From Chapter 5 it is clear that least and common weasels do usually take more small rodents, and fewer medium-sized rodents and lagomorphs, than stoats or longtails living in comparable habitats. Likewise, the stoats of smaller average body size living in the harsh northern lands do concentrate or. small rodents much more than do the large British and European stoats. But these comparisons can be tricky, because predators living in different places do not always have the same opportunities to choose between large and small prey to the same degree; one of the reasons that Arctic stoats eat fewer rabbits than British ones is that they meet fewer. The best way to look at the size relationships between predators and prey is to compare the diets of male and female weasels belonging to the same species and taken from the same population.

Remains of large prey, e.g. lagomorphs, are in fact more often found associated with male common weasels than with females, although the difference is not always statistically significant (Day, 1968; Erlinge, 1975; Brugge, 1977; Tapper, 1979). Unfortunately, although lagomorph hair is very distinctive under the microscope and unlikely to be misidentified, it looks the same in lagomorphs of any size (rabbits and hares, young and adults); and weasels of any size can scavenge on rabbits caught in traps or killed on the road.

Conversely, female common weasels do tend to concentrate more exclusively on small rodents than do males. In one analysis, in which I combined the results of several British studies to give a total of 512 items from weasels of known sex, 266 of 387 items identified in males were small rodents (69 per cent), compared with 73 of 89 items in females (82 per cent), and this difference was significant (King, 1977). Small rodents are not often stolen from traps (although this does happen, greatly to the annoyance of the trapper: Lightfoot and Wallis, 1982) or found dead on the road; and weasels of both sexes are able to kill small rodents of all ages equally well. Female weasels tend to spend more time hunting in tunnels than the males do, so they are perhaps more likely to find small rodents than lagomorphs as potential meals.

In Britain and Europe, female stoats tend (not always significantly) to eat fewer lagomorphs than males, and it is usually assumed that female stoats would be less able to kill a rabbit or hare than males. But perhaps female stoats in those countries eat fewer lagomorphs because they can make a good enough living on small rodents without the extra effort of tackling large prey. Female stoats in New Zealand do not have that option. They do eat some small prey (mice and insects) more often than males, but they also take larger prey, the lagomorphs and rats, as often as males. If rabbits attacked by stoats die mainly from fright, the size advantage of male stoats may not be all that relevant: it would presumably be just as traumatic for a rabbit to be attacked by a stoat of any size.

7 The impact of predation by weasels on populations of natural prey

The popular picture of the weasels (see Chapter 2) is rather different from the real one. No doubt a vole would agree with the description of a weasel as 'the Nemesis of Nature's little people', but the ecologist has the advantage of not having to see the weasel from the viewpoint of the vole. In a face-to-face encounter the odds are usually in favour of the weasel, but the weasel has first to make the encounter, and in this, the long-term odds are certainly in favour of the vole. Besides, the meeting of a single vole and a single weasel tells us nothing about the impact of weasels on the numbers of voles, since the fates of populations cannot be gauged from the fates of individuals. Therein lies one of the main reasons why predation by weasels, or any other predator, is such a tricky subject to investigate. The converse questions, of estimating the effect on weasel populations of losses to larger predators and to gamekeepers, are equally difficult, for the same reasons.

PROBLEMS OF STUDYING PREDATION

Mathematical models and computer simulations of predation are rather more common than field studies. The reason is that scientists are human beings, and they like to be sure of getting interesting and reliable results, preferably in the shortest time possible and without getting wet too often. Field studies on predators, such as weasels, do not meet these requirements, for four reasons.

First, weasels are vastly less abundant than rodents, which means that samples of weasels will be modest unless a very large study area is used, and even so results are very uncertain. A project on weasels is usually much more of a gamble than a project on voles — my own first year as a research student on weasels was very nearly my last. Second, predation is not a fixed process, which, like a chemical reaction, reliably reappears whenever and wherever it is observed. The interactions between predator and prey are flexible, and the outcome variable from year to year and place to place. Third, one cannot deduce anything about predation from watching the weasels on their own: one has to study the prey as well, and this of course doubles the work. One must count not only the number of adult prey present but also the number of young born and when, the numbers added to the population and subtracted by all causes, not to mention local and seasonal variation in all these things. A proposed study on weasels which cannot be done at the same time and place as a separate one on the prey usually involves too much work for one person, and can be tackled only by a team. Fourth, all known techniques for counting small mammals are inaccurate, and errors of estimation will increase at compound interest through the series of calculations needed to estimate predation rates. Moreover, a weasel's estimate of the number of small mammals available will include, for example, nestlings and transient and trap-shy individuals that are missed by the human observer.

It is very important to realise the difference between a study of predation and a study of the food habits of predators. Predation is a matter of rates and relative numbers, and its results can be understood only in terms of whole populations, not only of the predator and of its prey, but also of its competitors and its enemies, and its response to changing conditions. A record of a weasel killing a blackbird is a valid observation of the behaviour of at least that weasel; a list of the prey identified in the stomachs of 1,000 weasels can be a valid estimate of the food habits of the population from which those 1,000 weasels came; but unless the densities of weasels and prey available in each case is known, and the relative importance of other predators and prey in the same area, neither is a study of predation. The difference can be illustrated in terms of a familiar analogy, shopping. Clearly, the stock of a certain item of goods in a shop does not depend only on the number removed by shoppers, but on its price and replacement rate and on a host of other interactions involving the whole local shopping centre. Table 7.1 summarises some of these interactions, and introduces some useful shorthand terms than cannot be avoided in any discussion of predation.

The problem of studying the impact of predation by weasels on their prey has been tackled in four ways. All are inaccurate to some extent. The first is an indirect method: if the daily food requirements of individual weasels are known, the researcher can either estimate how much of a known loss could be accounted for by weasels eating prey at that rate, or else compare how much loss could be inflicted by weasels compared with the amount needed to reduce prey of a known density by a given amount (which of these two estimates is made depends largely on what sort of information there is about the prey). This assumes that weasels kill a certain number of prey per day, but they do not — they kill as many as they can catch. The second is the direct method of counting the number of prey alive and then counting the number of them removed by weasels. This method can be sabotaged by spectacular errors of assumption or census. One early study used unrealistically high figures for the density and productivity of least weasels, and was led to the conclusion that the weasels had eaten over three times more voles than were present (Golley, 1960). The opposite error can be equally large if the number of voles removed is estimated from analyses of the weasels' diet, since weasels may kill and cache many more voles than they eat. The third is the simplest and most difficult to interpret: simply removing the weasels and observing the prey. Unless the experiment is carefully controlled, it is usually impossible to attribute any change in the

Table 7.1 The ecology of predation explained in terms of an analogy with shopping

Concept	Predation	Shopping
1. The prey	Voles	'Morningmunch' breakfast cereal
2. The predators	Weasels	Shoppers
3. The locality	A whole ecosystem	A town
4. The habitat	A particular field	A particular shop
5. Prey spectrum	Total local fauna	Total stock of shop
6. Prey available	Subset of (5) within killing range	Subset of (5) affordable
7. Prey selected today	Subset of (6) according to the opportunities and needs of the day	Subset of (6) according to the opportunities and needs of the day
8. Searching time	Time to locate vole	Time to find right shop and right shelf
9. Pursuit time and killing power	Ability to catch and kill vole	Ability to find item and pay
10. Prey replacement rate	Reproduction rate of voles plus recruitment rate of population	Manufacturer's production rate plus buying rate of shop
11. Risk factor	Chances of injury to weasel during kill	Chances of overspending
12. Penalty for misjudging (11)	Death	Loss of face and credit
13. Preference for	Most vulnerable of those worth while	Best quality of those offered cheap
14. Functional response	Increase in voles taken per weasel with increased density/availability	Increase in items bought per shopper with increased opportunity
15. Numerical response	Increased breeding success of weasels with vole density	Increased number of shoppers with increased opportunity
16. Surplus killing/cacheing	Killing above requirements and storing surplus when opportunity offers	Stocking up on specials
17. Alternative prey	Shrews	Grapefruit
18. Specialist	Weasel willing to search for voles rather than eat shrews	Shopping around for Morningmunch
19. Generalist	Weasel willing to eat shrews when voles scarce	Person of wide tastes
20. Impact of predation Nil	When (14) and (15) much less than (10)	Supply exceeds demand
Controlling	When (14) and (15) exceed (10)	Demand exceeds supply

numbers of prey to predation rather than to umpteen other possible causes. The fourth is the theoretical approach of manipulating numbers in computers. These results are helpful and realistic in direct proportion to the amount of information about real animals incorporated.

All of these methods have different combinations of advantages and disadvantages, and all have been tried somewhere. Comparing the results shows clearly that the effects of predation by weasels certainly need not be the same in all situations. At one extreme are the weasels that spend most of the year hunting under deep or prolonged snow cover in the arctic and alpine grasslands; at the other, those that are part of a community of predators hunting in temperate forests and farmlands.

WEASELS HUNTING ON ARCTIC AND ALPINE GRASSLANDS

Weasels evolved in the cold, windswept open spaces of the Pleistocene glacial tundra, and their speciality is hunting the various species of voles (especially *Microtus*) and lemmings that are also well adapted to living there. In summer these prolific little animals make networks of runways through the matted felt of dead grass stems on the surface of the ground, and pull the green stems down through the tangle from below. Voles and lemmings are the favourite prey of all the cold-climate predators — hawks, owls, foxes, martens — but most of these have to hunt them through the curtain of grass. Only the small northern weasels can follow them along their runways and into their nests. In winter the migratory raptors move south and the snow protects the small rodents from foxes and martens. Weasels alone continue to hunt them as efficiently as ever, throughout the long dark winter.

In many places the populations of voles and lemmings display spectacular fluctuations in abundance every 3–4 years. In the summers that the rodents are increasing and at high density, raptors flock to kill huge numbers of them, and bring up large broods of hungry young; carnivores breed well too, including weasels. The combined functional and numerical responses (defined in Table 7.1) of all them increases the toll many fold. But no predators can outbreed voles and lemmings at that stage, so the rodents can still more than replace the losses. The crunch comes in the following winters, when the rodents are no longer breeding and food is getting short. When the larger predators have gone, the weasels carry on, searching out the diminishing numbers of rodents with deadly determination. The rodents have no defence against predators that can follow them right into their last refuges. The weasels' relentless pursuit prevents the remaining rodents from recovering, and is halted only when their own numbers are cut down by starvation. When the weasels become scarce, the surviving rodents have a breathing space to build up their numbers again. Many ecologists now consider that the population fluctuations of the northern voles and lemmings are caused largely by continued heavy predation during the winters of the decline phase, due mainly to weasels (Pearson, 1985; Hansson and Henttonen, 1985; Henttonen *et al* 1987; Sonerud, 1988). To prove this idea, it is necessary to calculate the numbers of rodents eaten by weasels during the very season when field work is most difficult. Fortunately, there is an easier way.

The nesting behaviour of small northern mammals offers a unique opportunity to estimate predation rates. In order to survive the winter, each vole or lemming must retreat to a winter nest of shredded grass stems under the snow. Weasels use the nests as temporary headquarters for several days, and leave evidence of their stay in the form of scats and left-overs. This nest-raiding technique can be very profitable, especially with sociable voles which huddle together for warmth. One study of the overwintering habits of radio-tagged meadow voles (*Microtus pennsylvanicus*) in New York (Madison *et al*, 1984) was wrecked by a stoat which got into the enclosure. It killed more than half the tagged voles and took over a nest, lining it with fur and carrying back to it the voles it had killed, complete with their transmitters.

On the bare Arctic tundra the large overwintering nests made by breeding female lemmings are easy to find in the first few days after the thaw. Maher (1967) found 153 lemming nests on Banks Island, in the Canadian Northwest Territories, of which he reckoned 20 per cent had been occupied by stoats, and he believed that the stoats were responsible for the low density population of lemmings of 1962–3. Nearly twice as many (35 per cent) lemming nests were raided by least weasels at Barrow, Alaska, in 1968–9, and in the following year the lemmings were so scarce that the number of nests found by McLean *et al* (1974) dropped from 770 to 0.

In the high Sierra Nevada of California, Fitzgerald (1977) worked in alpine meadows buried under 1–3 metres of snow from late November to mid April every year. He used a most economic technique based on the assumption that the weasels usually carry back to their nest the voles they have killed nearby. The weasels seldom eat the front of the vole's skull, including the large incisor teeth, and so a count of the pairs of incisors left in a nest which has been occupied by a weasel (Plate 11) will give a rough idea of how many voles were killed, and this number can be expressed as a percentage of the total population of voles present in the autumn. Fitzgerald found that the stoats and longtails living on the meadows removed up to half the overwintering population of montane voles (*Microtus montanus*) in the three winters 1965–6 to 1968–9, and after the winter of heaviest losses the voles were reduced to very low numbers (Table 7.2). His data support the idea that the hidden work of weasels under the winter snow tends to exaggerate the 3–4 year population fluctuation of voles, by deepening and extending the low phases.

In northern Europe at least, it is clear that all the species of small rodents living in one locality generally reach low density at the same time, along with the shrews (Henttonen *et al*, 1987; Sonerud, 1988). This can be taken as confirmation that intense searching by hungry weasels willing to kill any small animal they meet is the cause of the 3–4-yearly low periods there too. It is hard to think of anything else that could synchronise the fluctuations of a whole community of unrelated small rodents with different population dynamics. In northern North America, however, the ten-year cycle of the snowshoe hare dominates the community dynamics of small mammals, and its effect on weasels may be very different.

Table 7.2 Impact of predation by stoats on overwintering *Microtus montanus* in the Station Meadows (14 ha), Sierra Nevada (Fitzgerald, 1977)

	1966–67	1967–68	1968–69
Mean no. voles/ha in autumn	25	83	127
No. vole nests/ha	23	65	85
Total no. nests examined	292	783	793
No. stoats resident	3	1	4
% nests occupied by			
stoats	28	5	13
longtails	2	2	4
No. voles killed by			
stoats	159	46	225
longtails	5	13	91
Mean no. voles/ha next spring	10	23	<2
% total losses attributed to weasels	>80	13	54

WEASELS HUNTING IN TEMPERATE FARMLAND AND FOREST

In most temperate habitats there is a much greater variety of prey than in the far north and at high altitude. There is also a larger community of predators to hunt them, many more of which are resident all year round. There is no prolonged snow cover and savage cold to give the weasels a virtual monopoly on hunting voles in winter; on the contrary, the weasels not only have to share the rodents with larger predators, they also have to watch out for themselves (Figure 11.7).

The population fluctuations of voles in temperate habitats seldom reach the spectacular amplitudes typical of the far north, but there is often enough to make a lot of difference to the hunting prospects of the predators. Conversely, the impact made by predators on the voles depends on, among other things, whether or not the voles are breeding. For example, one of the earliest studies, by Lockie, Charles and East (1962) in a young plantation in Scotland, concluded that in late winter predation was the most important single cause of mortality for the voles (*Microtus agrestis*), responsible for a reduction of the total population from about 225 voles/ha in February to about 112/ha in April. But when the voles started breeding in earnest, the combined force of predators (common weasels, stoats and short-eared owls) could not cope with the rapid production, and the numbers of voles soared despite the losses.

Goszczynski (1977) describes how a team of Polish workers, interested in the causes of the population fluctuations of the common vole (*Microtus arvalis*), did essentially the same job but in more detail and on a very much larger scale. Their study area totalled over 3,000 ha of mixed arable land, including 13 per cent woodland, and they examined the diets of martens, foxes, badgers, feral cats, and four species of hawks and owls as well as of common weasels. The study ran for three years (Table 7.3) and covered a complete vole cycle, from a low in late 1970, through the peak in 1971 (>330 voles per ha) to the next low in 1973. The proportion of voles removed by all the predators combined was high to start with, when the voles were scarce, and about three-quarters of the total mortality of the voles at that time was due to predation. But by the time the voles had reached their peak they were so abundant that predation could account for very few of their numbers and less than half of their mortality, even though by that time all the predators were living almost entirely on the voles, and some of them, including the common weasels, had also increased in numbers. But as the voles declined, the predators were still numerous; the ratio of numbers ceased to favour the voles, and the increasingly desperate predators were searching out almost every single vole that was left.

The total predation pressure on the peak population of voles, expressed in energy units, was estimated at 31 per cent. The common weasels' share in it was calculated at 11 per cent, which put them in third place after foxes (37 per cent) and feral cats (29 per cent) in the number of common voles eaten. But the team had trapped common weasels only locally (30 traps over 150 hectares) and their figure for the average density of common weasels over the whole area of one per 397–456 ha was (by their own admission) a considerable underestimate. My guess is that the real contribution made by common weasels to the toll could have been much higher, especially when the numbers of voles were declining.

Table 7.3 Impact of the total community of predators (including common weasels) on *Microtus arvalis* and woodland rodents (*Clethrionomys glareolus, Apodemus flavicollis*, and *A. agrarius*) on 3,100 ha in Poland (Goszczynski, 1977).

| | VOLES | | WOODLAND RODENTS | |
	Density/ha	% mortality due to predators	Density/ha	% mortality due to predators
Autumn 1970	11		34	
Winter 1970–1		79		74
Spring 1971	32		9	
Summer 1971	333	20	7	33
Autumn 1971	332		43	
Winter 1971–2		11		41
Spring 1972	42		14	
Summer 1972	40	76	19	42
Autumn 1972	17		11	
Winter 1972–3		89		95
Spring 1973	1		2	
Summer 1973	9	>100	9	97

North Farm, a game estate in Sussex, was the site of long-term research on partridges and their predators by G.R. Potts and his team from the Game Conservancy (see Chapter 13). Their study area was a large expanse (2,500 ha) of gently rolling chalk downland, mostly divided into huge arable or pasture fields. Patches of woodland and rough grass were left where the hillsides were too steep for the plough, and along the edges of tracks and beside fencerows. Field voles and common weasels both avoided the open fields, which were frequently rolled, mowed, or heavily grazed, so both lived together in the few undisturbed areas and could easily be censused there. Tapper (1979) followed the changes in their numbers from 1971 to 1976. The voles were declining at the beginning of the study, fell to very low numbers (about 20 voles per ha) in 1973, shot up to around 300 voles per ha in 1974–5, and declined again in 1976. The numbers of weasels caught followed the numbers of voles, but lagged behind by about nine months. The weasels ate about 3–4 times more voles in the years when they were most numerous (voles comprised 54 per cent of their diet in 1975, compared with 16 per cent in 1973: Figure 10.9), and also doubled their own numbers, so altogether the number of voles they could remove was increased almost tenfold. Although the combined functional and numerical response of the weasels certainly increased the number of voles killed with the density of voles (after a slight delay), the actual number killed could not be measured. There is therefore no way of estimating whether the increase in toll kept up with the increase in density. However, Tapper pointed out that 3–4-year cycles can be generated by mathematical models in which density-dependent mortality acts after a delay of nine months.

In some places the year to year population fluctuations of voles are hardly noticeable. For example, in southern Sweden the local populations of common voles and wood mice vary through the year, but hardly at all from one year to the next. On a 4,000 ha area of meadows and grazed pasture near Lund, common voles range from 8–10 per ha in May and June to about 50 per ha in August and September; they never reach the high numbers recorded by Goszczynski and Tapper. Erlinge *et al* (1983, 1984) set out to document the effects of the entire community of predators on the voles and wood mice. They estimated the number of rodents produced in 1975 and 1976, and the number that were eaten each year by the generalist predators (fox, feral cat, badger, buzzard and tawny owl) and by the predators that specialise on rodents (stoat, kestrel and long-eared owl). In both years the total number of rodents eaten roughly equalled the number produced. Even though rodents make up only about 15 per cent of the diet of the generalist predators, they accounted for three-quarters or more of the losses (Table 7.4). The stoats' share in the total was under 10 per cent. The losses due to the combined force of predators were especially heavy in early spring, when other favoured prey such as young rabbits were not available. The voles started their breeding season surrounded by persistent predators poised to snap up the young as soon as they emerged from their nests, and this delayed and reduced the rodents' recovery from the winter non-breeding period. Predation was also particularly heavy in autumn, because of the rapid functional response of the generalist predators to the increase in numbers of rodents through the breeding season. The net result was that rodents could never escape the attention of predators, because the generalists were always there, ready and waiting. Stoats in this situation were almost as much at risk as their prey; when the population of rabbits declined, the stoats were forced into severe competition with the generalist predators for the remaining rodents (see Chapter 10).

Like all students of predation, the Swedish team had to make a lot of

Table 7.4 Estimated annual production and mortality of *Microtus agrestis* and *Apodemus sylvaticus* on 4,000 ha of marshy meadows and pasture in southern Sweden (Erlinge *et al*, 1983).

	NO. PRODUCED	NO. EATEN PER YEAR BY PREDATORS			Proportion of total eaten by stoats
		Total	Generalists	Specialists	
Voles	171,400	156,865	120,700	36,165	9%
Mice	20,100	21,546	17,180	4,366	7%

assumptions, both in bridging the inevitable gaps in their field data and in interpreting their results. Not all ecologists agree with the conclusions they reached, and some (e.g., Kidd and Lewis, 1987) have said so. In the best traditions of scientific discussion, others can read both the doubts and the reply (Erlinge *et al*, 1988), and make up their own minds.

Wood mice are usually much less common than voles, and also perhaps weasels find them slightly more difficult to kill (see Chapter 6), so predators hunting mixed populations of voles and wood mice, such as those observed in Sweden, take many fewer mice than voles (Table 7.4). But on a 150 ha area of farmland in France, where Delattre (1984) was trapping, the combined density of all small rodents was very low, and a lot of those that were there were yellow-necked and wood mice (Table 7.5). In the first year, while voles were still in the majority, the common weasels in the area bred well and removed a substantial proportion (16 per cent per month) of the small rodents available. But in the second and third years, mice made up 80 per cent of the rodents present, and the weasels and their impact declined. Delattre suggested that common weasels are so closely dependent on voles that they cannot breed or maintain their populations on mice alone — even if these are relatively abundant.

In the days before combine harvesting, field crops were stacked into ricks in late summer, and dismantled only in autumn or winter when farm workers had time to do the threshing. A large, well-built corn-stack was a least weasel's idea of paradise; warm, dry, safe from larger predators and overflowing with thousands of rodents. Modern hay-barns are pretty good too, though not quite in the same class. Farmworkers have always welcomed weasels in a rick, believing that they will reduce the loss and fouling of the stored grain by rodents. The extent of their unpaid assistance was documented in the Mikhnov district, near Moscow, over the winter of 1948–9 by Rubina (1960). The density of voles in the fields in the previous summer was high, reaching 86 per ha in September 1948. The least weasels found good hunting outside, and by December, only 20 per cent of the ricks in the district had been visited by them. Over the winter the density of voles crashed, and by the spring of 1949 was down to 0.3 per ha. Fully 90 per cent of the ricks surveyed in March had been occupied by least weasels, and in nearly all of them the density of rodents was less than in the few ricks not visited (Table 7.6).

Table 7.5 Impact of common weasels on a mixed population of *Microtus arvalis*, *M. agrestis*, *Clethrionomys glareolus*, *Apodemus sylvaticus* and *A. flavicollis* on 150 ha of farmland in France (Delattre, 1984).

	COMBINED DENSITY/HA	RELATIVE PROPORTIONS		NO. WEASELS			LOSSES DUE TO WEASELS/MON (as % biomass)
		Apodemus	voles	M	F	preg	
Spring 1978	7.2	41	59	9	6	all	16
Spring 1979	6.2	81	19	5	2	1	10
Spring 1970	6.8	80	20	2	0	–	3

Table 7.6 Number of rodents found per 100 m³ of stack volume during dismantling of cornstacks in the Mikhnov region, near Moscow, in the winter of 1948–9 (adapted from Rubina, 1960).

MONTH	CROP	STACKS WITHOUT COMMON WEASELS			STACKS WITH COMMON WEASELS		
		No. stacks	No. voles	No. mice	No. stacks	No. voles	No. mice
Feb.	Oats	3	100	10	2	50	8
Mar.	Oats	1	80	7	3	30	2
Ap.	Wheat	1	50	1	1	20	0
Ap.	Rye	8	50	10	6	50	0.5

In the temperate woodlands in Britain, the population fluctuations of wood mice and bank voles are much less dramatic than those of field voles in arable land. Over twenty years in Wytham Woods the combined density of these two species ranged from 1 to 52 per ha, and these were the very exceptional figures which followed the upheaval of myxomatosis. In most of the 20 years the combined density has been about 10–30 rodents per ha (Southern and Lowe, 1982). Tawny owls and weasels were the two most important vertebrate predators in the wood, so my study was designed to complement Southern's work on the owls. A fellow student, J.R. Flowerdew, was using the same area for a study on the population dynamics of wood mice, and he kindly allowed me to use his figures for the densities of wood mice and bank voles.

In 1968–9 I estimated that the known resident weasels ate on average about 8–10 per cent per month (range 2–20 per cent) of each of the population of bank voles and wood mice. Even though these figures were considered to somewhat overestimate the number of rodents killed by weasels, they accounted for only a small proportion of the total number of voles and mice disappearing each month (Table 7.7), and perhaps only about 14 per cent of the total production of rodents in the wood (Hayward and Phillipson, 1979). Flowerdew also calculated the survival of wood mice by counting how many of his marked mice disappeared between one trapping session and the next: predation by weasels appeared to have little effect on how long the mice lived either.

Table 7.7 Combined impact of common weasels and tawny owls on *Clethrionomys glareolus* in Wytham Woods

Predators	Area	Consumption (% of rodents present)	Source
Tawny owls 1954–6	20 ha	15–33% per 8 weeks	Southern & Lowe, 1982
Common weasels 1968–9	27 ha	2–20% per 4 weeks	King, 1980b
Total disappearance rate 1968–69		12–55% per 5 weeks	Flowerdew, 1972 and pers.comm.

But the tawny owls were also taking a regular toll, and at times it was substantially heavier — up to 33 per cent per two months. The two sets of results refer to short periods that did not coincide, and both are approximate and full of assumptions, but at the moment no better ones are available. Southern and Lowe (1982) cautiously concluded that the combined predation by weasels and tawny owls together could have depressed the numbers of rodents, especially when they were already at low density. On the other hand. above a certain level of abundance of rodents the owls and weasels could no longer keep up, so their effect slackened off. This is the kind of inverse relationship that helps to exaggerate the fluctuations in numbers of rodents.

The Edward Grey Institute also uses Wytham as a field research area for ornithology, and their most famous study has been on the long-term population dynamics of titmice. These birds nest in natural holes in trees, but will readily take to artificial wooden nest boxes instead. Members of the EGI have recorded the nesting success of tits in Wytham since 1947. From 1964 onwards about 900 boxes, spread over the whole 240 ha of the estate, have been available to the tits, and for each box there are annual records of nesting success, including which nests were destroyed by predators. Common weasels are by far the most frequent raiders (Figure 7.1). Their depredations were not too serious until 1957, when the percentage of boxes raided jumped from 0–8 per cent per season to 46 per cent. Every year since then, up to half of the boxes have been raided. This can be very inconvenient for ornithologists making an intensive study of a few particular nests, and by the time I started working in Wytham the EGI people were thinking about taking steps to remove the offenders. But they later decided that the predation by weasels was part of the natural process they were studying, although maybe rather accentuated by the unnaturally high density of tit nests made possible by the provision of so many extra boxes. The weasels were therefore left alone, and the effect they had on the tits was analysed from the long series of past records.

The results showed that year to year variations in two factors alone were sufficient to regulate the population density of the tits: the size of their clutches, determined largely by food supplies, and hatching success, which is influenced greatly by predation by weasels. Earlier, EGI staff had noted that later and larger broods of young tits were more often found by weasels, perhaps because these young were less well fed and therefore more loudly calling for food. But in fact the extent of predation in any one year was affected mainly by whether the weasels were especially hungry, which happened in years when the small rodents in the wood were at low density during the nesting season (Dunn, 1977; Figure 13.6). The weasels sometimes also managed to catch the female bird on the nest (there is only one entrance to the nest boxes, and only the females brood the eggs), and this might explain why female tits live slightly shorter lives than males.

One might ask, why is the effect of weasel predation on the titmice apparently greater than on rodents in the same habitat? Perhaps because the nest boxes are conspicuous and easily found; the nests are available only over a short season; lost clutches are rarely replaced more than once; on average there are fewer nests than rodents per weasel (nests about 2/ha; rodents about 21/ha); and weasels are by far the most significant

Figure 7.1. A common weasel caught by an automatic camera in the act of raiding a nest box and removing a chick (redrawn from a photograph by C.M.Perrins, in Dunn, 1977).

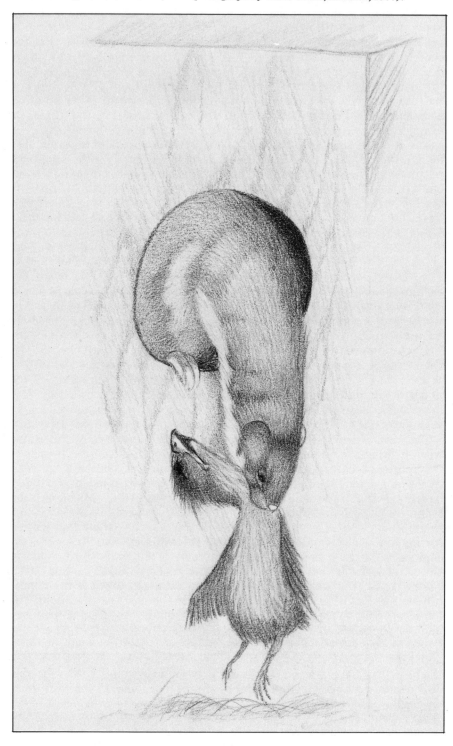

predator on tit nests, whereas tawny owls are probably more significant than weasels as predators of rodents.

Since the massive deforestation of Europe in historic times, rodents living in woodland have found themselves restricted to smaller and smaller islands surrounded by an expanding sea of farmland. Worse, Table 7.3 shows that the degree of attention paid by predators to these woodland rodents depends largely on events in the fields outside, so it is difficult to find a place to study weasel predation on woodland rodents undisturbed. Fortunately, there are large expanses of relatively untouched forest in New Zealand, populated by stoats, feral house mice and ship rats. The simple community of introduced mammals in southern beech (*Nothofagus*) forests has proved to be especially suitable for studying the biology of stoats and rodents, because there are few alternative prey, and the only other predators (feral cats, native owls and bush falcons) are all scarce there. Better still, there is great variation between years in the annual production of beech mast. The occasional huge crops set off a train of events that lasts 18 months and profoundly affects the density and population dynamics of both stoats and rodents.

I observed two consecutive seedfall events in each of two adjacent valleys (Figure 7.2). Most of the seed fell in autumn (March–June), and lay on the ground all winter. The density indices for the mice began to rise in later winter and spring (August and November). The mice bred all winter and into the following summer, although they stopped recruiting young into the resident population in late winter. The following summer, the number of stoats was much higher than in a normal summer, and they ate far more mice each than usual. I had no estimate of the actual numbers of either stoats or mice, so like Tapper I could make no direct estimate of the impact of predation by stoats on the peak population of mice, but there were some interesting differences between the two years which suggest that it might be substantial. In 1976–7, the stoats were counted by kill-trapping, so they were removed at first capture, but in 1979–80 they were counted by live-trapping, and then released to continue catching mice. The mice failed to reach the expected high summer densities, and declined sooner, in the year that the stoats were not removed. The same pattern was repeated in both study areas. This was quite contrary to expectation, since the seedfall in 1979 was even larger than in 1976, so much so that the mice were still uninterested in baited traps in the late winter, and the density index taken then was a considerable underestimate. In both summers the stoats increased their consumption of mice by 3–5 times, and their own numbers by the same amount. The predation pressure on the mice therefore must have increased by a staggering amount, somewhere between five- and thirtyfold. I suggest that the pattern in Figure 7.2 amounts to strong circumstantial evidence that the huge numerical and functional responses by stoats, applied together at the time that recruitment among the mice had already begun to fall, acted to reduce and shorten the post-seedfall irruptions of the mice. The mortality among the stoats at that time was very high (see Chapter 11), and normal conditions were restored within 18 months of the seedfall.

Weasels seldom persist in hunting prey at low density unless they have no alternative. The only temperate habitats where the choice is severely limited and emigration impossible are on small islands. Weasels arriving

Figure 7.2. The impact of predation by stoats is implied by the difference between these two sets of density estimates for feral house mice in Fiordland, southern New Zealand (see also Figure 10.4). When the stoats were killed at first capture, the numbers of mice remained higher for longer than when the stoats were released alive (from King, 1983a, 1985). (a) Eglinton Valley; (b) Hollyford Valley.

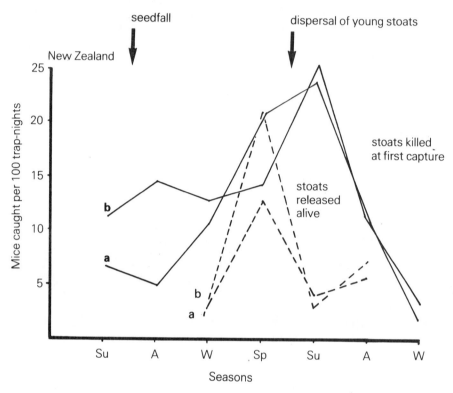

on an island can have a substantial impact, but this is a special case not typical of temperate habitats in general, and discussion of it is deferred to Chapter 13.

WEASELS AND OTHER PREDATORS COMPARED

In many ways, predation by weasels on small rodents is not quite the same process as that by wolves on deer, and some ideas developed from studies of larger carnivores cannot be applied to weasels. For example, wolves have to select the old, the sick, the disabled and the temporarily disadvantaged deer because the risk of injury in attack is very real. Over the long term the wolves tend to cull the unfit deer from the population. But the average mouse is no match for most weasels, so there is less need for predation by weasels to be selective. As Pearson (1985) put it, weasels do not wait until the meadows are overflowing with insecure or maladjusted voles; they can kill almost any vole with ease, and find them efficiently even when their populations are low. It is true that a 40 g female least weasel approaching a 60 g *Microtus* has to be cautious (R.A.Powell, personal communication), and so does any weasel attacking a well-grown rabbit, but on average the weasels can kill rodents more easily than wolves can kill deer. Both weasels and wolves try to get their living in the easiest way they can, but the weasel's advantage makes a difference to the results.

Other ideas on predation developed from studies of invertebrates are not applicable, either. Both invertebrate predators and their prey have a very short time between generations, and the rate of increase of populations of invertebrate predators is much closer to that of their prey than is that of any of the weasels (see Chapter 13).

Finally, the old idea of the 'balance of nature', of predators and prey living in a dynamic balance, is irrelevant to weasels. Weasel populations are seldom stable, for reasons explored in Chapter 10, and this ensures that no balance can be established, let alone maintained. Besides, the concept of the balance of nature is very difficult to define, and few ecologists now believe that any such balance exists.

8 Adjustable living spaces

Romantic poets who speak of the freedom of a wild animal or bird generally mean freedom from captivity in a cage. But there are other sorts of captivity, and some are worse (or at any rate, sooner fatal) than life in a cage. Few wild animals are free of the daily task of searching for food, and even fewer are free in the sense of being able to wander about wherever they like. Small animals such as weasels also have to keep constantly alert for danger, both from visible enemies and from more subtle hazards such as loss of body heat in winter.

A weasel may be safe from all these in its den, but it cannot stay there indefinitely. Sooner or later it must venture out to hunt and, in season, to search for a mate. The hungrier it is, the more time it must spend searching for food; the colder it is, the more time it will try to spend conserving energy in its nest. Least weasels and stoats living under the Arctic snows have to balance the opposite necessities of spending time outside hunting and inside keeping warm. In general, all weasels conduct their hunting and social affairs in the least possible space and time; for them, sleep is a positive defence against the twin enemies of cold and larger predators (Buckingham, 1979). Robitaille and Baron (1987) found a strong correlation between air temperature and the amount of time that stoats spent outside. Weasels range no further and hunt no longer than they have to, and as soon as their needs are fulfilled they return to one of their dens. Records of weasel home ranges and activity at different times and in different places therefore show enormous variation.

METHODS AND PROBLEMS OF DETERMINING HOME RANGES

The first requirement of field ecology is that one must be able to follow the movements of known individuals. Common weasels do have individually distinct belly patterns (Figure 2.4), but these cannot be distinguished except in the hand. The sight of a weasel in the wild is, though not all that uncommon, never close enough to read an eartag number. Weasels have few regular habits which offer an observer a sure ambush, and their nests are hard to find in most habitats. Snow-tracking (Plate 8), can give a lot of information without disturbing the animals at all, but it is not possible in mild climates, and has the disadvantage that there is no proof of which weasel made a given set of tracks. If tracks are found in the same area day after day, it is a fair bet that they were made by the same animal; but that is not the same as the certainty of identification offered by an eartag, especially since successive residents on the same ground tend to use the same dens and runways (Musgrove, 1951). The traditional way to observe weasels year-round in temperate habitats is indirectly, by catching them in live traps, marking them, and then releasing them in the hope of collecting a series of new location records.

Unfortunately, live-trapping weasels is often unrewarding, at any rate in certain places and in some years. To begin with, while one may fairly assume that where a weasel has been caught it must at least be present, the reverse is certainly not true. Weasels are able to learn to avoid traps; Cahn (1936) had a battle of wits with a stoat, which learnt from a single experience to avoid a further 32 carefully sited traps. Worse, weasels vary a great deal in the way they react to traps. Resident individuals, confident of winning any encounter with an intruder, tend to be bolder and less shy of traps than the non-residents, which are insecure and continually on the defensive. Also, females are more difficult to catch than males. A live-trapping study will therefore not sample the local population very accurately; while the male residents are being trapped day after day, and the female residents occasionally, many non-residents will pass through the area unseen and uncounted. Moreover, trapping is not an ideal method of working out the home ranges of any animals, because a resident held in a trap is unable to continue its normal life until it is released, usually many hours later.

There are two other methods of observing live weasels in the field, using different kinds of tracking. Both depend on trapping to start with, but once a weasel has been equipped with an identifying mark it is possible to follow it without interfering with its movements.

The simplest method is to give it a unique footprint by removing a toe (under anaesthetic, of course), and then setting out large numbers of tracking tunnels. In the system described by King and Edgar (1977), each tunnel has a pad of 'ink' and two papers sprayed with a chemical that reacts with the 'ink' to produce an indelible blue dye. Weasels find well-set tunnels irresistible, and this method can give a lot of records for each marked animal in a short time. On the other hand, the weasels will be recorded only in the places where the investigator has set tunnels.

A better method is radio-tracking, which is now a very sophisticated science in its own right, and has been applied to stoats in Sweden by Erlinge (1977a, 1979a) and Sandell (1986), to Irish stoats by Sleeman (1987), and to both stoats and common weasels in Scotland by Pounds (1981). It gives a much more accurate picture of the movements and activity of individual animals, although it is still important to be able to trap them whenever the transmitter is lost or the battery runs down. There can be problems in getting the transmitter collars to stay on for at least the life of the battery (average nine days for Erlinge, 1977a). The stoats dislike the collars and scratch at them at first; the weight (6–10 g) and bulk of the transmitter must be maddening for such a lithe animal. In time they seem to accept them, though it is not clear whether they are still able to hunt in all the usual confined spaces and behave completely normally.

Live-trapping takes some skill and a lot of luck. Traps have to be set in the kinds of places weasels are likely to visit (in stone walls and hedgerows, under stacks of wood or heaps of stones, in the roots of old trees, on fallen logs, alongside streams), and one soon gets an eye for suitable sites (Figure 8.1a,b). The trap I used has a treadle which can be weighted (Figure 8.1c,d), so that only animals heavier than, say, 30g can be caught. Mice and voles are much more numerous than weasels and as fond of exploring holes, so unselective wooden traps will often be blocked against weasels and damaged by gnawing. A larger trap suitable for stoats can be hand made from the plans given by King and Edgar (1977). Wire cage traps are cruel: they are too draughty to keep an active weasel warm during its enforced stay, and mortality in them is high. The captured weasels bite and pull at the wire, breaking their teeth and skinning their noses. Weasels really need the darkness and privacy afforded by wooden box-traps, and these should always be used even though they are heavier and less convenient for the trapper to handle.

In some habitats, it is so easy to put traps in places where weasels must find them (e.g. in stone wall country and along ditches and hedgerows), that results can be gained even if the traps are never baited, although baited traps tend to catch more often (King and Edgar, 1977). In woodland the sites have to be constructed more or less artificially, and well baited in order to attract a weasel's attention. In some countries (but not in Britain), traps can be baited with a live mouse, which both lures in the weasel and provides a fresh meal while it is waiting to be released (Erlinge, 1974). If traps are left locked open between trapping sessions, the weasels get used to being able to go in and out, and sometimes use them as temporary dens or foodstores; the residents are caught as soon as the traps are set, and some non-residents are caught that would otherwise have escaped attention altogether.

I believe (others differ) that live-trapped weasels are best handled under anaesthetic ether (Lockie and Day, 1963; Plate 12). It is easy to use, minimises both the fright to the animal and the risk of bitten fingers for the trapper, and simplifies the necessary recording procedures and the insertion of eartags (Figure 8.2). Resident animals do not seem to be put off from returning by the experience of being anaesthetised.

The simplest method of presenting the results of a trapping study is to map the trap sites visited by each individual, and then to join the outermost records. The area to be measured is that of the mimimum convex polygon that includes every trap visited, whether or not it also includes other traps not visited. This method grossly oversimplifies the real picture, since an animal's range is not merely two-dimensional. Weasels of all species commonly climb trees, and use some parts of their ranges much more often than other parts. Unfortunately, even a relatively successful live-trapping or radio-tracking study of weasels seldom provides enough information to allow the observer to do more than make a simple map.

Figure 8.1. Top and centre: Whitlock live-traps set out in woodland habitat (from King 1973). Bottom right and left: The tip-up mechanism of the Whitlock trap, demonstrated by a tame weasel (King, unpubl.).

Figure 8.2. Attaching a tag onto the ear of an anaesthetised stoat (photo courtesy C.D.MacMillan).

HOME RANGE IN COMMON WEASELS

The first live-trapping study of the home ranges and social organisation of weasels in Britain was done in a young pine plantation in the Carron Valley, Stirlingshire, by Lockie (1966). The trees were fenced off from stock, so the grass was rank and full of field voles. On his 32 ha study area (surrounded by about 800 ha of similar plantations), Lockie found ten male weasels, each jealously guarding a plot of 1–5 hectares (Table 8.1; Figure 8.3). Transient males (at least 20) passed through all year round, especially in late summer and again in early spring. These were usually caught only once; occasionally one would settle for a while, but its movements were much restricted, often to only one trap. The three resident females lived on much smaller areas (each was caught repeatedly in only one trap), and, unlike the males, they had no contact with each other; another six transient females were only ever caught once. The males defended their territories against each other, whereas the females had to defend themselves and their nests against the male owner of the territory on which they lived. This pattern is quite typical of weasels in general (Powell, 1979).

Lockie did not witness the setting up of the organisation of territories he found when his study began in November 1960. It remained stable until November 1961, but then the whole system broke down. Some of the residents died and others disappeared, and those that were left seemed to lose contact with each other. Over the next two years, to the end of 1963, enough common weasels entered the area to populate it, as it had been in 1961, ten times over, but there were never more than two there at one time, and the system of contiguous territories was never re-established. By the following May, the numbers of field voles were down to 44/ha, and the obvious conclusion is that the weasels dispersed in response to the lack of prey. But in fact the system broke down whilst the voles were still very abundant (almost 300/ha), and at a time when weasels are normally settled onto steady home ranges for the winter. Lockie concluded that there has to be some minimum number of weasels all present at the same time before a territorial system can be established. But this suggestion has been invalidated by later studies showing that stable ranges can be held by isolated weasels in no contact with neighbours. Meanwhile, there is no other explanation of Lockie's observation.

I began to work on the weasels of Wytham Wood in early 1968. Lockie's was the only previous study that had worked, so of course I copied his approach. But the situation in Wytham was quite different. Wytham was deciduous woodland, not open grassland, and the only small rodents common within its boundaries were wood mice and bank voles, whose combined density was always very much less than that of the teeming field voles of the Carron Valley. In the first six months of trapping in Marley Wood, the 27 ha patch of Wytham I had chosen, I caught only five weasels, one of them three times. But help came just in time. While I, in some depression, had taken myself off for a break in August 1968, the Wytham gamekeeper borrowed some of my traps and set them on my study area. When I returned, he informed me that he had caught four weasels in a week (and let them go, unmarked) so why was I having trouble? He had applied the old gamekeeper's trick of tipping the guts of a rabbit into a polythene bag, stirring the mess around with a stick, and wiping the fragrant aroma on the entrances of the traps. I wasted no further time before applying the same method, and by the time the field work part of the study ended, in June 1970, I had caught 37 common weasels, a total of 347 times.

Only four males lived in the wood at any one time, each occupying at least 7–15 hectares. Of the four, only one or two lived entirely in the wood, and the rest had part of their ranges outside. The females always had much smaller home ranges than did males; the four I managed to observe never used more than 1–4 hectares (Figure 8.3). Adjacent to the wood on one side was a young plantation, full of rank grass and field voles, rather like the Carron Valley. Some of the resident weasels with small ranges on the edge of the wood spent a lot of time hunting field voles in the plantation. I also found that there usually were weasels outside the wood, in the plantation and in the fields on the other side, but none of them ever visited the wood, and conversely, few of the residents were ever caught far from the woodland boundary. When a resident died, his home range was either shared out between the nearest neighbours, or a new weasel came in from outside. Conversely, if a resident had no neighbours, he might extend his ground if opportunity allowed. The resident animals were very well aware of their neighbours, and adjusted their behaviour accordingly. Excursions onto a neighbour's ground seemed to be carefully timed to coincide with his absence.

I always set the traps every third week, from Monday afternoon to Friday morning, visiting them morning and evening every day and

Table 8.1 Some representative estimates of weasel home ranges

Species	Country, years	Habitat	Sex	Area (ha)	Reference
Common weasel	Scotland, 1960–3	Young plantation	M F	1–5 <1	Lockie, 1966
	England, 1968–70	Deciduous wood	M F	7–15 1–4	King, 1975a
	Scotland, 1977–9	Farmland	M F	2.4 1.2	Pounds, 1981[1]
Least weasel	Iowa, 1925–57	Farmland	M+F	4–10	Polder, 1968
	Finland, 1952–58	Mixed	M F	0.6–3.0 0.2–2.1	Nyholm, 1959
Stoat	Scotland, 1977–79	Farmland	M F	254 114	Pounds, 1981
	Sweden, 1973–82	Pasture and marshes	M F	8–13 2–7	Erlinge 1977a[2]
	Ontario, 1973–5	Mixed	M F	20–25 10–15	Simms 1979a
	Switzerland, 1977–80	Alpine	M F	8–40 2–7	Debrot & Mermod, 1983
	Finland, 1952–8	Mixed	M F	29–40 4–17	Nyholm, 1959
	Russia, 1970–1	Meadows, scrub Forest	M+F M+F	11–69 120–124	Vaisfeld, 1972
Irish stoat	Fota I., Cork, 1985	Mixed	F M	2–22 11	Sleeman, 1987
Longtail	Michigan, 1940	Mixed	M+F	32–160	Quick, 1944
	Colorado, 1941–6	Mixed	M+F	80–120	Quick, 1951
	Kentucky, 1970–5	Farmland	M	6–24	DeVan, 1982
	Indiana, 1985	Mixed	F	41	Vispo, pers. comm.

[1] In the same area in 1971–3, Moors (1974) estimated male ranges of 9–16 ha in winter, 10–25 in summer, and female ranges of c.7 ha, but Moors allowed a 'corridor' along fencelines of 40 m, whereas Pounds allowed 10 m.

[2] Winter estimate; in spring and summer male stoats range much more widely, over areas measured at 105–2644 ha (Erlinge & Sandell, 1986)

Figure 8.3. The patterns of winter home ranges of male common weasels (a) at high density in a young plantation in Scotland, April–October 1961 (Lockie, 1966), and (b) at low density in deciduous woodland in England, January–February 1969 (King, 1975a). Both sets of data plotted by the simple but debatable method of joining the outermost traps visited by each animal.

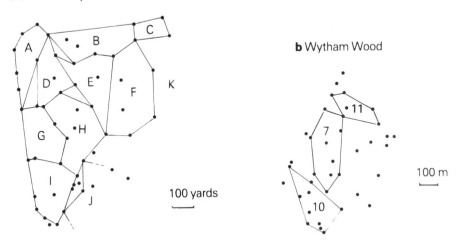

a Carron Valley

b Wytham Wood

100 yards

100 m

renewing the rabbit-gut scent as I passed each evening. I established this procedure in the belief that weasels are more active at night than by day. When I came to work out the results I was surprised to find that, at least in those animals at that time, the reverse was true. Although I did find a captured weasel more often in the morning (190 times) than in the evening (144), it took twice as many night-time as daylight hours before one of the traps caught a weasel, even though the bait on the traps was fresher then. Common weasels can see just as well by day as by night, and it would not be surprising if the Wytham weasels tended to avoid attracting the attention of tawny owls.

A resident common weasel might shift his range to another part of the wood, but when one disappeared it was usually because he had died, often after a substantial loss of weight. On average in Wytham, the resident males held their ranges for only about seven months. Since they leave the family group when they reach independence at about 3 months, this means that most of them lived only about a year or less, and a different set of residents was observed each year. Surprisingly, the weasels did not live any longer in the protection of Wytham (a reserve) than did those I collected from game estates, and this I put down to the poor food supplies in the wood. Small predators do not live off the fat of the land; for most of the time, life is more chancy for them than for their prey.

The common weasels in Wytham often used to travel along mole runs (Figure 8.4). One I released from a trap darted off and dived straight down a not very obvious mole hole with every sign of confidence and familiarity. That might have been a case of 'any port in a storm'; but in fact I had other, more convincing evidence that the Wytham weasels regularly ran along mole's runways and borrowed their nests. Among the fleas which I collected from the weasels while they were unconscious in

Figure 8.4. Common and least weasels seldom eat moles, but they frequently use mole-runs, and borrow the large and comfortable nests made by moles.

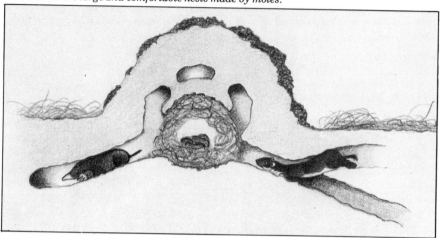

my hand were two species specific to moles and rare on all other small mammals (Table 11.6). The Wytham weasels very seldom ate moles, so they could have picked up these fleas only in mole nests and runways. Gamekeepers know well that common weasels can use mole runs to get into a rearing pen, and weasels are sometimes caught in traps set for moles.

In 1970, Moors (1974) decided to work on common weasels for his doctorate studies at Aberdeen, and in fact he was able to use some of the same live traps that I had just finished with only a few months before. He set them in the stone walls and fencelines around the pasture and arable fields of Miekle Tarty Farm, near the university field station at Newburgh. He found that the weasels lived mainly in the stone walls and surrounding long grass, and seldom ventured into the open fields. They could move very rapidly from one end of their ground to the other, often covering more than one kilometre in an hour. Counting only the used area (taken as a strip extending to 20 m on either side of the field edges, i.e., a 40 m corridor along each wall or fenceline), that is about the equivalent of an area of 9–16 hectares per male in winter, and about 10–25 hectares in summer. As before, the few females caught had smaller ranges, averaging only about 7 hectares (Table 8.1).

The difference in area estimates for summer and winter is due to an apparently regular seasonal reorganisation of home ranges. In both winters the male's territories were stable, and each animal stayed within his own area, but in spring of both years this settled pattern was totally disrupted. By April none of the known overwintered males was caught only on his old territory; many had disappeared and the rest were wandering widely. Things settled down again in late summer, when a new crop of juveniles appeared and contended for territories with the surviving adults.

Before Moors had finished his field work, Erlinge (1974) began a new study in a mixed-age coniferous and deciduous alder/oak woodland in southern Sweden. There was a rich field layer in all but the oldest spruce woodland, where the trees had grown thick enough to shade out the grass, and stone walls to provide the weasel's favourite refuges. Field

112

voles were common in the grass between the youngest spruce trees, and wood mice and bank voles in the alder/oak woodland, but there were very few small rodents at all in the oldest plantation.

As expected, the resident common weasels lived where there were most small mammals to hunt. When the study began, there were three resident males and two resident, breeding females, all in the grassiest areas; the alder wood was visited occasionally, but only by non-residents passing through, and no weasel was ever caught among the oldest spruces. The residents seemed content to remain on their chosen territories, although there were large areas of similar habitat all around each one, apparently vacant; four young and three adult males visited but did not settle. This arrangement persisted over the winter, and then, in spring, the resident males began to range further, covering larger areas and seldom staying in one place for long. In the following autumn, the stable territorial system was re-established, with five resident males, including only one that had been present when the study began. As before, the residents settled in the grassy areas and ignored the closed-canopy spruce woodland; but no breeding females, and fewer non-resident males, were caught in the second autumn. Erlinge does not say how large the males' territories were at any time, but mentions that the females' movements, even in spring, were 'less extensive . . . one female was trapped 29 times in March and April over an area of about 1.5 ha'.

The most recent study of home range in common weasels is one of the few to have applied the difficult technology of radiotelemetry to weasels. Pounds (1981) began his doctorate studies at Aberdeen in 1977, based at the same field station where Moors had struggled to make sense of weasel biology only a few years before. Pounds had the advantage of having many basic problems already solved; the techniques of live-trapping and of maintaining weasels in captivity were by then almost routine, and he also had a fair idea of the distribution and diet of the local weasels from Moors' work. So he was free to go beyond simple descriptive observation and start answering the really interesting questions which previous workers could only ask.

In the winters of 1977–78 and 1978–79, Pounds fitted seven male and two female common weasels with radios, and tracked each one for up to 28 days. As expected, they all used the stone walls and fencelines around the fields, and each had 2–5 dens and 3–10 daytime resting places scattered along its regular routes. Each had several favourite hunting areas, and would stay in one for a while and then set off on an apparently purposeful straight-line excursion to another one. The weasels could be active at any time, but the longer trips were undertaken more often by day than by night. Some of the hunting areas were exclusive, and others were shared, although not at the same time. Mostly they preferred to hunt along field margins or in rough grassland, avoiding the open fields and the scanty cover of wire fences. Only one male was seen hunting in an open turnip field, and that was during the harvest; he ran along the rows, pouncing on the small rodents disturbed by the workers.

The total areas calculated for the winter home ranges of these common weasels were very large; those of the seven males averaged 34 ha, and those of the two females, 38 and 12 ha. But the 'exploitable ranges', i.e., excluding the generally unused open fields, were 2.4 ha for males and 1.2

ha for females. The difference between the figures given by Moors and by Pounds for weasels observed in the same area only a few years apart is due to the difficulty of deciding how large a boundary strip to allow along the field edges (Table 8.1). Pounds confirmed much of what previous studies had already shown, from the clumsier method of live-trapping — that females occupy smaller areas, that weasels are capable of travelling surprising distances in a short time, and that they avoid each other if they can but are quick to replace each other in possession of favourable ground.

HOME RANGE IN LEAST WEASELS

The few studies of the home ranges of least weasels have all been done by snow-tracking. Snow makes live-trapping hazardous and tracking easy; an experienced and skilful tracker can read whole stories from snow.

Over a 13-day period from 20 December 1939, Polderboer (1942) recorded weasel tracks on his farm in Iowa. He found the trails and dens of four least weasels, and calculated that each occupied an area of less than one hectare. The weasels lived in the fencerows and slept in nests of grass and maize husks, originally made by mice, entered through burrows of 2.5 cm or less in diameter. Polderboer confirmed the identity of the animals making the tracks by trapping each one at its den in a steel trap. None of the dens was lined with fur or had a latrine nearby, which suggests that the weasels were not long-term residents, and that their real home ranges were actually larger than one hectare. Nevertheless, this figure entered the literature, at a time when hardly anything else was known about the ecology of least weasels, and on one occasion was used to calculate the average population density of least weasels, with comic results (see Chapter 7). A later estimate of the ranges of least weasels on winter-ploughed fields was 4–10 ha (Table 8.1). Their dens were concealed under the furrows, and they pursued mice and voles through the small spaces between the turf or stubble sods.

In Finland in the winters of 1952–8, Nyholm (1959) systematically observed the tracks left by least weasels in snow-covered fields and copses, and along the banks of rivers and lakes. He reckoned that least weasels ranged over less than 3 ha, although he remarked that it was difficult to determine the ranges exactly, because the weasels moved about so much under the snow. But, naturally, much depends on how hard it is to find food. In the Kola Peninsula, in the far north of European USSR, voles and least weasels were numerous in the summer of 1938. The voles crashed to very low numbers in the following autumn, and least weasels tracked during the winter of 1938–9 were hunting over extended home ranges of up to 10 ha (Nasimovich, 1949).

HOME RANGE IN STOATS

Probably more field work has been done on stoats than on any of the other small mustelids. The pioneering studies were all done by snow-tracking. Nyholm (1959) followed one stoat around its home range, which was divided into several separate hunting areas, visited in turn. Each area had at least one den or refuge, usually in a barn or a pile of logs, or in the banks of ditches. He tracked many other stoats as well, and calculated the home ranges of 63 of them (Table 8.1). They usually travelled about 500 m in a night; one ran 1.8 km within its own territory, and another, presumably a non-resident, almost 6 km.

Later Russian work also made use of snow-tracking. Vaisfeld (1972) mapped the home ranges of stoats in the provinces of Arkhangel and Kirov, in the very far north of European USSR. In the flat flood-plains of the great northern rivers, the stoat's trails were concentrated around patches of scrub. Every home range (varying from 21 to 69 ha) had at least some scrub cover; no stoats lived out in the open meadows. In some areas, the scrub had been cleared so as to extend the meadows, and there were windrows of bulldozed scrub piled up for burning. These windrows provided even better cover and food for small mammals than the natural scrub, so were greatly favoured by the stoats. At the beginning of the winter of 1970–1, 18 stoats lived on 80 ha of this habitat (i.e., averaging 1 per 4 ha). Within a few months, 15 of them had been caught by hunters. The three that remained lived in one corner, on home ranges of 11,13 and 17 ha — not so as to avoid the hunters, but because human disturbance (the piling up of the scrub) had so increased the prey resources of that area.

Erlinge (1977a) observed the home ranges of stoats in southern Sweden, at first by live-trapping, and later by radio-tracking. The main study area was a 4,000 ha expanse of pasture, wet meadows and marshes, crossed by streams and stone walls. The stoats were concentrated in the most favourable spots, in the marshes and along the stone walls where small mammals were most abundant. There were four main groups of residents, separated from each other by unoccupied open fields; stoats from one group seldom crossed over to visit another except in spring. Each group included several adult males and females plus a larger number of juveniles of both sexes. Surveys during snowy periods confirmed that the trap captures reflected the real distribution of the animals.

Home ranges were set up in late summer, as the year's crop of juveniles entered the population and sought to establish themselves for the winter. Males and females lived separately, with little contact; the females sometimes used part of an adult male's range, but avoided him whenever possible, while the juveniles kept well clear of his area altogether. The females' ranges were generally well spread out and they had little to do with each other. They did patrol their ranges, and on one occasion two happened to be at a common boundary at the same time, but they got no closer than 60 m before moving away in opposite directions. Females generally spent a lot of time in deep rodent tunnels (Erlinge, 1977b). Males were more often in at least indirect contact with their neighbours. Two males whose ranges overlapped spent a lot of time in the boundary zone. There were never any signs of fighting or chasing or other direct confrontations, but the boundary was obviously set by social contacts between the two males. Adult males whose ranges included or overlapped those of one or more females confidently moved around wherever they pleased, since they were always dominant over the females — except, perhaps, when a male visited a female's den. Then she would react with a defensive hiss or threat call, and he would retreat.

All the resident stoats tended to hunt over some parts of their ranges more than others, usually in short bursts of 10–45 minutes separated by longer periods (3–5 hours) of rest. The central area was visited almost every day, and the rest every few days. Parts of the area were ignored altogether. The stoats obviously concentrated on the places where rodents were most abundant, but they had to cover more ground, and spend more time hunting, when rodents were scarce. They tended to be nocturnal in winter and diurnal in summer, and this change was connected with a pronounced seasonal reorganisation of stoat society.

In spring the settled system of winter ranges gradually broke down, just as it does in common weasels. Some males disappeared, and others set off on long excursions (up to 5–6 km) or stayed at home but moved about far more actively than before (Sandell, 1986). It was mainly the dominant males that left their territories and wandered widely in spring, whereas the lower-ranked males stayed put. Erlinge and Sandell (1986) suggest that the reason for this change in behaviour is that the decisive resource for males in early summer, receptive females, is more widely dispersed and less predictable and defensible than the decisive resource during the winter, usually food. The dominant males can probably be sure of gaining access to any females they can find (Erlinge, 1977c), so they can score the most matings by searching the largest possible area. But the receptive period of the females is very short, and the wanderer may well turn up at the wrong time. The lower-ranking males cannot dispute the possession of a female if it comes to a fight, but by staying close to a female's den they could be on the spot at the right moment. Females are also more diurnal in summer (Debrot et al, 1985), but they make the change later than males because in spring they spend more time in their nests, saving energy for pregnancy. The pronounced differences in activity patterns of males and females in spring cause strong seasonal swings in the sex ratio of stoats caught in traps.

Large stoats, such as those in Scotland, can range over enormous areas, which are very hard to document. Pounds radio-tracked a single male over 254 ha in ten days, and three females averaged 114 ha. Lockie's 32 ha study area was too small to host more than one male stoat, and the 20 ha it regularly visited was obviously not the whole of its home ground. At the other extreme, the smaller stoats of Ontario and Switzerland have ranges nearer those of common weasels, which are possible to measure by live-trapping (Table 8.1).

HOME RANGE IN LONGTAILED WEASELS

Polderboer et al (1941) found the trails and dens of four longtailed weasels on an Iowa farm. They reckoned that, at that time, each longtail seldom travelled more than 100 m in any direction from its primary den, so their trails rarely crossed. Each had access to as many as five or six food caches within this distance. Polderboer dug out the dens, and found layers of rodent fur, skins and skulls, and heaps of scats — all the signs of an established resident weasel. But he could not make accurate estimates of the longtails' home ranges, and the assumption of a radius of activity of only 100 m seems rather low for such energetic animals.

On 260 ha of farmland near Ann Arbor, Michigan, Quick (1944) mapped 52 trails made by four longtails in early 1940. Each weasel had a primary den, and hunted within about 300–600 m of it; the average length of the 52 trails mapped was 2 km, ranging from 20 m to 5.5 km. The longtails ventured out even when it was very cold (including once when it was −20°C), but not every night; they would sometimes stay in their dens for days. Quick calculated the areas of their home ranges assuming they were roughly circular and centred on the primary den (Table 8.1). The ranges overlapped, but the four rarely crossed trails on the same day. When they did meet, each weasel took care to leave its mark. Once, two trails met at a post on a fence corner; each weasel deposited a scat (Figure 8.5) and then went its separate way. A month later, the trails met again at the same post, and then ran along the fence together for about 20 m. Unfortunately, snow-tracking does not show whether the animals that made crossed trails actually met, nor what sex they were.

Quick (1951) also snow-tracked longtailed weasels in Colorado, and found rather similar home ranges (Table 8.1). Glover (1942) snow-tracked longtails in Pennsylvania, and found that, in a single night's excursion, 11 males ventured out 18–773 m, average 215 m, from their dens, and 10 females, 6–433 m, average 105 m. There is hardly any other information available on longtails, except a passing reference by Svendsen (1982) to unpublished data showing that the average home range size in longtails is 12–16 ha. But there have been at least two attempts to observe them by radio-tracking.

DeVan (1982) trapped seven male longtails in northern Kentucky (Table 8.1). One of them was trapped on two occasions, 18 months apart; this male, both times, plus one other male, was also radio-tracked. The weasels hunted through the brushy overgrown vegetation along creeks and in patches of woodland, and seldom crossed the open fields. Each had at least one well-hidden den. One of the radio-tracked males was observed over two weeks in January–February 1975. He used to come out of his den, on the bank of a dry creek, about two hours after sundown, and hunt up and down the creek for about 75 m each way, often revisiting the den for 2–10 minutes at a time during his active period of about 5 hours. The other radio-tracked male was followed over three months from November 1974. He once left his den and travelled to another den 850 m distant, robbing a baited trap on the way; thus well supplied, he then stayed in the second den for the whole of the next day. But occasionally the weasel can have the last laugh. One, tracked to a burrow in an overgrown field, apparently stayed there without moving for three days. DeVan grew suspicious, and finally dug out the burrow. In a grassy vole nest at the blind end he found a few drops of blood, some vole fur, and the transmitter; but the weasel had gone.

DeVan caught only males; the only other longtail I know to have been radio-tracked was a 133 g female. Conrad Vispo (personal communication) followed her for almost two months in October and November 1985 (a total of 348 tracking hours), in a nature reserve in Indiana (Table 8.1). She too was fairly strictly nocturnal. She nearly always came out at about sunset, around 5 pm, until about 9 pm when she returned to the den and rested until about 11 pm. After that she was active on and off for the rest of the night, especially during the last couple of hours before dawn. Unusually short excursions were often due to the weather; a heavy shower, or a passing cold front bringing a sudden drop in temperature, would drive her back to the shelter of one of her dens. During the two months she was located at seven different dens, all below ground and most in remnant patches of oak woodland.

SCENT COMMUNICATION

Weasels are solitary animals for most of the year, but that does not mean that they are totally non-sociable. Weasels have to be well aware of their neighbours, even if only to avoid them. They keep in touch with each other by a well-developed system of scent communication — an efficient mechanism for small animals living on large home ranges covered with thick vegetation. Under snow the conditions are ideal for scent communication — cool, dark, windless, humid and quiet.

Hidden under the tail of a weasel is a pair of large, muscular sacs, in which is stored a substantial quantity (up to 100 ml in male stoats) of musk, a thick, rather oily yellowish substance with a powerful and unpleasant smell. The musk is produced in modified skin glands, which are grouped together at one end of the sac and empty into it. Musk is a complex substance, but the important components are lipophilic compounds of low molecular weight, several containing sulphur (Brinck *et al*, 1983). When the musk is exposed to the air, it is metabolised by bacteria into various carboxylic acids, perhaps in different combinations according to which bacteria are present.

Voluntary muscles control both the openings of the glands and the walls of the sac, so a weasel is able to produce musk at will. Normally, only a little is secreted at a time, but a severely frightened weasel is able to expel the entire contents of the anal sac at once — the famous 'stink-bomb' well known to careless trappers. Perhaps the effective defence system of the skunk evolved from such a beginning.

All mustelids have a system of anal glands, constructed slightly differently in each genus. The anatomy of the scent glands gets progressively more complex in a series from *Meles*, through *Lutra* and *Martes* to *Mustela*, which seems to be the most advanced of all (Stubbe, 1970, 1972). Weasels also have smaller glands in the skin of the body, especially along the belly and flanks, and on the cheeks.

Weasels regularly mark their home ranges by depositing scent from these glands in strategic places. Like most carnivores, they also make use of two other strongly scented substances, scats and urine. For example, in the course of travelling around his home range, a typical male would seldom pass a place where he has previously found or deposited a scat without visiting it again, carefully sniffing, and then turning and depositing a new one — often with an expression of fierce concentration (Figure 8.5). Scats may be found singly along trails, sometimes in different stages of weathering, suggesting regular marking of familiar routes; they are obviously powerfully attractive to any weasel using the same path, because they make good bait in live-traps (Rust, 1968).

The various forms of marking behaviour have been closely observed in captive Swedish stoats by Erlinge and his colleagues (Erlinge *et al* (1982). Besides depositing scats, stoats make use of two main kinds of body scent, produced in the anal glands and in the smaller skin glands, and spread around by special behaviour patterns called 'anal drag' and 'body rubbing'. A stoat performing anal drag presses the anal area to the ground, with his tail raised, and wriggles forward, pulling himself along

Figure 8.5. Scats are objects of great interest and usefulness to weasels, and are carefully placed in strategic positions around a resident's home range.

with his forelegs. Females do it too, and also young as soon as they begin to move about outside the nest. The idea is to permeate the whole of his home area with his own scent, to mark new objects encountered and to cover over the marks made by other stoats. They will do it when they are alone, and at any time of day.

Body rubbing, by contrast, is used as a threat signal, especially by a dominant of either sex during an aggressive encounter with a subordinate. The dominant vigorously stretches himself out along logs or stones, scraping the scent from his cheeks and sides against them (Figure 8.6). He does the same thing when he deposits a kill in a cache or when he takes over a den formerly occupied by another stoat. The message is definitely a belligerent one, rather than the mere labelling of property.

It seems, from watching the reactions of one weasel to marks made by another, and the way that weasels use these cues to space themselves out with minimum open conflict, that the scents of each are not only individually distinguishable, but also very informative. For example, a subordinate stoat faced with the scents left by a body-rubbing dominant reacts with obvious fear. It shows various signs of uneasiness and anxiety; it gives the little trilling call which imitates the cries made by juveniles and which would mollify the aggressive reactions of the dominant if it were still within earshot; and it will search around for a way to escape. By contrast, a dominant stoat will show no obvious reaction to the marks, apart from marking over them. Dominant individuals also set marks more often than subordinates, because they are more self-confident.

Figure 8.6. Resident weasels also deliberately rub their body scent on prominent objects around their home range, as a sign of ownership which is recognised and understood by intruders.

The world of a weasel is full of meaningful scents, which are just as informative in total darkness as in full sunshine, and whose message lasts longer than those of the fleeting visual images on which we rely. The chemical composition of the secretions produced in the scent marking glands of weasels can be displayed by gas chromatography. If scent marks really do convey important information between individual weasels in the wild, as field and behavioural observations imply, the chromatograms should show subtle differences between individuals, consistent over time in the same individual; and indeed, they do (Brinck *et al,* 1983).

The component molecules separate out according to their weights, and the patterns produced show distinct differences from one animal to the next. Better still, the differences reappear in successive samples from the same animal. The origin of the differences is uncertain. Perhaps the molecules of one animal's musk are structurally different from those of any other, or perhaps each animal has a unique combination of bacteria producing a different set of metabolites of musk (Gorman, 1976). Either way, it seems likely that, to a stoat, scents are as unique as faces are to us. Like faces, scent marks give one weasel a lot of useful information about another — not only its sex, identity, social status, and breeding condition, but also the probable outcome of a confrontation. The advantage of scent marks is that they persist for some time, so that the owner of a home range is able to give out information to potential intruders in many places at once. The intruder, on the other hand, has the information on which to decide whether or not to risk an encounter with his unseen neighbour. Stoats can fight ferociously, and are well able to injure each other, so it is an advantage to a stranger to assess the likely outcome whilst escape is still possible. In fact, avoidance and retreat are much more common than all-out offence in deciding the local dominance hierarchy and distribution of individuals. But running battles do happen, especially in spring. Vernon-Betts (1967) gave a particularly vivid account:

During the last week in April I was driving down a lane when I saw two weasels fighting on the grass verge. I stopped the car within a few feet and watched them for several minutes fighting with the concentrated ferocity of a couple of bull terriers. After some time . . . one got his grip at the side of the neck and the other was trying to break loose. The break came and both animals darted behind the car out of my sight. I was about to get out when they reappeared on the road about 10 yards in front of me. I released the brake and free-wheeled after them as they conducted a running fight for more than 100 yards down the road . . . eventually we reached a hairpin bend and both animals went onto the verge opposite a kissing gate in the hedge. Through the gate I saw a hunting cat with ears pricked advancing on tiptoe; clearly it could hear the squeaks of the weasels but had not yet seen them. Suddenly the pursuer saw the cat and made a run for the hedge . . . The pursued ran for the gate and apparently straight into the jaws of the cat . . . When I reached the gate, only the weasel was to be seen, white belly up, paws in the air, a bright bead of blood behind one ear and apparently dead. I picked it up . . . It was an undoubted male, and the same size as its antagonist. I began to carry it back to the car. As I was passing through the gate I noticed its belly was pumping up and down; after a further two steps it gave a violent wriggle so that I dropped it. It hit the ground running and darted into the hedge where it immediately burrowed into a pile of dead leaves . . . Half an hour later I returned the same way, and, though I stirred the leaves with a stick, there was no sign of it.

This extraordinary incident illustrates not only a particularly vigorous territorial dispute between males in the breeding season, but also the so-called 'sham-dead' trick of weasels in response to immediate mortal danger. It may be, as some believe, a deliberate defensive ploy, but others interpret it as the effect of violent exertion on a brain already under pressure from parasitic worms (Figure 11.10).

When weasels are living at high density and have a lot of close neighbours, they do spend time patrolling their boundaries, and encounters between a resident and an intruder are more likely. For example, Lockie (1966) had already inferred, from the distribution of trapping records, that the resident common weasels he was observing were working to keep others off their 'own' ground. Then he actually saw it happening:

I . . . once [saw] a territory holder escort a transient from its territory . . . Both animals suddenly appeared running towards me, the chaser shrieking now and then. They paid no attention to me and passed close by. At the known boundary of the territory the owner broke off and returned into his territory where he was shortly after trapped and examined. The other animal kept running and disappeared from view a quarter of a mile down the track. I was unable to catch and examine the chased weasel, but since none of the known residents was missing I presumed it to be a transient. On another occasion I trapped a transient stoat which squealed as it came out of the anaesthetic . . . Immediately the presumed owner of the territory appeared racing towards me apparently to see what was happening . . .

Lockie recognised that such incidents were rare, and it is certainly in the weasels' interests to avoid them by use of more subtle means of communication.

The word 'territory' is appropriate for an exclusive, defended area, whereas it is better to use 'home range' when there is considerable overlap and tolerance between neighbours. Weasels seem to display all variations from one extreme to the other. I tend to call them home ranges, because it is not always possible to say to what degree each resident's ground is defended, and there is nearly always some degree of overlap between neighbours — indeed, there has to be a common zone where each can deposit scent marks for the other to find. Once established, resident animals patrol their ground more or less regularly, setting and renewing scent marks in the course of each hunting expedition. The only criterion that matters is that the resident has priority of use of the area.

The amount of effort a resident makes to evict intruders depends on whether or not the resources contained on his area are defensible. If they are widely scattered, too much energy would be required to maintain an exclusive area, and the chances would be high that the owner could not detect all intruders anyway. Males will therefore maintain strictly exclusive territories only where prey are concentrated, especially in winter when they are not interested in searching for females. In spring the same males may completely change their behaviour. Females seem to stick to familiar ground all the time, and their problem is not, or not only, to evict other females but to watch out for the males that use the same ground. They can be just as intolerant of each other as males, but meet less often.

THE HOW AND WHY OF HOME RANGES

How do weasels determine how big a home range they need, and why do they bother?

The size of the area a resident weasel hunts over depends on the density of the local small rodents. For example, male common weasels in the Carron Valley, at the time the field voles were very abundant (110–540/ha), did well on home ranges of only 1–5 ha; those at Wytham, where wood mice and bank voles were much scarcer (together only 21-39/ha), had to hunt over much larger areas and were still perpetually hungry (King, 1975a). When the density of these woodland rodents fell still lower, in 1977–80, the resident weasels simply disappeared. Those were the years an unlucky doctoral student, Hayward (1983), had chosen to repeat my study, in the same places and using the same techniques. During the twelve months after August 1978, despite intense effort, he caught no residents at all and only three non-residents, once each. He came to the wry conclusion that even established weasel populations are liable to local extinction when prey resources collapse. He was not the first to work out this important piece of information the hard way.

If prey density is the most important consideration deciding home range size, the weasel's own body size is probably the next one. Weasels often have to operate their energy budgets with rather little to spare, especially in winter, and their ability to cover a lot of ground increases as they get larger. By contrast, the smallest weasels are able to exploit small rodents most efficiently, and so can make a living on a small patch of ground on which a larger one, excluded from tunnels, would starve. The home range estimates compiled in Table 8.1 are influenced by a host of different variables, but there is still a general correlation between the size of the weasel and the area it occupies. Every study shows that the ranges of females are smaller than those of the males of the same species, measured at the same time and place. The ranges of common and least weasels are clearly smaller than those of stoats and longtails; the smaller local races of stoats (e.g. in Ontario) have the smallest ranges of that group.

Why do weasels bother to establish a home range and try, to varying degrees, to keep others out of it? There is no certain answer, but we can make a few suggestions. First, a reliable stock of prey is a weasel's security, for overwinter survival and for future breeding success. A female needs a certain minimum density of voles available before she can successfully rear a litter, perhaps about 10–15 rodents per ha in common weasels (see Chapter 10). Since rodents are not evenly spread throughout all parts of any habitat, a weasel will obviously stick to a good area when it finds one. The supply of rodents is not reliable for long, but then, most weasels do not live for long. Second, weasels are vulnerable to larger predators, and the best defence against attack is to have an intimate knowledge of one's own ground, the position of every refuge, and the safest, quickest way to get to it. Third, energy conservation is all-important to weasels in winter, which means that there is a high premium on efficient hunting (see Chapter 2). A weasel that knows exactly where to go to find a meal is more likely to be able to meet its needs and get back into its warm nest in the least possible time. As so often with weasels, the huge cost of living in a small, thin body affects almost everything they do.

9 Reproduction

Reproduction, and survival between reproductive seasons, can be taken as the two main aims in life for any animal. The details of the reproductive machine — the anatomy of the organs, the whole complicated process of the production and care of the young, and the extent to which this process can be adjusted to the prospects of success — are matters of intense importance to individual animals, and are always under the unrelenting scrutiny of natural selection. This chapter gives a simple description of the machinery; variations in its performance, which profoundly affect the population dynamics of weasels, will be taken up in Chapter 10.

THE REPRODUCTIVE ANATOMY OF WEASELS

The gonads of both males and females are quite simple, and look somewhat alike in all species of weasels. The testes are oval sacs within the furry scrotum. The coiled tube of the vas deferens leaves the epididymis, at the distal end of the testis, and ascends back into the body cavity again. The penis is stiffened by the baculum, a small rod-shaped bone attached to the pelvis by muscles at one end, which acts as a rigid support during copulation. The urethra fits within the groove on the underside of the baculum, shown in Figure 9.1. Normally the whole apparatus is hidden inside the body, and in living animals the baculum can only be felt through the skin along the midline from the small tuft of hair at the orifice to just forward of the testes. But when the baculum can be dissected out, as from carcasses, it becomes one of the most informative items of a weasel's anatomy.

There are two reasons for this. One is that the shape and size of the baculum are certain characteristics of the species (Figure 9.1), so an incomplete skeleton of a male can often be identified from the baculum alone. All are roughly the same in general design — they have a more or less straight shaft, with a curve at one end and a knob at the other. But the baculum in *nivalis* is relatively short and thick, and the distal curve is a distinct hook; in *erminea* and *frenata* it is longer and more slender, and the distal curve is more gentle and sometimes forked. The second reason is that, within one species, the baculum is a useful indicator of

Figure 9.1. The bacula of male weasels are diagnostic of both age and species (after Burt, 1960).

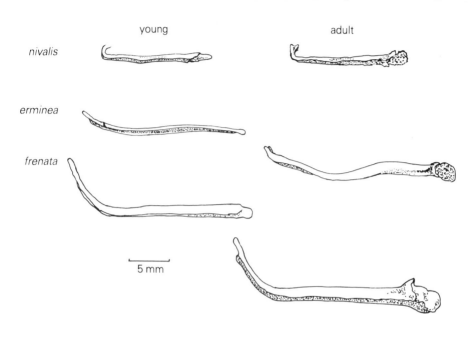

Figure 9.2. The weight of the baculum has long been a useful method of distinguishing subadults, but these bacula, all of known or part-known age, show that baculum weight continues to increase for several years, perhaps throughout life (data for New Zealand stoats from Grue and King, 1984).

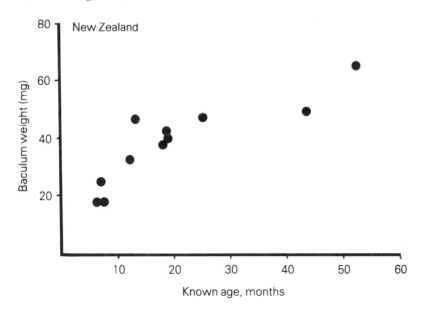

age. Wright (1950) showed, by a series of laboratory experiments, that the development of the baculum is controlled by androgens. The knob is characterisic only of adults; juveniles have only a thin shaft hardly broader at the end than along its length. In males castrated as juveniles, the knob did not develop at all. The essential role of androgens in this development was proven by the classic reverse experiment — castrated juvenile males treated with implants of testosterone propionate developed nearly normal knobs. In intact males, the knob first develops at puberty and continues to grow in size, and therefore in weight, for several years at least, and probably throughout life (Figure 9.2). Presumably the strengthening of the bone stimulated each breeding season by testosterone has a cumulative effect.

In stoats and longtails it is possible to define the minimum baculum weight beyond which a male can be classed as adult, although the actual threshold figure depends on general body weight. For example, in the small male stoats of northern Ireland (average body weight 233 g), the minimum baculum weight of adults was 30 mg (Fairley, 1971); in the larger males from Holland (284 g) it was 32 mg (van Soest and van Bree, 1970); in the large males from New Zealand (324 g) it was 38 mg (King and Moody, 1982). In the smaller subspecies of longtails the bacula are smaller than in the larger subspecies (Wright, 1947). In *erminea* and *frenata* the weight of the baculum clearly distinguishes the young males, but in *nivalis* there is a smooth transition from the juvenile form and weight (Table 9.1).

Table 9.1 Baculum weight in relation to age and species

	nivalis	*erminea*	*frenata*
Young	5–21mg	10–30mg	14–29mg
Adults	15–59mg	50–89mg	53–101mg
Locality	Britain	Britain	Montana
Reference	Hill, 1939	Deanesley, 1935	Wright, 1947

The uterus is a simple tube with two branches (usually called horns) joined together at the base and pressed against the dorsal side of the body cavity. The ovaries are quite conspicuous, round and flattened and rather yellowish, lodged in the free ends of the two uterine horns. The ova develop in follicles just under the surface of the ovary, and when they are ripe, the follicles burst and the ova are released to pass down the Fallopian tube to the uterus. Preserved uteri betray no sign of whether they are carrying young, or have done so before, until embryos become visible, as evenly spaced swellings, about three weeks before full term. The uterus does enlarge somewhat before oestrus, but this phase is short-lived and seldom observed. Oestrus is best detected externally, from the swollen, moist, doughnut-shaped vulva.

The mammary glands are set towards the rear of the long abdomen, and are invisible except during lactation. The nipples are tiny pimples hidden under the fur, both in juveniles and in adults until shortly before a litter is born. The nipples of adult females which have recently suckled

1. *Adult common weasel (C. Buckingham)*

2. *The ability of weasels to forage under the snow is the key to their survival in the far north (R.A. Powell)*

3. Irish stoat (Fr Doolan)

4. Common weasel showing its individually distinct belly pattern (C. Buckingham)

5. North American stoat in winter pelage, known in the fur trade as ermine (R. A. Powell)

6. *A weasel cannot curl its long body into the spherical shape which most efficiently conserves heat; the best it can achieve is a flattened sphere (C. Buckingham)*

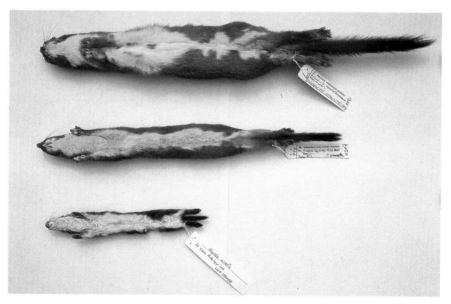

7. *Study skins of females of the three species of weasels from Pennsylvania, one of the few places where all three co-exist. Top: longtailed weasel from Franklin Co., 17 January 1979, head and body length unrecorded, tail 129 mm. Centre: stoat, Adams Co., July 1971, head and body length 297 mm, tail 91 mm. Bottom: least weasel, Mercer Co., 5 July 1979, head and body length 164 mm, tail 26 mm. Specimens from the Vertebrate Museum, Shippensburg University, Curator G.L. Kirkland (Author)*

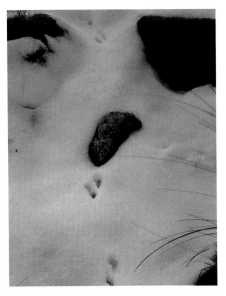

8. *Snow-tracking is a very useful method of observing the activities of weasels in cold climates, that is, over most of their range (Author)*

9. *Male least weasel killing a vole (R.A. Powell)*

10. *The Irish stoat is capable of killing a rabbit, but it is risky for smaller weasels to tackle large prey (Fr Doolan)*

11. Vole nests that have been occupied by weasels during winter are lined with fur inside, and can easily be found and counted after the thaw (B.M. Fitzgerald)

12. A young female stoat, anaesthetised for tagging and handling, lying on her field record card and about to wake up (Author)

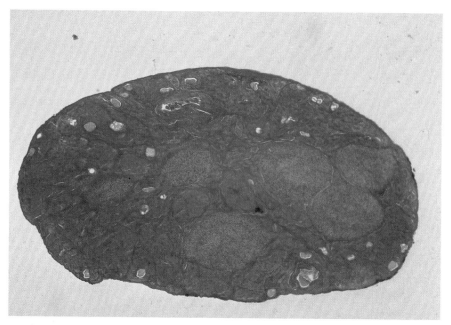

13. Cross section of the ovary of a stoat, showing five small corpora lutea of delay, plus the edge of a sixth (Author)

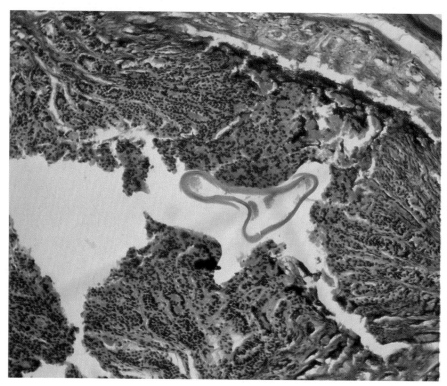

14. Cross section of the uterus of a female stoat during the period of delay. Part of a free blastocyst is shown, slightly distorted by processing (Author)

15. *Female common weasel suckling young, ten days old (C. Buckingham)*

16. *Young stoat, four weeks old showing the temporary mane (E.G. Neal)*

17. *Young stoat, seven weeks old, (E.G. Neal)*

18. *A large male stoat killed by a New Zealand falcon,* Falco novaeseelandiae *(A. Cragg)*

19. If there is a stoat nearby, a common weasel keeps under cover and maintains a sharp lookout, escaping at the earliest opportunity (C. Buckingham)

20. Fred Allen, one of the gamekeepers at North Farm, Sussex, resetting a Fenn trap that had caught a stoat (The Game Conservancy)

young remain elongated for some months, but those of adults which have lost their young or failed to rear them remain practically invisible. Female stoats and longtails usually have four or five pairs of nipples, and common and least weasels have three or four pairs. Only those nipples that are being suckled remain active, so fewer than the total possible number will be visible on a female with a small litter.

The most useful feature of the reproductive anatomy of females, for the researcher at least, is the corpus luteum (Plate 13). Each ovum released at ovulation leaves a space behind, which is quickly filled with a dense mass of hormone-producing cells. These are slightly yellowish in colour and are clearly visible to the naked eye, hence the name 'yellow bodies'. One corpus luteum forms for each ovum released. Their function is to produce the hormone progesterone, needed to maintain the pregnancy. The beauty and usefulness of the corpora lutea lies in the two facts that ovulation in weasels has to be induced by copulation, and that each corpus luteum marks the site of an ovum that has been released. Hence, counting corpora lutea is a convenient way to estimate which animals have mated, plus their total potential fecundity, and these are very important data for population studies (see Chapter 10).

MATING BEHAVIOUR IN ADULTS

Mating is a very vigorous affair in all weasels. It has to be, because, in adults at least, the stimulus of copulation is needed before the ova can be released. All attempts to stimulate ovulation by injection of gonadotropins, the hormones that usually have this effect in other animals, have failed (Gulamhusein and Thawley, 1974; Rowlands, 1972), and the ovaries of unmated females have no corpora lutea.

The female is subordinate to the male for most of the year, and normally avoids him, but she is well able to reject unwanted suitors with displays of ferocious aggression. Only when she reaches full oestrus will she accept a male's advances. He approaches cautiously, rubbing himself on the ground with twisting movements, and making excited trilling calls. If she answers in kind, the brief courtship begins. They sniff at each other, trilling incessantly, and follow each other around. If she is fully receptive, or if it is not the first encounter between the pair, she may leap playfully around him, whereupon he immediately grabs her by the scruff of the neck while she remains passive (Figure 9.3). First encounters require somewhat more lively negotiation before getting to this stage, but the result is the same. He then grasps her round the chest with his front legs, never letting go of her neck with his teeth; she may break loose from the leg grasp, but not from the neck hold. He drags her about until he is in a position to arch his supple back and make pelvic thrusts, usually while half lying on his side. The baculum ensures that she is well stimulated, and that intromissions can be energetic, prolonged (up to three hours, with alternate periods of thrusting and resting), and frequent (up to several times per hour). Afterwards the partners may rest, together or separately, and may repeat the procedure over the next two or three days. However, the female may accept other males she meets during this period; she has no noble ideas about loyalty to one partner. Indeed, for captive breeding programmes Wright (1948) advocates introducing several different males to an oestrous female one after

Figure 9.3. Ovulation in weasels is induced, so the female has to be well stimulated. The baculum enables the male to maintain the extended and vigorous intromission required.

another, until her heat subsides, as a means of ensuring success. But since she probably does not ovulate until the second or third day after mating, the males that meet her on those days have more chance of fathering the litter.

Mating success is all-important to the male; it is his only passport to representation in the next generation, since he takes no part in rearing the young (see Chapter 12). So he attempts to find as many mates as possible each season, though the best way to do that depends on his age and social status (see Chapter 8). For the female, mating is only a dangerous preliminary to the real business, the rearing of the young, and as soon as her short period of heat is over she rejects the male with squeals and savage bites. There is no pair bond of any kind; indeed, the adults appear to have as little to do with each other as possible.

Even in captivity, where mating encounters are set up in decent isolation from the possibility of interference from other males, some individual males are consistently uninterested or ineffective in achieving matings and others equally consistently successful (Don Carlos *et al*, 1986). Likewise, Müller (1970) found that some captive females rejected all males, refusing to mate at all, and even willing females did not necessarily accept all males offered as partners. Breeding weasels is therefore a somewhat unpredictable business, and allowance has to be made for individual variation in both sexes.

THE SEXUAL CYCLES IN ADULTS

Common Weasels

The breeding season in common weasels is long (Figure 9.4). In Britain, males have enlarged testes and are fecund from February until some time between the end of August and the beginning of October. The testes regress in autumn, but never relapse into complete quiescence since the early stages of spermatogenesis can be found in the cells throughout the winter. However, there are no spermatozoa in the epididymes from November to January inclusive, so there is a definite infertile period in winter. Adult females start coming into heat in February, though they do not necessarily conceive then. They go into anoestrus in September, earlier when they are in poor condition.

Implantation in common weasels is direct, that is, the fertilised zygote proceeds straight through the stages of development (or, if there is any delay, it is too short to be significant). The gestation period is therefore about the same as the time it takes the embryos to develop, about 35–37 days, and the ovaries contain corpora lutea only when the female is carrying actively developing young. Pregnancies may be observed at any time from March to August, and the first litters are born in April. Rearing takes at least nine weeks, so one full cycle takes about 3–4 months (Table 9.3). When voles are numerous, adult females will come into oestrus again when the previous litter has been weaned, by about the end of May. The corpora lutea of the first pregnancy persist well into the second, so females breeding for the second time in a season, with two sets of corpora lutea in the ovaries, may be found from June onwards (Deanesley, 1944; King, 1980c). The second litters are born in about July or August, and the mother may still be suckling in October (Delattre, 1983).

Common and least weasels are alone among carnivores in their ability to produce second litters, later in the summer, in response to a glut of food. Well-fed females in captivity can easily be persuaded to produce three litters in a season. In the wild, two litters is about the most the females can manage, and then only when hunting is exceptionally easy. It is not correct to assume, as in some models (see Chapter 12), that they produce two litters every year. On the other hand, when food is very scarce, adult females in the wild may not manage to produce any surviving young at all. So there is enormous variation in the pregnancy rate and in the length of the breeding season in common weasels, from 7–8 months in vole peak years to total failure in crash years.

Least Weasels

The breeding cycles in least and common weasels are broadly similar. The gestation period is about the same (34–36 days), and both have direct implantation, but there are two very interesting minor differences. In both, the normal spring breeding season can be extended during vole peaks, but, so far as we know, common weasels never continue right into the winter. But least weasels in North America have been reported as pregnant or with small young in most months of the year (Hall, 1951; Heidt, 1970); and in the tundra they definitely continue to breed under the snow well into the winters of lemming peaks (Fitzgerald, 1981). This is less surprising than it sounds, because in fact the conditions in the far north for breeding of both small rodents and of weasels are much more favourable in winter than in spring (Chernov, 1985). Once the snow pack is established, the subnivean space provides a reliable refuge, with near constant conditions and shelter from large predators. But in spring, the melting snow often floods the burrows and nests, drowning nestlings,

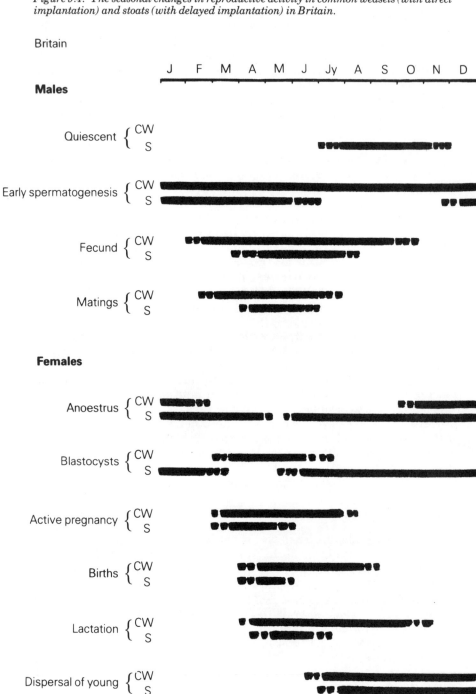

Figure 9.4. The seasonal changes in reproductive activity in common weasels (with direct implantation) and stoats (with delayed implantation) in Britain.

blocking access to food, and exposing small animals to windchill, late frosts and hungry predators. All the same, the subnivean temperature is still near or below zero, and female least weasels breeding there must be under considerable thermal stress whenever they leave the safety of their fur-lined dens. The effort they are prepared to put in conveys some idea of the urgency and importance of breeding success to small, short-lived animals.

The second difference between least and common weasels was pointed out by Frank (1974), who kept large numbers of them in his lab at Braunschweig, in West Germany. In each of three successive years, a wild-caught least weasel produced three litters, mostly common-least hybrids. The periods of pregnancy (5 weeks) and of rearing (8–9 weeks) were the same as he recorded in pure-bred common weasels kept in the same conditions. The difference was that the least female came into oestrus again only 5 weeks after the previous litter had been born, whereas none of the common females did so until 9–10 weeks later. Hence the least female was able to start the gestation of the second litter during the rearing of the first, and she completed the production of two litters in 5.5 months instead of the 7–8 months needed by the common females. Frank emphasised that this happened regularly, and suggested that it might be an adaptation to give least weasels maximum productivity in the short summers of their northern home. This seems at first glance a reasonable suggestion, except that, since least weasels are able to continue breeding into the winter when conditions permit, there seems no need for them to hurry to finish breeding by the end of the summer. On the other hand, if their breeding cycle is less closely controlled by season than in other weasels, they would be free to respond to a vole peak whatever the time of year, and more rapidly than other kinds of weasels can. Then the speeding up of the production process in least weasels would be more a matter of competitive advantage (see Chapter 12) than of adjustment to short northern summers.

Stoats

The reproductive cycle in stoats is quite different from those of common and least weasels (Figure 9.4). First, in both sexes the cycle is strictly controlled by the season, or more precisely, by the changing ratio of light to dark hours. This control is fixed, and cannot be overridden even in years when the countryside is teeming with prey. Second, there is an obligatory delay in the development of the embryo, which starts about two weeks after fertilisation. By this stage it has travelled down the tubes from the ovary, developing rapidly as it goes into a hollow ball of 100–200 cells, a blastocyst, until it has reached the uterus. In common and least weasels (and most other mammals) it then implants itself in the wall of the uterus and proceeds to develop to full term. But in stoats and longtailed weasels, it merely stops developing, and floats free in the uterus for the next 9–10 months (Plate 14). Not until the days begin to lengthen again in the following spring does it reawake and continue with its progress as if nothing had happened. Delayed implantation is one of the most fascinating puzzles among the many presented to us by the weasels (see Chapter 12).

Immediately after the winter solstice, the males begin to prepare for the spring breeding season. From February to April the testes enlarge rapidly, stimulated by a massive rise in the level of testosterone in the blood (Gulamhusein and Tam, 1974). The fertile season in adults is well defined, from May to July; then the testes regress more slowly and are quiescent until November. The regressed testes of adults in autumn and winter are still distinctly larger than the undeveloped testes of subadult males at the same season. The first signs of spermatogenesis appear in December, though there are no spermatozoa in the epididymes (i.e. the animals are incapable of fertile matings) until May.

The control of the female cycle is rather more complex (Figure 9.5). Throughout the long period of delay, the corpora lutea are small (0.7–0.8 mm across) and produce the small amounts of progesterone needed to maintain the blastocysts. If the ovaries and their corpora lutea are removed during delay, the blastocysts decay (Shelden, 1972). As the spring evenings gradually draw out, the increasing ratio of light to dark hours passes some more or less definite threshold, and this triggers a response in the pituitary. It begins to produce larger amounts of a gonadotropin (probably luteotropin); the corpora enlarge to 1.2–1.3 mm across, and the level of progesterone in the blood suddenly rises. It prepares the uterus for implantation, and also stimulates development of other essential organs, such as the nipples. About ten days later the blastocysts implant, spreading themselves out evenly between the two horns of the uterus (migrating from one to the other if need be), and the embryos complete their long-interrupted growth in another 28 days. The number of implanted embryos is often less than the number of corpora lutea, though there is much annual and local variation (Table 9.2).

As with the moult cycle, the ultimate control of implantation is by day length. The immediate control of the activities of the cells is by hormones, but it is day length that turns them on and off. Captive stoats can be induced to implant and produce their young at the wrong season by adjusting the ratio of light to dark hours over their cages to that typical of spring, but not simply by injecting what appear to be the right hormones (Wright, 1963; Mead, 1981). In places where the winter coat is normally white, it is easy to tell when a female is about to produce her young, without disturbing her, because the moult and the breeding cycles respond together to changes in day length. The birth may be expected about 22–25 days after the first brown hairs begin to appear on the female's nose (Ternovsky, 1983).

It is possible to estimate the expected date on which a given set of foetuses would have been born by calculating their average weight and inserting it into the formula provided by Hugget and Widas (1951): $\sqrt[3]{W} = a(t-t_0)$, where W is the average weight of the foetuses of one litter, a is the specific foetal growth constant, and t is the age of the foetuses from conception. The plot of weight against age is linear from t_0, the intercept on the time axis. The original formula applies to all mammals, but I worked out the application of it to New Zealand stoats, in which the young are 3–4 g at birth (King and Moody, 1982). I substituted appropriate values for a and t_0, and rearranged it to give t as a negative value, days before birth:

$$t = (\sqrt[3]{W}/0.063) + (16-40)$$

Because birth weight is one of the variables in the equation, the figures given here might need to be adjusted for local races of smaller body size, in which the newborn young are under 2 g (Table 9.3).

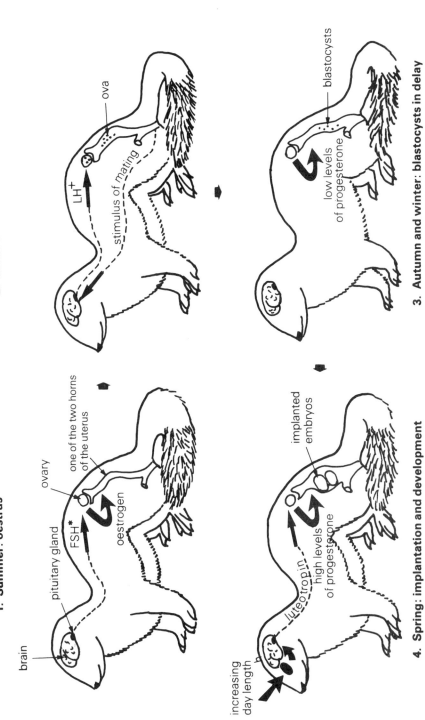

Figure 9.5. Control of the seasonal reproductive cycle in the female stoat.

1. **Summer: oestrus**

brain

pituitary gland

ovary

one of the two horns of the uterus

FSH*

oestrogen

2. **Summer: ovulation and fertilisation**

LH+

ova

stimulus of mating

3. **Autumn and winter: blastocysts in delay**

blastocysts

low levels of progesterone

4. **Spring: implantation and development**

increasing day length

luteotropin

high levels of progesterone

implanted embryos

* FSH = Follicle stimulating hormone
+ LH = Luteinising hormone

Table 9.2   Litter size in weasels

Species	Data from	Country	Mean	Range	Reference
erminea	corpora lutea	UK	10	6–17	Rowlands, 1972
		NZ	10	3–20	King & Moody, 1982
		Sweden	9	5–15	Erlinge, 1983
	blastocysts	Sweden	7	1–15	Erlinge, 1983
	embryos	UK	9	6–13	Deanesley, 1935
		NZ	9	6–13	King & Moody, 1982
		Siberia	11	1–17	Ternovsky, 1983
	births	New York	6	4–9	Hamilton, 1933
		Germany	6	4–9	Muller, 1970
		Siberia	7	1–14	Ternovsky, 1983
		USSR	9	2–18	Heptner *et al*, 1967
nivalis	corpora lutea	UK	7	4–11	Deanesley, 1944
vulgaris	embryos	Poland	5	4–7	Jedrzejewska, 1987
		UK	6	4–7	King, 1980c
	births	UK	5	2–7	East & Lockie, 1964, 1965
		NZ	5	3–6	Hartman, 1964
nivalis	embryos	Alaska	10	7–16	Fitzgerald, 1981
nivalis		Mongolia	12	5–19	Heptner *et al*, 1967
		USSR	7	4–10	Danilov & Tumanov, 1975
	births	Finland	4	4–5	Blomquist *et al*, 1981
		Michigan	5	1–6	Heidt, 1970
frenata	?	N. America	7	2–9	Heidt, 1970

The critical change in day length which sets off the processes leading to implantation is reached earlier in places at lower latitudes than at places nearer to the poles; hence the young are born earlier in warmer climates. For example, in New Zealand we collected stoats from places spanning a range of latitudes from 38°S, where implantation starts at about the end of August, to 45°S, where it starts about 10–15 days later. The estimated range of birth dates was from late September to mid October in the North Island, and from mid to late October in the South Island (Figure 9.6). The equivalent dates in the northern hemisphere would be, say, March in France, early April in England and late April or May in Scotland. In the USSR the range of birth dates recorded by Aspisov and Popov (1940) was from late March in the Ukraine (45–50°N) to early May in Tatary (55°N). There is of course some local variation, spanning about three weeks in any one place, but compared with many other small animals, including both common and least weasels, the season of births in stoats is quite closely synchronised. Day length also controls the seasonal development of the testes in males (the spring rise in testis weight is conspicuously later in higher latitude males), and the spring moult, which is also later at higher latitudes. In fact, the whole suite of related spring activities is closely co-ordinated by the neuro-endocrine system and adjusted to the expected environmental conditions.

While the young are still suckling, the mother stoat comes on heat again. Oestrus normally follows littering in the adults, and preparations for it are therefore also controlled by day length. When the days reach a

Figure 9.6. The date of implantation in stoats is controlled strictly by day length, so the date of birth of the young is significantly related to latitude (from King and Moody, 1982).

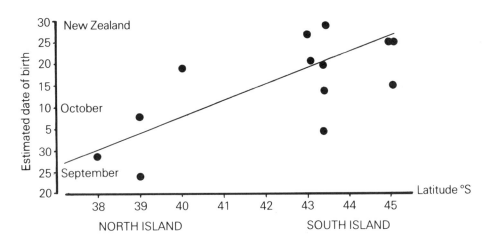

certain length, the pituitary hormone follicle stimulating hormone (FSH) stimulates the ovary to produce oestrogen, which prepares the vulva for mating. But an oestrous female will not ovulate until she is mated, and will remain on heat (with swollen vulva) until she is. The pituitary will not release the hormone luteinising hormone (LH), necessary for ovulation, until it receives the nervous signals from the vulva. Three captive females I kept in isolation were still on full heat some three months after the normal season, and had no corpora lutea. It is therefore easy to tell the state of any given female, because as soon as she is mated, the swollen vulva subsides and a fresh set of corpora lutea appears in the ovaries. The corpora lutea persist for most of the year, whether or not any young are eventually born, and there is no overlap between successive generations of corpora lutea, because they degenerate before the next oestrus. By mid-summer, practically all wild females (>99 per cent) are pregnant, carrying a new set of blastocysts and showing no signs of recent oestrus. If oestrus is brief and synchronised by day length, the males must be very efficient at finding receptive females. The proverbial English description of a particularly persistent human suitor as 'a bit of a stoat' (Drabble, 1977) is obviously quite a compliment. Meanwhile, post-partum oestrus and prolonged delay in implantation means that almost all female stoats are pregnant almost all the year round. If there were a prize for the sexiest animal, the stoat would surely win it.

There are two persistent myths about the breeding of stoats, which have confused people for many years even though there is no real evidence that either is true. The first is the idea that females ovulate spontaneously throughout the year but do not conceive until the spring. This story arose because Ruth Deanesley, who undertook the first intensive study of the reproductive cycle of stoats (published in 1935), did not know about delayed implantation, so she interpreted the corpora lutea of delay as infertile ovulations. Alerted by Wright (1942), she later re-examined her material, and published a correction (1943); but the earlier paper was so good in every other respect, so thorough and so much more widely read than the correction, that the mistake continued to be repeated in general reference books for the following thirty years. The second is the idea that, although most females conceive during the main breeding period in summer, those that miss out get a second chance in spring, and litters conceived then develop directly, with no delay in implantation (Watzka, 1940; Kopein, 1965). There is no evidence for this, either from examination of the reproductive state of large samples of wild-caught females or from extensive observation of the mating behaviour of stoats in captivity. However, there is a possible explanation for the observation that some females are apparently ready to mate in spring or early summer, before any young conceived the previous year could have been born. Females which lose their litters for any reason do come into oestrus early. It would be possible for these to be fertilised as soon as the males are ready, which could be 6–8 weeks before the successful breeders reach post-partum oestrus. But they still have to wait until the following year to produce their young, after an unusually long period of delay.

Longtailed Weasels

The breeding cycle in longtails is the same as that in stoats (Wright, 1947, 1948, 1963), except in one respect. The young are born in April or May, but post-partum oestrus in the female longtail is inhibited by lactation. Unless she loses her litter, she does not return to heat until June, July or August (according to location), rather later in the season than does the female stoat. Females that lose their litter very early in the season can be ready to mate again as early as mid March (DeVan, 1982). The males are fertile from March to September.

As in stoats, the spring moult is an accurate herald of the breeding season. Both male and female longtails are sexually inactive whilst in their white coats. From the time the brown hairs begin to appear, it takes about 21 days to the implantation of the blastocysts, and about 47 days to the birth of the young. Any female remaining white unusually late in the season may be confidently assumed to have resorbed her litter. In males there is a significant correlation between the rise in the weight of the testes and the beginning of the spring moult. For these and other reasons, longtails are apparently not difficult to breed in captivity, and have proved themselves useful research animals, especially in studies of endocrinology and photoperiodism.

THE DEVELOPMENT OF THE YOUNG

From Birth to the Opening of the Eyes

Well before the young are due, the mother weasel must find a safe, warm nest for them. She does not make one of her own, since weasels do not burrow, but then, she does not need to. It is a simple matter to find a ready-made nest, and if the owner is still at home it may find itself unwillingly providing board as well as lodging for the weasel family. The best dens are the ones made by an animal of the right size; small rodents make good dens for least weasels, but stoats and longtails look for a den made by larger rodents or rabbits. It needs to be well away from the danger of flooding, and thickly insulated with dry grass and leaves. The mother often improves the lining with fur plucked from dead prey, although she does not take it from her own belly fur as doe rabbits do. Nests built under good cover, such as a pile of rocks or logs, are especially attractive since they are safe from the prying paws of larger predators. When she has found a den, the mother weasel collects a store of food and then retires to await the birth.

Infant weasels look rather alike in all species, both in their appearance at birth and in their early physical development. They are all born completely helpless, and all grow in the same way, but least and common weasels develop more rapidly than stoats and longtails, and they reach the milestones of development at younger ages (Table 9.3). For example, although young stoats are born larger than young common weasels, they then fall behind and are 6–8 weeks old before they are again larger than common weasels of the same age.

The new-born young weigh 1–4 g, and at birth or soon after their pink skin is covered with a fine, pale natal down, which gives them a silvery appearance. They do not grow the characteristic brown and white fur of adults for several weeks. The eyes can be seen only as indistinct bluish-black dots crossed by the sharp horizontal line of the tightly closed eyelids. The ears are very small, pressed against the side of the head, and a waxy deposit can often be seen in the ear channels. They can easily be told from infant rodents, because they already have the long neck of the weasel kind; the front limbs seem to be placed almost halfway down the total length of the head and body. All four limbs are short, weak and hardly jointed, but already furnished with broad paws, and the very short toes have fine well-developed little claws. The prominent ribs make the tiny bodies (the width of a pencil) appear to be closely segmented; Ternovsky (1983) commented that 'in appearance they are reminiscent of large ants'. The tail, little longer than the limbs, is cone-shaped. The urethral opening of the males lies halfway between the navel and the prominent anus; the vulva of the females lies directly in front of the anus.

The new-born young have no teeth, but powerful equipment and instincts for sucking. The jaws are relatively shorter than those of adults, and a massive shovel-shaped tongue takes up most of the space inside the mouth. Left alone, they lie in a heap together, crawling under each other to avoid disturbance; if one is separated it immediately tries to struggle back into touch with the rest. Almost from birth they can produce a fine chirping sound, usually a sign of protest or distress. Most observers report that at this stage, males and females are roughly the same size, and both are, on average, equally represented. The litters of common and least weasels tend to be somewhat smaller (usually 4–8) than those of stoats and longtails (usually 6–12: see Table 9.2), for reasons explored in Chapter 12.

At first the nestling weasels have no proper fur and cannot maintain their own body temperature. When the mother is not in the nest they huddle tightly together, but even so, if their body temperature drops too far (below 10–12°C, according to Segal, 1975), the young go into a temporary cold rigor. Their pulse and breathing slow, their metabolism and growth slip into a lower gear, and they become stiff and cold to the touch. The effect is somewhat like hibernation, except that it is rapidly reversible as soon as the mother returns. The reason seems to be connected with energy conservation. When the mother is with them, she

Table 9.3 Development of young weasels (from Hamilton 1933, Sanderson 1949, Hartman 1964, East & Lockie 1964, 1965, Heidt et al 1968, Heidt 1970, Müller 1970, Blomquist et al 1981, and Ternovsky 1983)

Stage	Least weasel	Common weasel	Stoat	Longtailed weasel
Total gestation	34–6 days	35–7 days	220–380 days	205–337 days
Birthweight	1–2 g	1–3 g	1–3 g small races 3–4 g UK, NZ	3–4 g
Birth coat	naked	naked	fine white hair on back	fine white hair all over
Growth of mane	none	none	14–21 days	none
dorsal fur	18 days	21 days	21 days	28–35 days
black tail tip	none	none	42–9 days	21 days (?)
Teeth, milk	11–18 days	14–21 days	21–8 days	21–8 days
permanent	4–6 weeks	8–10 weeks	10 weeks+	10 weeks+
Opening of eyes	26–30 days	28–32 days	35–42 days	35–37 days
Eat meat	3–4 weeks	3–4 weeks	4–5 weeks	4–5 weeks
Lactation lasts	4–7 weeks	4–12 weeks	7–12 weeks	5–12 weeks
Play outside nest	4 weeks	4 weeks	5–6 weeks	5–6 weeks
Kill prey	6–7 weeks	8 weeks	10–12 weeks	10–12 weeks
Adult size, M	3–6 months	3–6 months	12 months	12 months
F	3–4 months	3–4 months	6 months	6 months
Sexually mature, M	3–4 months	3–4 months	12 months	12 months
F	3–4 months	3–4 months	4–6 weeks	3 months

provides both warmth and food, and they cuddle up close to her and channel as much as possible of the energy she provides into growth (Figure 9.7, Plate 15). When the mother is away, if they tried to maintain normal temperature they would have to draw, from their own meagre resources, energy to keep themselves warm which might otherwise be used for growth. The advantage to the young of not attempting to keep warm when left alone is that they save energy for growth, and reduce the chances of running out of energy altogether, even for staying alive, before the mother comes back. The disadvantage is that, if hunting is bad and the mother has to be away a lot, the young have few chances to grow at all, and may end up permanently stunted, or dead.

Figure 9.7. A mother weasel must spend as much time as possible with her young while they are very small, because when they get too cold they stop growing.

Unweaned nestlings spend virtually all their time asleep. They squeak and chirp in response to disturbance near them, but otherwise they wake up only to suckle and to defecate. The nest is kept quite clean because the mother licks up the faeces of the young — indeed, they apparently perform this service for each other. They make no attempt to leave the nest, although the mother may move them if the family is threatened by any interference or by bad hunting in the immediate vicinity. Then she carries each one in turn by the scruff of the neck (Figure 9.8), darting through the undergrowth to the new den, leaving it there and returning for the others. Michael Hitchcock, a Middlesex keeper, described to me how he was standing by a pile of rotten logs when a common weasel came out, studied him for a few seconds at a range of one metre, then went in and emerged carrying a tiny blind young one by the neck, which she took along the hedgerow out of sight. She returned and repeated the procedure with a total of six young. After the first one Hitchcock kneeled down by the burrow and watched the operation from a distance of 40 cm; he was struck by the total fearlessness of the mother weasel in her domestic crisis. The young remain limp and passive whilst being carried, and make no sound unless the mother grabs them in the wrong place (e.g., by the ear). German observers call this condition *tragschlaffe*, and point out that it can also be seen in adult females being carried about by a male during mating.

Figure 9.8. The mother weasel carries her kits in the typical carnivore way, grasped by the scruff of the neck.

When the young are a few weeks old (Plate 16), their milk teeth begin to come through, razor-sharp miniature editions of the adult meat-eater's teeth. Weaning is a gradual process in young weasels; whilst still blind and deaf, they chew vigorously on mice which are opened for them, or on small pieces of meat, skin or bones, although they may continue to suckle for several more weeks. They begin to be aware of their surroundings, and they respond to squeaking noises or to human speech by raising their heads, opening their mouths and hissing faintly. Some will make feeble attempts to strike if provoked. They try to get to their feet, usually collapsing again immediately. Crawling begins as an unsteady exercise in circles, but before long they learn to crawl short distances, in a more or less straight line, before the mother retrieves them. From about the time that meat enters the diet, they learn to defecate outside the entrance of the nest, and the weight difference between males and females becomes noticeable.

From the Opening of the Eyes to Independence

Around the time that the eyes and ears open, nearly always in the females first, the behaviour of the young weasels changes as they begin to perceive the world around them. Within a few days they are actively exploring outside the nest, and the mother no longer attempts to keep them all together. They are still a bit wobbly on their feet at first, especially the hind feet, but they can run along at least as quickly as mice. They now depend much more on the animal prey supplied by their mother than on her milk, and in the wild would soon be weaned, although captive young ones may continue to suckle for as long as the mother will let them. Their appetites are stupendous — each one is soon eating as much as half its own body weight per day. Their mother may have a struggle to provide such largesse, so there is plenty of incentive for the young, as soon as they attain sufficient co-ordination, to start providing for themselves.

The milk teeth are used for chewing on carcasses as soon as the deciduous carnassials (the third upper premolars and the fourth lower premolars) have erupted. These appear at about three weeks, and are replaced by the permanent teeth about two months later. Both sets of teeth erupt in a predictable sequence. The permanent carnassials, the fourth upper premolars and the first lower molars, are last in place (Hall, 1951). Killing behaviour is not learnt, and although the first attempts are clumsy, the young quickly improve with practice. Some people maintain that the mother will bring a live but disabled rodent to the den and use it to teach killing technique to the young. I doubt this, since the hunting methods of weasels do not include any complex acquired skills (as in, say, the big cats), and the family life of weasels is too brief to give the young much chance to improve their proficiency under tuition. Besides, young which have been separated from their mother at an early age are soon as expert as any others. Of course, the young of nearly all carnivores play with their littermates and with their prey, practising the crafts of their trade; but that is not the same thing as the mother deliberately teaching them.

Within another few weeks the young are more or less fully mobile and their motor co-ordination is improving daily. Standing up on their hind legs and jumping over obstacles are among the last of the typical weasel skills to develop. By this time the young are fully furred and able to maintain their own body temperature, at first only inside the nest but later also outside it. They follow their mother on short hunting expeditions, dodging from one hiding place to another. If one falls behind it will call loudly with the infantile begging cry; the mother answers by trilling to show the lost one where she is, or if necessary she goes back to pick it up. At any disturbance the mother hisses furiously, which causes the young to 'freeze' and keep under cover. The mother is totally fearless whilst she has young, and will perform feats of amazing courage, threatening any animal, however large, that gets in her way. Human observers, if unobtrusive, are simply ignored. Michael Hitchcock also told me that he was, on another occasion, standing by a hedge when he heard loud, high-pitched squeaking, coming closer. Eventually a family of common weasels appeared, but he could not count the number of young as they were moving about so fast; some of them actually ran over his boot. Another gamekeeper described to me how he had seen a 'rope' of common weasels — a parent and a group of young in single file — crossing a country lane. Galen Burrell (in Hirschi, 1985) watched one mother stoat with her family of young in the alpine meadows of the Colorado Rocky Mountains:

Grasping the plump vole in her mouth, she carried it about 100 m to the far corner of the rock pile . . . Here she was greeted by eight young stoats. The nearly full-grown youngsters, mewing and chirping softly, excitedly sniffed their mother, one another, and then the breakfast vole. The stoat family disappeared into their burrow. I . . . waited . . . The mother reappeared. Standing on her hind legs she first scanned the surroundings, ignoring me, and then chirped. Eight heads popped out of the burrow. In a rushing stream of bodies the young ones followed

141

their mother down the mountainside . . . [She] was keenly aware of the whereabouts of all her children. As they flowed down the mountain they would suddenly pile up behind an obstacle — usually a rock that was just too big for them to leap over. Curiosity also seemed to divert them from their mother's trail, and she was forever returning to pick up stragglers. Grasping each one by its neck, she would drag it back to its brothers and sisters. Then the entire family would move on . . . [They reached] a safe new hiding place . . . Without pausing to rest she slipped away. [She killed a pika] 50 m away from her young ones. With a tremendous effort she dragged, pushed and sometimes carried the pika (which was twice her size) a short way towards [them, then] she pushed the pika under a rock. Then she headed up the slope towards the place she had hidden [a deer mouse killed earlier the same day]. Despite the time that had passed, she remembered exactly where the mouse was, picked it up and carried it back to her hungry children. Not long after that the mother stoat moved her brood up to where she had stashed the pika. Darkness fell as the family consumed their meal under the cover of their rock fortress . . .

This extraordinary account gives a vivid picture of the flexibility of behaviour which allows a mother weasel to make choices according to circumstances — e.g. to bring the young to the kill if the kill is too heavy to carry to them. It also underlines the energy invested by the mother in her young, and the enormous commitment of time and effort it takes for her to rear them alone.

In the wild family parties of 3–6 stoats or more may be seen moving about together in early summer, most often in June and July. As they get older they scamper about, chasing each other and making high-pitched squeaking and whistling noises. Usually only one adult is seen with a group of young, presumably the mother, but there are records of family parties accompanied by two adults. By the time they have hunted together for two or three weeks, the young have got their permanent teeth and some experience in using them, and they are ready to set out on their own. Families kept together in captivity have to be separated at this stage, as they become increasingly intolerant and irritable with each other.

In 1976–8 I organised a reporting system whereby vistors to national parks in New Zealand sent in a record card for every stoat or group of stoats they saw (King, 1982a). The visitors reported seeing stoats in groups only from October to February, most often in December and January. This neatly confirmed what we already knew from trapping studies: young stoats were seldom caught in any numbers before the end of December, and were most numerous in January when the families break up and the young disperse. Erlinge (1977a) observed the same thing in June in Sweden.

Age and Size at Puberty

Young common weasels born early in the season, especially when food supplies are good, grow very rapidly. Early-born young of both sexes can be physically and sexually mature by the age of about three or four months. In mid or late summer (July–August), they may be taking full part in reproductive activities on equal terms with the adults, and in vole peak years their contribution is extremely important (see Chapter 10). In most seasons, though, the young females either fail to conceive, or lose their litter at a very early stage, and the average young common weasel does not breed successfully until the following year.

By contrast, in young stoats and longtails the development of young males and females is radically different (Figure 9.9). Young females reach puberty as nestlings, and then grow to their full adult size by the autumn, when they are about six months of age. Young males stop growing in autumn, and remain immature and distinctly smaller than adults throughout their first winter. In spring they reach puberty, and then suddenly put on a great spurt of growth. They are indistinguishable from older adults by the time they are 13–14 months old and the breeding season is well under way.

Figure 9.9. The different growth patterns in male and female stoats (from King and Moody 1982).

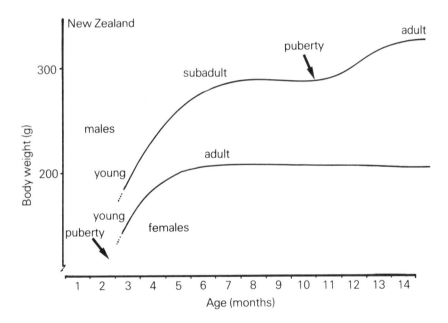

The precocity of the juvenile females is the most extraordinary thing about the development of young stoats. While they are still in the nest, in fact while they are still blind, these tiny unweaned babies become reproductively mature, and are fertilised by an adult male, probably the same one that serves their mother. It passes belief that the large and aggressive males can mate with infant females without damaging them, yet it is clear from many observations of captive matings that they do so, and not just occasionally but as typical and normal breeding behaviour which leads in the following year to a litter of typical and normal young. Ternovsky (1983) described a remarkable but not exceptional case:

The youngest female was 17 days old on the day of mating (25 May 1980), was 112 mm long, was helpless, deaf, blind and toothless; she was feeding on her mother's milk and could move only slightly by crawling. Her body mass (18 g) was 13 per cent of her mother's body weight and only 6 per cent of the body weight of the male. Coitus lasted only for one minute. Spermatozoa were present in a vaginal smear. On 22 May 1981, after 337 days, this female gave birth to 13 young and fed them successfully.

Considering the enormous difference in size and strength between an adult male and a juvenile female, one might regard this behaviour as an animal version of rape, but that idea would be wrong. It seems that the juvenile females are not only willing to co-operate with the male, they are eager to do so. The arrival of a male (or perhaps more specifically, his scent) stimulates a sexual reaction in blind and deaf female young. They call to him with high-pitched trills and chuckles, grading into the typical adult nuptial cooing signal. They grab onto him as he passes by, or crawl after him, interfering with his mountings with both their mother and sisters (Müller, 1970; Don Carlos et al, 1986). This does not sound like coercion, and indeed it is not. It is in the young female's interests to mate with a male that is strong enough to overcome her mother's defences and enter the nest; and the lack of a year-round pairbond, and the short average lifespan and rapid replacement of locally resident males, reduce the chances of mating with her own father.

Adult male stoats can tell the sex of a juvenile as soon as they have grabbed its neck, and they usually drop the males at once. How they know which is which is a mystery, except that it will certainly be a response to some kind of scent signal. The only clue is that young stoats develop a prominent mane of brown hair on the nape of the neck at about three weeks old (Plate 17). It was first described many years ago (Bishop, 1923; Hamilton, 1933), but its function has never been explained. Perhaps it contains glands that produce a scent distinctly different in males and females.

Ternovsky (1983) described one case in which the adult male mated with all four young females in a litter of eight, and killed all four males. One might ask why the adult males do not make a habit of this, since presumably it would be in their interest to remove potential future rivals. But if the old male lived that long he would be well able to drive the youngsters away to try their luck elswhere, and meanwhile, restraint might be worthwhile on the offchance that he might be killing his own sons.

Juvenile female longtails are also precocious, though not to quite such a dramatic extent. They are 3–4 months old, weaned and almost full grown before their mother comes on heat again between June and August and the adult males are permitted to approach the family. Only then are the young females mated. Young longtails do not develop a mane, as do young stoats, and this difference supports the idea that the function of the mane has something to do with helping the adult male stoats to identify their infant mates. There is no obvious reason why the young female longtails do not also mate as nestlings.

By the time they leave the family group, virtually all juvenile female stoats and longtails will be fertilised. Even in very large samples of trapped stoats it is unusual to find even one young female without corpora lutea. But the additional energy required to maintain the blastocysts is slight, so they do not add much extra burden to the young females as they complete their own body growth. The young males of both species are more conventional; they breed first when they reach adult size as one-year olds.

Dispersal

Most families break up when the young are 3–4 months old and fully capable of looking after themselves. Then the young leave the mother's home range to find one of their own. The young females tend to settle down nearby, usually less than 5–6 km away (Erlinge, 1977a; Debrot and Mermod, 1983); 16 of the 18 young females observed by Erlinge (1983) in Sweden did so for life. Young males, however, may travel extraordinary distances in a very short time. In one New Zealand study, in December and January of 1979–80, six of 65 young males caught in live-traps and eartagged were known to have travelled at least 6 km, 8 km, 12 km, 15 km, 20 km, and 23 km. These were only the minimum, straight-line distances between known capture points; the real distances, running in and out and round about as stoats do, must have been much greater. And they were covered remarkably quickly: 12 km in 27 days plus a further 3 km the next day; 20 km in five days plus a further 4 km in the next two days; and 23 km in 39 days (King & MacMillan, 1982). Similar feats have been recorded even in the smaller weasels. One stoat tagged in Alaska turned up 35 km away, though in the six months between the capture records it must certainly have travelled much further (Burns, 1964). These long treks by young males are no doubt encouraged by intolerance from the established adult males, which tend to move about less once they are established on a home range. But the adults tolerate the young females. Obviously, it is in the interests of the local resident adult male to drive out the young males and accept the young females, which next season will be his potential rivals and mates respectively.

10 Populations: density and productivity

Because weasels are predators, they are necessarily rare — much more so than the voles, mice and rabbits on which they prey. In a meadow, there are from hundreds to thousands of grass plants for every field vole, and from scores to hundreds of field voles for every weasel. On the other hand, because weasels are the smallest of the warm-blooded predators, they are much more common than the foxes, feral cats, hawks and owls that also eat field voles. It is therefore often possible to collect large samples from populations of weasels.

One might expect from this that the population dynamics of weasels would be among the best studied of all carnivores, but that is not so. Weasels are too small and secretive to be observed directly (except in occasional lucky glimpses), so systematic study of them has to be done indirectly, by routine trapping. The techniques were worked out in the last century by gamekeepers and fur trappers, but not applied to scientific studies until recently. More important, weasels are unreliable. They are not evenly distributed in all habitats, and even where they do live, they may be abundant one year and scarce the next; these variations make it hard to plan a study. Many hopeful researchers and students have put in weeks or months of fruitless field work, often in places where weasels were known to have been present at some previous time.

ESTIMATING DENSITY

The usual method of estimating density is to use live-traps to capture, mark and recapture repeatedly the resident individuals of a given area. Not every resident will be caught during every trapping session, but it is usual to assume it is still there provided it is caught again in a later session. The simplest way to estimate the population density is the 'calendar of captures' method, which compiles regular totals of the number of residents known or assumed to be present each session. Unfortunately, live-trapping is very labour-intensive, so it is usually possible to cover only a relatively small area for a rather short term. This means that the population estimates are so much affected by statistical errors that they may be quite wildly wrong. More sophisticated methods

146

designed to overcome this problem usually demand far more data than any live-trapping study on weasels can supply.

Over the long term, controlled trapping with Fenn traps (Figure 13.7) can give a lot of information useful to population studies. This method is much less laborious than live-trapping, so can be conducted over a wide area. The traps are set out evenly, baited and checked daily, and operated in the same way and for the same number of days per session regularly all the year round. The theory is that, if the trapping operation has been absolutely consistent, and the living weasels of all ages and both sexes are caught at the same rate (or at least, that differences between them are constant), then changes in the number of animals killed, and in the proportion of each age and sex, probably do reflect real changes in the density and population structure of the animals available to be killed. It is important to spell out this rather obvious assumption, because much depends on it, and it is not always as true as it sounds. For example, if the traps are baited, it could be argued that when more weasels are caught it is because they are more hungry, not because there are more of them. Baited traps do catch stoats more often than unbaited ones, but both show the seasonal variation in capture rate which reflects a real variation in density (King and Edgar, 1977).

A simple method of expressing the relative density of weasels caught on standardised lines is to calculate the number of captures per 100 trap-nights, or C/100 TN (one trap-night equals one trap set for 24 hours), allowing for unavailable traps. For example, take a line of 150 traps, checked daily for three days. At the end of the session, the results could be tabulated as in Table 10.1. The real density cannot be worked out from the density index, but the correlation between them is fairly good, at least until C/100 TN exceeds about 20. For stoats the figure seldom exceeds 7/100 TN. Erlinge (1983) tested the accuracy of livetrap-night indices on a population of stoats of known density, and concluded that they are a reasonably reliable guide.

Table 10.1 Calculation of a density index from Fenn trapping results

	A traps untouched	B stoats caught	C rats etc caught	D traps sprung, empty	E $\dfrac{B+C+D}{2}$	F 150 $-E$
Day 1	144	2	4	0	3	147
2	139	5	4	2	5.5	144.5
3	144	3	2	1	3	147

Although 150 traps were set for 3 nights, the total number of trap-nights is not 3 × 150 (=450), because every trap that is set off, by a stoat or by any other animal, cannot catch again until it is reset. Assuming that, on average, each sprung trap is out of commission for half a night, half a trap-night is subtracted from the total for every trap sprung, for whatever reason. The corrected total number of trapnights is the sum of column F, that is, 438.5; the total number of stoats caught is 10; the density index is 10/438.5 x 100 = 2.28.

VARIATION IN DENSITY

The local distribution of weasels is closely related to that of their favourite prey. They haunt places where small rodents or rabbits may be found, such as hedgerows, stone walls, haystacks and rough grassland; they avoid places with little cover for themselves or their quarry, such as ploughed fields and open-floored woodland. Their home ranges are smaller in places and habitats rich in food, and their overall local density greater (Table 10.2). For example, tracks of stoats in the snow can be found much more often in habitats rich in small mammals, such as among the poplars and willows along river banks and in meadows overgrown with scrub, than in mature spruce forests or open fields.

Table 10.2 Some density estimates for weasel populations

Species	Habitat	Density of weasels	Reference
Stoats	Southern Sweden, autumn 1974–79		Erlinge, 1983
	average over rough pasture	3–10 per 100 ha	
	in marshy areas where water voles abundant	up to 22/100 ha	
	Ontario, all year 1973–5		Simms, 1979a
	average, including arable, short pasture, forest	6/100 ha	
	overgrown pasture and shrubby areas only	10/100 ha	
Longtails	Pennsylvania, January–March 1942		Glover, 1942
	scrub oak—pitch pine forest	12/100 ha	
	Michigan farmland, January 1937	3/100 ha	Allen, 1938
Common weasels	Poland, mixed farmland, all year 1971–3	1–7/100 ha[1]	Goszczynski, 1977

[1] The authors acknowledge that this is probably an underestimate.

Weasel populations are linked to those of their prey in time as well as in space, and their variations in density with time are by far the more dramatic of the two. As in all animals that breed seasonally, including the small mammals on which they depend, the number of weasels in a given place is highest in mid to late summer, at the end of the breeding season. At this time the young are leaving their mother's protection and learning to fend for themselves. In a typical year there will be easy prey available for the young weasels at first — young rabbits and rodents which, like themselves, are new to independent life, and inexperienced in avoiding predators. However, as the winter draws on and food becomes scarcer for everyone, the autumn influx of young animals — rodents, rabbits and weasels alike — fades away. By early spring the twin scythes of starvation and predation have cut down the local populations of both predators and prey to their seasonal minimum.

However, superimposed upon this regular variation between seasons, there may also be variations between years. Even in a favourable habitat, the local prey species have good seasons and bad ones, and the numbers of prey available at a given season are also typically unstable from year to year, and the number of weasels follows suit. Small prey species affect small weasel species, larger prey affect larger weasels.

DENSITY VARIATION IN STOATS

In the days when ermine was an important fur resource, Russian scientists concerned with managing the fur harvest invested years of work in the study of population variation in stoats. They calculated the relationship between the number of ermine skins harvested each year and the fluctuations in the local populations of small rodents and water voles. The pattern was quite clear, even from the somewhat rough and ready density indices used and the considerable number of complicating factors. Over the whole Kamchatka region, the yield of stoat skins from 1937–38 to 1963–64 varied from 4,000 to 12,000 per year. The peak years came about every 3–4 years, usually lagging a little behind a peak in the numbers of small rodents. In some local districts within the region, the most productive years exceeded the worst by 15 times, even up to 50 times in others; and the best years for stoats and sables (another important fur-bearing mustelid) usually coincided (Vershinin, 1972). On the wide flat flood-plains of the Volga and Kama Rivers in central European Russia, where the main prey of stoats is the water vole plus a variety of smaller rodents, the correlation between the numbers of water voles and of stoats caught was very close; so much so, that the yield of ermine pelts each winter could be forecast merely from the number of water voles collected in the previous June (Figure 10.1) — unless a low period for water voles coincided with a peak in numbers of small rodents.

The importance of water voles in determining the population density of European stoats was confirmed by the work of Claude Mermod and his students Sylvain Debrot and J.M.Weber at the University of Neuchatel in Switzerland. They live-trapped stoats in two valleys in the Jura Mountains (Figure 10.2). In the Brévine valley (at >1,000 m altitude) there were 1,875 ha of pastures, open fields and forest. Peatbogs in the valley bottom and 86 km of stone walls offered plenty of shelter for stoats. When Debrot's study began in the summer of 1977, the density of stoats was high (6.8/100 TN) and they ranged almost everywhere except in the forest. But the density of stoats declined drastically over the following two summers to 0.7/100 TN in 1979, and those that were left became more or less restricted to the bogs. The number of stoats trapped on the main study area dropped from more than 50 to only 3 over this period.

The reason for the crash was that 1975 had been an extraordinarily good year for water voles, which then disappeared over the next couple of years and remained scarce for several more. When water voles were abundant, the Brévine stoats fed almost exclusively on them, and thrived (probably reaching their highest numbers in 1976); but when the water voles disappeared, the stoats followed suit. Debrot (1983) showed, from game and fur records covering the surrounding district and extending

Figure 10.1. In the Tatar Republic (USSR) during the 1930s the relationship between the annual harvests of ermine and of water vole furs was so reliable that Soviet scientists could predict the next season's crop of ermine from the number of water voles collected a few months previously (from Aspisov and Popov, 1940).

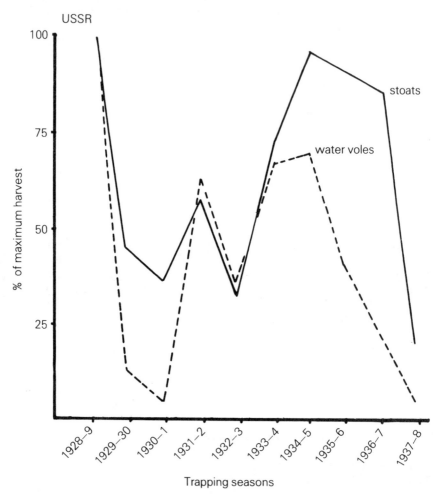

back to the 1950s, that the relationship between the numbers of stoats and of water voles in that area was quite general (Figure 10.2). Each population peak of water voles (about every five years) was followed within a year by a peak in numbers of stoats. By contrast, in Debrot's second study area, the Val de Ruz, 616 ha at 700 m altitude, where prey resources were more diverse and less variable, the density of stoats remained fairly stable, averaging 2.6/100TN over the three years from April 1978. The stoat's diet in this area included more wood mice and birds, and fewer water voles, than at Brévine (Debrot and Mermod, 1981).

The data on the stoat population of the Val de Ruz were extended until early 1985 by Weber (1986), and his figures are added to Figure 10.2. Both authors used the 'calendar of captures' method of counting resident stoats, but Weber's monthly estimates have been converted to three

Figure 10.2. On one of Debrot's two Swiss study areas, the alpine Brévine Valley (a), a sudden decline in numbers of stoats followed a population crash among water voles, visible in regional hunting statistics (inset). At lower altitudes, e.g. in the mixed farmlands of the Val de Ruz (b), populations of both voles and stoats are more stable (redrawn from Debrot, 1981 and 1983, and Weber, 1986).

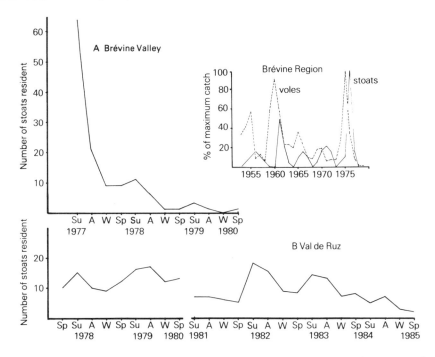

monthly averages to match Debrot's data. The numbers of water voles were again high in 1982, but the response in the Val de Ruz stoats was far less drastic than had been observed at Brévine.

The stoat's capacity to increase in numbers when water voles are abundant was demonstrated convincingly on the island of Terschelling, off the coast of Holland (van Wijngaarden and Bruijns, 1961). In 1931, about 9 stoats were released on the island, which multiplied to at least 180 by 1934 (see Chapter 13).

In Britain, stoats are larger than in Switzerland, and eat rabbits much more often than water voles (Figure 5.2). Rabbits were introduced to Britain in Norman times, and have been common for only the last 200–300 years, whereas stoats probably arrived thousands of years ago, among the very first post-glacial colonisers. For almost all the time that stoats have lived there, Britain has been largely forested, and the diet of stoats in those days must have been very different from what we see now. Instead of rabbits there would have been red squirrels, and field voles would have been less often found than bank voles and wood mice. Since red squirrels and forest rodents are always less abundant than rabbits and field voles, it seems likely that the deforestation and changes in agricultural practice which have favoured the small mammals of open country must also have allowed a considerable historical increase in the average density of stoats.

Rabbits do not normally show the great ups and downs in numbers that water voles do, so the extent of the stoats' dependence on them was unknown until 1953–55. In those two years, myxomatosis invaded Britain, and about 99 per cent of all rabbits died (Sumption and Flowerdew, 1985). The consequences were sensational, for the vegetation, for small rodents and for their predators. One of the few predator-prey studies that was already in progress at the time, on the tawny owls in Wytham Woods, documented spectacular swings in density of rodents and in the breeding success of the owls over the next few years (Southern, 1970). No one was in the process of making a population study of stoats in Britain at the time, but there was another source of information available, which showed the impact of the invasion on stoats very clearly.

The vermin books of well-organised game estates often contain long sets of figures showing the numbers of predators killed every year. Stoats are traditionally among the gamekeeper's greatest enemies, and every one killed is recorded with satisfaction. But in the years immediately after myxomatosis, stoats practically disappeared from the countryside and from the gamekeeper's gibbets. Vermin bag records from estates all over the country showed the same remarkable exodus, as is illustrated on a Suffolk estate in Figure 10.3. For example, on one Hampshire estate of 1,600 ha, only 13–58 stoats were killed each year from 1954–60, compared with 136–302 each year in 1947–53 (Anon, 1960). On a Norfolk estate of 9,300 ha, the tallies dropped from 409–1013 a year before the epizootic to 40–257 afterwards (King, 1980c). For the next 20 years stoats remained scarce. From the early 1970s the rabbits began to recover, followed by the stoats, but each new outbreak repeats the original pattern (Figure 10.3).

Figure 10.3. The vermin bag records of a Suffolk estate illustrate well the close relationship between stoats and rabbits in much of England (data from the Game Conservancy, courtesy S.Tapper).

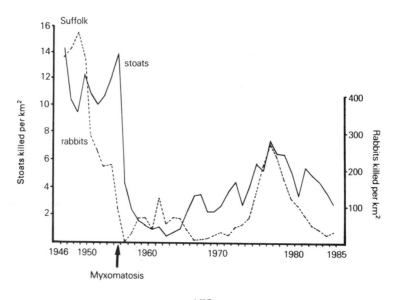

The same response has followed drastic reductions in numbers of rabbits in other countries, though not always for the same reasons. In Sweden, the numbers of stoats fell after a decline in rabbits even though Swedish stoats are smaller and eat rabbits less often than those in Britain (Erlinge, 1983). In this case the decline in stoats was attributed to intense competition for voles from the many other generalist predators on the study area. New Zealand stoats are large and eat many rabbits, but there is no myxomatosis there. Rabbits are usually controlled by poisoning or shooting, and the effect of a successful campaign on the local stoats is rather similar to that of myxomatosis elsewhere (Marshall, 1963).

The general conclusion, that the population density of stoats is controlled by variations in the density of their prey, is inescapable — but the mechanism by which it worked was, until recently, unknown. There was an early clue in the 1943 report by Popov that, in 1937–8, when stoats were numerous in the Tatar Republic (in the USSR) the proportion of young in the fur trapper's catch rose to 65 per cent, but when stoats were scarce (1939–40), it dropped to 19 per cent. But the reasons for this change remained unexplored. Since then, three very different studies have attempted to answer that question. In New Zealand, I used regular Fenn trapping to sample stoats living in three simple forest communities. In Sweden, Erlinge (1983) used live-trapping and radio-tracking to follow the fortunes of the members of an undisturbed population of stoats living on a large area of pastures and marshes over six years; and in Canada, Raymond and Bergeron (1982) used live-trapping to do the same on a smaller area of arable farmland over three years. Such different approaches will obviously produce very different kinds of information. For a start, the habitats occupied by the stoats observed, their average body sizes and the prey resources available to them, were wildly different in the three countries. The most significant contrast, though, is in the virtually opposite methods used, but this is in fact an advantage. There are some kinds of data that can be got only by watching undisturbed live animals (e.g. the home ranges and behaviour of individuals); and some, equally important, that can be got only from systematic examination of large samples of carcasses (e.g. the fecundity and mortality rates of populations). The impressive thing is that the results complement each other, and can be integrated to give us a fascinating general view of the way stoats adapt their lives to the resources at hand.

Demography of Stoats in New Zealand Beech Forests

In New Zealand, all the land mammals common in the forests are introduced, and there are relatively few of them (see Chapter 5). The stoat is usually the commonest and often the only carnivore. Native raptors (a harrier hawk, a bush falcon and an owl) are scarce. This animal community is not 'natural', but at least it is very simple, and that makes it easier to see what is going on; in particular, the sequence of events is seldom influenced by competition at any level.

I was interested in documenting the responses of the forest rodents and mustelids to the masting cycle of the southern beech (*Nothofagus*) trees. My main study areas were two mountain valleys in Fiordland National Park, in the far south of the South Island. Every 3–4 years there is a massive seedfall, and tonnes of food is dumped on the forest floor in autumn and early winter. In both forests, 1976 and 1979 were masting years (Figure 10.4). Over the next few months the number of young mice caught on my standard traplines suddenly soared, not only because more were born but also because more survived to enter the traps. Further, the adult female mice continued to breed well into the winter, instead of stopping in autumn as usual. By the spring (September) there was an extra large group of young parent mice already breeding and producing the first of the summer generations. By early summer (November) the mice had reached the relatively high population densities, for the season, of 10–20 mice/100 TN.

For the stoats living in the same forests, life was suddenly much easier than usual. For the next few months they had a feast; stoats of both sexes and all ages ate mice much more often than usual in the summers after a heavy seedfall. But, more importantly, the variation in the supply of mice in these forests had an effect on the stoats out of all proportion to the contribution of mice to the stoat's diet. In non-seed years the density index for stoats (averaged over the three months of each season) ranged from 1–2 C/100 TN in summer down to zero in winter. But in the summer after a big seedfall, the density index for stoats shot up to 5–6 C/100 TN. The increase in numbers of stoats caught in post-seedfall summers was directly related to the density index for mice at the same time (Figure 10.5).

I worked out the sequence of events as follows. The number of young that can be produced by any population of animals in a given season depends on four things: (1) the number of females in breeding condition; (2) their fecundity, or the mean ovulation rate per female; (3) their fertility, or the mean litter size per female; and (4) their productivity, or the number of young reared to independence over the whole local population. The number of female stoats in breeding condition can be taken as 100 per cent every year, since almost all females of all ages are fertilised by the end of each breeding season (see Chapter 9). We can therefore ignore the first point, but the others are all important.

Figure 10.4. The variation from year to year in the numbers of feral house mice and of stoats in two southern beech forests in New Zealand. The arrows show the years in which the beech trees produced a heavy crop of seed (from King, 1982b, 1983a).

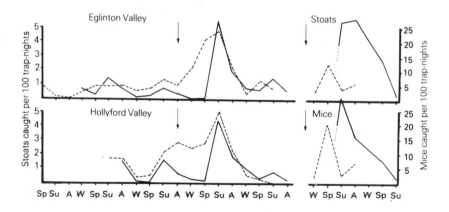

Figure 10.5. There is a direct relationship between the number of mice and of stoats in New Zealand beech forests in summer (from King, 1983a).

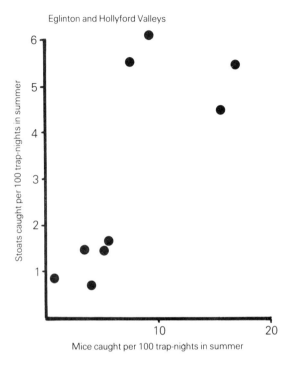

Eglinton and Hollyford Valleys

Fecundity is easy to measure, by counting the corpora lutea in the ovaries. By contrast, fertility is very difficult to measure in stoats, because it is impossible to collect large samples of pregnant females or to find breeding dens to observe. This is frustrating, because variation in fertility is probably the key to the whole process. Productivity is also very variable, but easily deduced from the age structure of the summer population. So we have the beginning and the end of the story, but there is a gap in the middle. Still, we can see enough to work out the general outline.

Environmental conditions, especially the nutritional state of the female stoat, control the number of young produced each season by a simple, energy-saving and effective mechanism. The females cannot increase their fecundity in a good year, as common weasels do. The potential number of young stoats born in any given year is already set by the number of ova shed in the previous year, and delayed implantation fixes the cycle regardless of food supplies. The female stoats have no opportunity to increase that number even in a bonanza season. The only thing that can happen is a *decrease* in the mortality of the young at all stages of their life, from implantation of the blastocysts to independence. When food is short, some blastocysts fail to implant, and/or some of the embryos are resorbed before reaching full term, and/or some of the young born die as nestlings. When food is abundant, fewer potential young are lost at each stage. To follow the process, we need to calculate how many young start off each year as ova, and then how many fall aside at implantation, in the uterus, at birth, in the nest, and during the transition to independence.

Fecundity. Of the 451 female stoats collected in good condition during the main period of delay in implantation, December–July inclusive, all but two had the small corpora lutea of delay — that is, all but these two had been mated. The odd ones had not merely failed to find a mate, because they were not still on heat. They were the exceptions that prove how rare any kind of reproductive inefficiency is in stoats. In the rest, the number of corpora lutea, each representing one ovum released during the previous mating season, were counted by serial sectioning. The corpora are rather large, so if an ovary is cut into eight slices, each corpus luteum appears in at least two, often three or four, cut surfaces. (In practice, of course, each ovary was cut into about a hundred very thin sections, and we looked at every eighth or tenth one.) The corpora can be counted quite easily by plotting on paper the position of each one as it appears and disappears through the series. The process was rather like calculating the number of prunes in a small pudding cut into eight slices. Adding the count for the two ovaries from one female gives the fecundity of each individual, and averaging these gives the mean fecundity per female for the population that season.

The number of corpora lutea per female varied from 0 to 19, but the average number per sample was remarkably constant through the year, in different years, and in different areas. The young females tended to be slightly more fecund than the adults, but not significantly so; and in each area there were some individuals with very high counts in some years and none in other years. But these variations were minor; the local averages varied only from 8 to 10, and the general average was 9.7. The number of corpora in the two ovaries of one female were inversely related — when one had more than the average, the other had fewer.

Fertility. Fertility is harder to calculate. We had hardly any information on litter size calculated from embryos, and none at all on nestlings. The whole study turned up only 13 pregnant females, of the 641 collected, and these had from 6 to 13 embryos, average 8.8. So there had already been some loss from ovulation (average 9.7) to implantation. In 8 of 10 pregnancies, the number of foetuses was fewer than the number of corpora lutea. Moreover, not all the blastocysts that had implanted would have developed to full-term young, since some had died and were being resorbed back into the mother's body. In 5 out of 12 pregnancies, at least one embryo was resorbing; in one, 7 of the 8 embryos were reduced to simple swellings, leaving only one normal embryo almost at full term.

If things get very bad, a female can resorb the entire litter, and then appear in the spring with no sign of having produced any young at all. Because the season of births is quite well synchronised by day length (Figure 9.6), and >99 per cent of females are fertilised each season, it is possible to predict the stage in the reproductive cycle that each female should be in at any given time. Females that are not pregnant or lactating at the expected date can be assumed to have lost their litters entirely, either by total resorption, or in the nest soon after birth. Some are already fertilised for the next season, months before the successful females. In our samples these were nearly always found in beech forests in the crash seasons the year after a good seedfall. The mortality of embryos is not always so drastic, but the net result of it is that fertility is usually, perhaps always, lower than fecundity. Deaths among the small nestlings, which we know nothing about but which surely must happen, would add to these losses.

Productivity. The final step in the long process of producing the annual crop of young stoats is the rearing and training of the young for independence. This phase takes about 2.5–3 months, and we have practically no information on it. Scientists studying other kinds of predators, especially raptors, do well at this time, since the nests are conspicuous and the young are easily observed. Those who choose to study stoats have to wait until the young are ready to show themselves. By midsummer they are moving about and exploring the world, including the tempting wooden tunnels housing the traps. The number of young stoats caught per hundred trap-nights is an indirect measure of productivity, not per female but of the population sampled.

In poor years, fewer than one young stoat is caught per 100 TN; in good years, more than 6/100 TN. Do these differences reflect real changes in fertility from year to year and not, for example, changes in trappability among the members of a population producing a constant number of young? Yes, because the number of adults caught varies much less between years. There is a relatively steady number of breeding adults every season, producing many young some years and few in others (Figure 10.6). The good years are those when a high proportion of the fertilised ova survive to become live, independent young stoats. Since the energy demands of a lactating female stoat may increase by 200–300 per cent (Müller, 1970), the chances of the young surviving increase in direct proportion to the mother's chances of being able to find so much extra food and still have time to keep her young warm. Conversely, in the bad years, about the same number start out but few get there. Because many females get only one chance to breed, and never 'know' whether conditions in the spring will be good or bad, it makes sense to adjust the effort made to the chances of success, and to defer making that adjustment for as long as possible. If, by the spring, things look unpromising, it may be better to save energy and produce fewer young, or even to wait and hope to survive till next year rather than take a chance and lose all.

The Link between Reproductive Success and Food Supplies. The graded mortality through the breeding cycle clearly has something to do with the nutritional condition of the female, but exactly what is unclear. Perhaps female stoats feeding mainly on mice get some kind of stimulus not received by females living on other foods. Could it be that the body of a whole mouse (skin, bones, guts and all) contains essential elements not found in the meat taken from larger carcasses? Could it be that a female stoat gets some kind of behavioural cue from the excitement of making frequent kills or of carrying and handling a whole prey animal? I could only make suggestions like these from my field results, but since then, some results from a captive breeding programme for stoats run by Don Carlos *et al* (1986) at Minnesota Zoo have supported them. Apparently, the females were at first fed on tinned cat food, but none produced young. The next year, one was transferred to a diet of freshly killed laboratory mice, and she produced young while another one kept on the old diet failed. Later, two more females put on the mouse diet were successful.

The female stoats I examined were more fecund (had a higher average

Figure 10.6. Most of the huge numbers of stoats caught in post-seedfall summers were young ones (white bars), whereas in non-seedfall years, very few were produced (data from King, 1981a). Young: 3–5 months old. Adults (grey bars): over 15 months old.

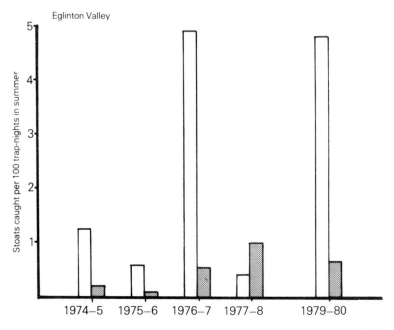

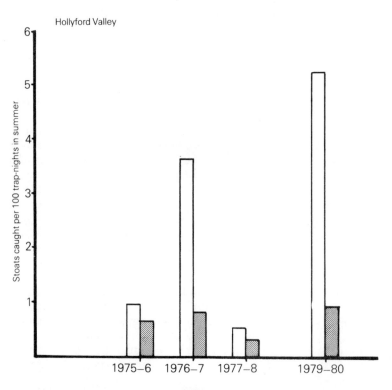

ovulation rate) in the breeding seasons when mice were abundant, and perhaps this is also an effect of good feeding. But this higher fecundity has *no* effect on the number of young produced in the following season, which is controlled by food supplies at the time of implantation and onwards. It is easy to jump to the wrong conclusion, that fecundity and productivity should be linked; in some animals they are, but in stoats they are not.

In beech forests, therefore, the effects of a seedfall are rather like those of a stone dropped in a pond. The mice react to the seed, and the stoats react to the mice. The whole chain of reactions takes less than a year, from the March, April and May of the main seedfall to the following December and January when the season's crop of young stoats disperses. The simplest explanation is that the productivity of both mice and stoats in these habitats is generally held in check by a shortage of food, especially protein, for the very young. Food resources for stoats in these beech forests are normally sparse. After a seedfall, there is a sudden glut of protein, and the main effect is a sudden improvement in the survival of the dependent young stoats. (Young mice survive better too, though it is not yet certain whether this is directly or indirectly due to the seedfall.) The reason why the density of stoats varies so drastically in these beech forests is that the seedfalls provide enormous stimulation at relatively long intervals. Density is increased hugely by the herds of young produced in a seed year, but very few of them survive the three or four years until the next one, so density declines quickly after each peak and remains low in the meantime. The great advantage of New Zealand beech forests in working out these relationships is that they are relatively simple habitats, and the differences between seed and non-seed years are so clear-cut.

Demography of Stoats in Canada

For the smaller races of stoats living in open habitats right across Europe and North America, the most important prey is usually the local species of *Microtus*. Changes in the numbers of specialist vole predators, such as common weasels and the smaller races of stoats, usually turn out to be linked to the widespread changes in abundance of voles, from great scarcity one year, through enormous abundance and back again 3–4 years later.

In southern Quebec, a three year live-trapping study attempted to document this relationship, on two 90 ha areas of arable farmland about a kilometre apart. Raymond and Bergeron (1982) estimated the density of meadow voles (*Microtus pennsylvanicus*) and other small rodents, and caught, marked and released 94 stoats, in the years 1978-80. In each area, changes in the numbers of voles were reflected in the numbers of resident stoats caught in autumn, particularly in the numbers of juveniles. It appeared that the alternative prey available (other small rodents and shrews) was sufficient to enable most of the females present each season at least to attempt to breed whatever the density of voles, because nearly all (18 of 21) showed signs of lactation in early summer. However, the close link between vole density and the number of juveniles caught in autumn suggests that the litters that were produced did not survive well unless voles were abundant. As in New Zealand, although for different reasons, the population dynamics of the stoats and the small rodents were unstable and closely linked, probably by the same mechanism.

Demography of Stoats in Southern Sweden

Because field voles are important prey, not only to stoats but also to most other carnivores and raptors living in the same area, their 3–4-year population fluctuations have profound consequences throughout the grassland community, and they have been the subject of years of research by field ecologists attempting to explain them. But in the area where Sam Erlinge and his students had been observing stoats for years, the field voles showed only a fairly predictable seasonal variation in numbers, with rather little variation between years. Erlinge and his colleagues were interested in the possibility that the voles in that area might be prevented from increasing to peak numbers in favourable seasons by steady, year-round predation by a whole host of predators (see Chapter 7). They were also interested in the relationships between the different kinds of predators competing for the field voles, and in the effect this competition might be having on the population dynamics of the stoats. One can hardly imagine a set of circumstances for stoats to live in (habitat, prey resources, competitors) more radically different from those in my New Zealand study area. Contrasts like these are an opportunity to understand the population dynamics of these adaptable predators.

The main prey available in Erlinge's 40 km^2 area, of open fields with interspersed copses and marshes, were field voles, wood mice, water voles and rabbits. The predators hunting them were stoats, foxes, feral cats, badgers, polecats, common buzzards, tawny owls, longeared owls, kestrels, and common weasels. By a huge effort of teamwork, Erlinge *et al* (1983, 1984) managed to document the numbers and annual breeding success of most of these predators, and also to estimate the density of prey available to them and roughly how many of each prey were taken by which predators (Table 7.4).

The part of this census work concerned with stoats was done by live-trapping in March and April (to estimate the number of adults present before the breeding season) and from August to October (to estimate the number of young produced). Over the six years of the study, 142 individual stoats (75 males, 67 females) were marked and released (Erlinge, 1981, 1983). Snow-tracking in winter helped to confirm that the trapping data did reflect the real distribution and numbers of the stoats, even though not all individuals were caught. Erlinge estimated the number of stoats present in various ways, not all of which agreed, but the general pattern was very clear; the stoats were at higher density at the beginning of the study than at the end (Figure 10.7). The figures suggested that about 45–50 individuals were present in the autumns of 1974 and 1975, and about 35 in 1976. After 1977, the data became too few to calculate actual numbers, but by autumn 1978 there were probably less than half the number of individuals that had been present in 1974–5.

Two important prey were also censused twice a year throughout the study. The figures for field voles drifted slowly upwards, in almost direct opposition to those for stoats; the figures for rabbits declined sharply, closely following those for stoats. Rabbits were counted because they are a key resource for the larger, generalist predators living on the same area, but they were not often eaten by the stoats, which are rather small in Sweden (though not as small as in Canada) and are rodent specialists. The third most important prey, the water vole, apparently remained fairly stable throughout the study.

Erlinge calculated the breeding success of the population from his live-trapping records. There was no opportunity to estimate fecundity, but that did not really matter. The corpora lutea counts that were available showed that potential litter size in Swedish stoats is close to the average (Table 9.2), and it is probably safe to assume that mean fecundity is as constant from year to year there as anywhere else. So the start of each season's production saga is almost certainly the same as in New Zealand. There is no way to tell whether the following stages are the same, but presumably they are, because by the time the young stoats appeared in the traps, their numbers had been drastically cut down. The vital difference was that there was no positive relationship between the numbers of field voles and the production of young stoats each season. In four of the five years observed, the stoats produced more young in seasons when the field voles started breeding early and fewer when they started late; in the fifth year the voles started early but the stoats had their worst season. If these data are representative, the surprising conclusion must be that field voles in this area do not influence the breeding success of stoats.

But there was another relationship between rodent numbers and breeding success, demonstrated in space rather than in time and involving water voles rather than field voles. The isolated water-meadows and marshes scattered through the study area, somewhat like islands in a grassy sea, harboured more voles of both kinds than the open pastures surrounding them. Moreover, the marshes were not all the same; in some, only field voles were common, and in others, there were water voles too, which were sometimes more abundant than field voles. Both kinds of voles are among the stoat's favourite prey, but the water vole provides a larger packet of food for the effort of making a kill, so, given a choice between them, the water vole would probably always be preferred. Erlinge found that the breeding females living in the marshes in which water voles were abundant produced more young females (27 young to 11 adults caught, mean 2.45 per adult) than those which had only field voles (14 young to 16 adults caught, mean 0.88). The difference between these figures was not significant overall, and there are some problems with presenting the data as ratios of young to adults caught (e.g. they may not be caught at the same rate), but it seems likely that breeding success was generally higher in the marshes with plenty of water voles. In the hedgerows on nearby farmland, breeding success was about the same as in marshes without water voles (7 young to 7 adults, mean 1:1).

As in all weasels, the success of each breeding season was closely reflected in the age structure of the population in the following autumn. Erlinge's data (Figure 10.7) show that the years when stoat numbers were high were also the years with the highest proportion of young in the autumn catch. The years 1976, 1977 and 1978 were poor years for recruitment, and in fact the population was by then not replacing itself. Decline was inevitable; yet the numbers of field voles, usually regarded as the stoat's most important resource, were if anything increasing. What was the cause of this apparent contradiction?

Figure 10.7. The total number of stoats present on Erlinge's study area each year was closely linked with the breeding success of the previous summer, as reflected in the proportion of young (white bars) in the autumn population (after Erlinge, 1983). Age classes as in Figure 10.6.

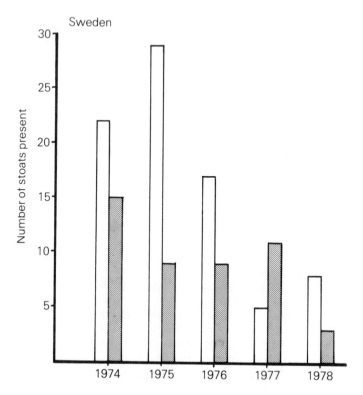

The Swedish stoats lived in a diverse community including many alternative prey, but they had to share their main foods, small rodents, with many other predators. Erlinge's team concluded that the pressure exerted by the whole community of predators on the small rodents was so great throughout the winter, when the rodents were not being replaced by breeding, that by spring there was often little food available for the female stoats. Only in places with augmented supply, such as in the marshes with water voles, were a female's chances significantly improved. The general increase in the numbers of field voles through the study was not enough at the critical times to make any difference. The main reason for this was, they suggested, that as the numbers of rabbits decreased, the other predators had to hunt more intensively for field voles. The decline in rabbits was not crucial in itself, since the small Swedish female stoats seldom killed rabbits. But Erlinge believed that the increase in competition for voles, caused by the decline in rabbits, was the reason for the poor breeding success and, in due course, the decline in stoats. Sometimes the other predators also affected the stoat's breeding success more directly. Remains of stoats were found in the pellets of raptors, and two nests of breeding female stoats in meadows were dug up by some predator.

Erlinge's study and mine, both dealing with practically the same problem, were published in the same journal and in the same year. Both papers were the culmination of many years' work, some previously published, but neither of us knew the details of the others' thinking. Yet we independently came to the same general conclusion, from radically different study areas and data, that the stoats in each area were limited in numbers by shortage of food. In reaching those conclusions, neither of us could escape certain assumptions and limitations in sampling design, and we both had to make the usual regrettable compromises between the ideal and the practicable. But from a different area again, the data of Raymond and Bergeron (1982) fit the pattern, and so do most other data on the population biology of stoats. The means by which food shortage affects density seem to be the same in all three study areas reviewed here — by increasing the mortality rate of the young at each stage of their development from the maximum potential set in the previous year. However, the especially interesting thing is that the shortage of food is apparently due to different processes in each population. According to the authors of each study, in bad years the large New Zealand stoats starve because there is simply no food available; the medium-sized Swedish stoats starve because the available food has been eaten by other predators; the small Canadian stoats starve because prey other than voles are present but too large or too scarce to support them.

DENSITY VARIATION IN COMMON WEASELS

Game records show enormous variations in the numbers of common weasels killed (Figure 10.8). Occasionally, common weasels are capable of quite startling irruptions, up to a five-fold increase in numbers over the previous year, and the best-known of these was clearly related to the huge increase in food supplies for common weasels that followed the arrival of myxomatosis. When the rabbits had gone, grass and herbs previously kept nibbled constantly short flourished as they never had before, and the densities of small rodents reached record levels, followed by the common weasels. The contrast with the effect on stoats (Figure 10.3) is remarkable.

Since the exceptional post-myxomatosis peak, lesser variations in the population density of common weasels have become clearer. They are also linked to the availability of small rodents, especially voles. The best proof of the connection comes from North Farm, the Sussex game estate described in Chapter 7. The numbers of common weasels caught followed the numbers of voles, but a little later (Figure 10.9). The same pattern is probably repeated all over the country. For example, in the records plotted in Figure 10.8 there is a rise in common weasel numbers about every third or fourth year (up to twice the previous year's number), suggesting that those were the years when field voles were abundant.

These variations in the density of common weasels come about because shortage of food has the same controlling effect on the productivity of common weasels as it has on stoats. Breeding is a hugely expensive undertaking for the smaller weasels. The average British male common weasel, weighing about 120 g, has to find nearly 2 g of suitable food per hour, or 40 g per day every day. The extra activity connected with the spring mating season must increase this requirement, though by how much is unknown. For a female averaging about 60 g, the daily

Figure 10.8. The number of common weasels killed by gamekeepers increased suddenly after the arrival of myxomatosis, and on average remained much higher than previously until the mid 1970s, when the rabbits and stoats began to return (data from the Game Conservancy, courtesy S.Tapper).

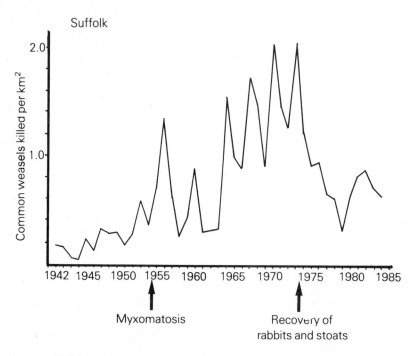

Figure 10.9. The numbers and breeding effort of common weasels on Tapper's study area in Sussex were both closely related to the supply of field voles (from Tapper, 1979 and Anon, 1981).

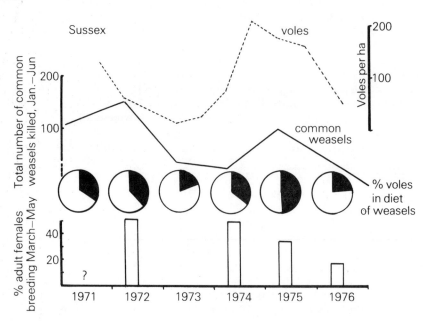

requirement is normally almost 1 g per hour, or 22 g per day. Her needs increase only modestly (6–7 per cent) during gestation, but soar to 80–100 per cent extra during lactation (Hayward, 1983), to about 70 per cent of her own weight daily. In colder climates, and when the young are nearing weaning, the additional demand is even higher, reaching up to 5–6 times her own needs, or up to twice her own weight daily.

Because reproduction is so very energy-intensive, there is a minimum density of available prey below which it is not possible to raise a litter. For common weasels this minimum appears to be about 10–15 voles per hectare (Erlinge, 1974; Tapper, 1979; Delattre, 1984). The effects of a bad season, increasing the mortality of the young at each stage from implantation to independence, work the same as in stoats; in vole crash years the breeding success of the adult females is poor, and the few young females that are born do not breed themselves till the following year. For example, on Tapper's study area in Sussex (Figure 10.9), voles comprised between a quarter and a half of the weasels' diet in 1972 and 1974, and at least half the females caught were breeding; in 1973 and 1976, the weasels had to turn to other foods, and few or none managed to breed. The total failure of an entire year's reproduction in a small, short-lived animal such as the common weasel has a serious effect on population density. When it happens on more than a very small scale, the result will be local extinction of that population.

On the other hand, common weasels can respond to increases in food supplies much more rapidly than stoats. Some idea of the speed of this reaction, and of the following decline, can be gained from a study done by Delattre (1983) in the foothills on the French side of the Jura Mountains. At 600–1,000 m altitude near Levier, field voles staged a population irruption in the summers of 1979 and 1980. Delattre reckoned that in August 1980 the density of field voles was 100–200 per ha. The inevitable crash, over the winter of 1980–1, was so complete that by May 1981 the field voles were down to less than a single individual per hectare. So the period of plenty was short, but while it was on the response of the common weasels was spectacular. Delattre caught none on his 100 ha study area in August 1979 and only two outside it. But at the end of 1979 resident weasels moved in, and increased in numbers throughout 1980. In that season, two cohorts of young were produced; the first appeared from May to August, and the second from September to November. Some of the females captured in October 1980 were still suckling. By May of 1981, 19 individuals were living in the area. Two months later, only one was left.

In a bumper season for small rodents, therefore, common weasels increase their reproductive output as do stoats, but by a different and far more effective means (Table 10.3). Potential litter size in common weasels in Britain is generally rather less than in stoats (Table 9.2). But in good seasons, the best that the stoat can do is to decrease juvenile mortality, whereas the common weasel not only does that but also has the option to increase fertility, and that leads to far more rapid population increase despite the smaller average litters. The difference is due to the key part played by the young females.

Young common weasels of both sexes can breed in the season of their birth, and delayed implantation does not restrict them to only one litter a year. In a vole peak year, the adults present in spring produce their first

Table 10.3 Effects of delayed implantation on response of populations of stoats and common weasels to variation in food supplies

	Stoat	Common weasel
Delayed implantation?	Yes	No
Fecundity	High (6–13)	Low (4–8)
Earliest possible age of female at 1st littering	12 months	3–4 months
Life span	<1–8 years	<1–3 years
Response in good years	Much of high potential fecundity realised in single large litter; but increase in fecundity impossible	Additional summer litters produced (2nd litter in adults, 1st in early-born young females); ? also increase in fecundity possible
Response in bad years	Increase in prenatal and nestling mortality	Decrease in fertility of adults, no summer litters
Reference	King & Moody, 1982 King 1981a, 1983a	Tapper 1979 King, 1980c

litter in about May. Abundant food means that the effort of providing for the litter is not too debilitating for the mother, and there are fewer losses than usual among the young. In August or September the mother produces a second litter, which means that she has doubled her fertility for the season — something a stoat cannot do — but that is not in itself the cause of the difference in productive capacity between common weasels and stoats. The really important difference is that by midsummer the early-born young female common weasels have several times the numbers and only half the mortality rate of the adult females, yet are equally mature. So the breeding stock in late summer contains many more females 3–4 months old than 15 or more months old. As in stoats, the autumn peak population is made up mainly of young animals, but in common weasels, the great majority of these were produced by the early-born young females of the same breeding season. In ideal conditions, a single adult female common weasel could have 30 descendants by the autumn, if she bore two litters of six herself and the three early-born females produced six each: $12 + (3 \times 6) = 30$. This astonishing reproductive capacity is more than sufficient to account for the sudden irruptions of common weasels reported during vole peak years.

DENSITY VARIATION IN LEAST WEASELS

The least weasel is often considered rather a rare species, since it is usually less well represented in museum collections than the two larger American weasels. However, in some years least weasels can suddenly become very abundant, only to disappear again just as quickly. The earliest evidence for this erratic behaviour came from fur buyers' returns. Mr Fryklund, a fur buyer from Minnesota interested in natural history, recorded the species of weasels he handled every year. He offered a better than average price to trappers for whole weasel carcasses, and was well known in Roseau County, so the local trappers brought to him all the weasels they caught. From 1895 to 1927 he handled only seven least weasels; in the winter of 1927–8, three; from November 1928 to April 1929, with about the same opportunity to recieve specimens as before, he got 59; from August 1929 to May 1930, 84; and from 1930 to 1935, three. In his 40 years as a fur buyer, Mr Fryklund handled 166 least weasels, 143 of them in the two years 1928–1930 (Swanson and Fryklund, 1935).

In North Dakota in 1969–70, the same thing happened again. Wildlife biologists working on the food habits of the red fox noticed that least weasels suddenly began to turn up in the fox dens they were excavating. (Foxes will kill least weasels but seldom eat them, so most of those collected by a hunting fox will be left at the den.) Also, fur buyers reported more least weasels than usual in those two years, and several least weasels were found dead on the roads. Altogether, Lokemoen and Higgins (1972) accounted for six least weasels from November 1968 to June 1969; 54 in the same period in 1969–70, and eight in 1970–71. This irruption of least weasels apparently followed a population increase in meadow voles, *Microtus pennsylvanicus*. Likewise, no least weasels were recorded in Missouri and south-western Iowa until 1963. Small rodents were abundant in 1966–68, and in two months of intensive trapping in early 1968, Easterla (1970) caught 8 least weasels in one 6 ha field.

It is during these periods of high density that least weasels may disperse into new areas. For example, they were unknown in Kansas until 1965, but since then have been dispersing south, presumably stimulated by periodic surges in numbers (Choate *et al*, 1979). In the last few years they have continued on and reached eastern Oklahoma, some 300 miles further south. On the other hand, when the small rodents fail, least weasels simply disappear. The years of scarcity outnumber the years of abundance for least weasels, which explains why such sudden changes in the distribution or numbers of these normally seldom-seen little animals are so remarkable.

At Barrow, on the north coast of Alaska, the population cycle of the brown lemming has been observed since the early 1950s. Whenever least weasels are seen or caught they are also recorded. Of 66 least weasels collected over the 20 years after 1953, 48 came from lemming peak years (McLean *et al*, 1974). The response of least weasels to a lemming peak is presumably the same as that of common weasels to a vole peak, but the results can be even more startling. Not only can least weasels have an oestrus during lactation, so producing several litters in very quick succession (see Chapter 9), but, like the stoats of the far north, they are also capable of producing very large litters in lemming years (Table 9.2). Similar population fluctuations of least weasels in northern and eastern Eurasia have been observed, in relation to the density and distribution of rodents, for many years (Nasimovich, 1949; Rubina, 1960).

DENSITY VARIATION IN LONGTAILED WEASELS

Much less information is available on the density and population dynamics of longtails, even though they are quite a common species. Their general density on Simms' (1979b) study area in Ontario was much less (averaging 0.5 /100 TN) than that of the much smaller stoats (averaging 2.6/100 TN). Because they have a more generalist diet and a less extremely opportunistic life-style their numbers may be relatively more stable than those of the smaller weasels; on the other hand, they probably still respond to a glut of small rodents just as the other weasels do. Edson (1933) reported that after a heavy crop of vetch seeds in the autumn of 1931, there were many mice about over the winter. In May of 1932 he caught a longtail in a trap set for mountain beavers, followed by another nine by October.

11 Populations: lifespan and mortality

There is a general relationship between size and lifespan in wild animals. Mice and voles seldom live more than a few months, whereas bears and elephants can live for 40–50 years or more. Weasels as a group are small relative to all other carnivores, and indeed, also to many other mammals. We expect, then, to find that all weasels are relatively short-lived, but that within the group, stoats and longtails will live longer than common and least weasels. The best data available are from stoats and common weasels, so most of what information we have comes from them.

METHODS OF AGE DETERMINATION

The only method of determining the age of a weasel that can be really accurate is continuous observation of a marked individual from the time it was recognisably juvenile, which can best be done in captivity or in conjunction with a successful live-trapping study. For unmarked dead animals collected from the wild, the only methods that are reasonably safe to use are those that have been calibrated against a set of specimens of known age. To my knowledge, two such sets have been collected. The first is the property of Fritz Frank of West Germany, a set of skulls of 26 male and 18 female common and least weasels and their hybrids bred under semi-natural conditions in his laboratory. The other set comprises 22 skulls of wild and wild-caught captive stoats from New Zealand. From these two sets of material, two rather different methods of age-determination have been tested; one based on observation of changes in the shape of the skull and the baculum, and the other on sectioning of the canine teeth. Each has its usefulness, and each complements the other to some extent.

The date-skull-baculum (DSB) method which I developed from Frank's material is simple, requires no special equipment, and is most useful for distinguishing young animals, not yet full-grown, among a set of skulls that must not be damaged (Figure 4.1). The development of the post-orbital constriction, allied with several other anatomical features known to be related to age, can be used to classify wild-caught common weasels into two, or at most three, year-classes. It is very reliable for the first 6–8 months after the young begin to appear in the population, though less so in late winter and spring. The skulls of stoats and longtails show the same developmental changes, although they span a longer period than in common weasels, in proportion to the slower development of larger animals (Table 9.3).

The disadvantage of the DSB method is that it cannot distinguish between the year-classes of full-grown animals. If histological machinery is available and destructive processing is permitted, it is far better to use the more complicated but reliable method of counting cementum layers in the teeth.

The teeth of mammals are anchored in their sockets by a hard substance, cementum, which is strengthened with new layers year after year. Thin sections of the teeth can be stained to show the cementum lying around their roots, and within it the edges of the annual layers showing up as dark lines in a paler field (Figure 11.1). The technique of counting the cementum lines in order to find an animal's age in years has become routine, provided that it can be proved first that the lines really are annual. I am sure (1980e) that the equally obvious lines in the superficial bone of the jaw are not annual in common weasels.

Since it is relatively easy to catch and identify young stoats in the summers after a beech seedfall, I planned to mark and release a cohort of young known to have been born in the southern summer of 1979–80 and retrieve them over the next few years. By August of 1981 I had 22 stoats of known or part-known age: 14 that had been marked as young of the

Figure 11.1. Cross section of the canine tooth of a female stoat from Denmark, killed in June at age five years and one month. Note five annual layers in the cementum (photo courtesy H.Grue).

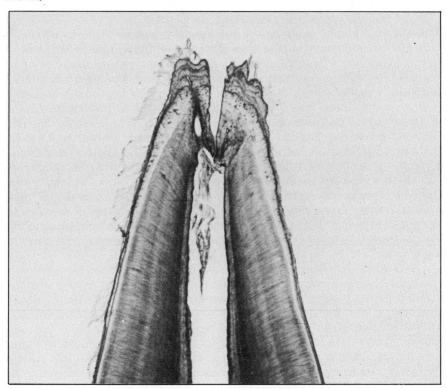

year, and 8 that had been marked as adults. I sent this material to Helen Grue in Copenhagen, coded so that she did not know which animal was which. In every case the number of lines she reported corresponded exactly to the number expected. We assumed from this that the lines are annual in stoats, both in New Zealand and in previous studies which have determined the ages of stoats from cementum lines without being able to confirm their meaning. The lines are always formed in autumn and winter, so the date of death is required before the age of a given specimen can be determined. The same method can be applied to common weasels, though for them it still lacks calibration.

The ages of living stoats and longtails can be classified in the summer months when the young are still visibly immature (males with small testes, females with no obvious teats); but the ages of living common and least weasels, other than kits, are impossible to determine with any confidence.

The problems of deciding how to classify the ages of common weasels are a little different from those of classifying stoats, because of the different reproductive cycles of species with and without delayed implantation. In common weasels the annual cohorts of young are added to the population over a long period, and there can be six months' difference in age and reproductive maturity within one season's crop. The physical distinction between young and adult blurs quickly in common weasels, and never could be defined in reproductive terms. By the end of the breeding season the generations may appear to overlap. However, the compensation is that these small weasels are short-lived; the young ones are usually vastly in the majority, and can be distinguished from the smaller numbers of second-year and older animals. In many studies, division into two age-classes, while not ideal, may be enough.

By contrast, the production of young stoats is relatively closely synchronised by day length, so each annual cohort is more distinct. The young of both sexes can confidently be separated from the adults until well after the end of the breeding season, and the young males are clearly recognisable until shortly before the next season (Figure 9.9). However, stoats are longer-lived, and for them, separation of the young animals by cranial features is not enough; tooth sectioning of the adults is necessary. Since this is a time-consuming and expensive operation, it is economic to use skull and baculum characters to exclude the young of the year from the list of specimens to be sectioned.

ESTIMATING HOW LONG WEASELS LIVE

There are two ways to work out the natural lifespans of wild animals. The first is to catch a group of new-born young, mark them and return them to the wild, and then watch them from a distance to see what age each one is when it dies from natural causes. It is not difficult to catch young weasels in box-traps and mark them with tags or clips on the ears, but keeping track of them afterwards is very difficult indeed, especially the young males which may disperse over great distances in their first year. The other way is to collect a large sample of dead weasels, taking care to make the traps equally available to both sexes and all ages, and then work out what age each one was when it was killed. It is not difficult to kill weasels in steel spring-traps, but determining their ages has been, until recently, very difficult, especially in the adults. Both methods will give a table listing the numbers of animals in each age-class, though tables derived by the two methods have different mathematical properties.

There are, of course, problems with both methods. For example, if kill-trapping is used, the complete age structure can be obtained from one or a few samples; but if kill-trapping affects the distribution of ages in the target population, data from a previously untrapped population may be different from those from regularly trapped populations. Conversely, if live-trapping is used, the sampling method has minimum effect on natural age structure, but how can the ages of the oldest adults be known unless the study goes on for long enough to follow them all to the end of their natural lives? And how can one tell if an animal that is not recovered has died or merely moved elsewhere?

Another serious problem arises from the instability of many weasel populations. In habitats in which productivity and density vary greatly from year to year, the young entering the population vastly outnumber the breeding adults in good seasons but scarcely match them — or even fail to appear altogether — in poor seasons; it then becomes important to separate data from high and low density years for analysis. A third important source of confusion is the season of the year at which the sample was taken. Consider two samples, one collected soon after the end of the breeding season and the other in winter. The first will probably show a far higher proportion of young to adults than the second, because in late summer there will be many more newly independent young about than if sampling is delayed until overwinter mortality has begun to take its toll of them. Yet the dynamics and productivity of the two populations could easily be the same. Finally, all data on age distributions derived from trapping refer only to individual weasels that survive at least to trappable age; they do not take into account the young that die at birth or in the nest. If the number of these were known, the mean ages would be much lower, and the mortality rate of the first year-class would be much higher. Omission of this information is not serious provided one remembers that all such statistics apply only from the age of independence.

The first method was applied by Erlinge (1983) to six years' worth of data on live stoats in southern Sweden (Table 11.1). The data are set out as a declining total : x animals to start with, of which y are still present a year later, and so on. There are two obvious problems. First, if any animals had stayed longer than six years, they would not have been detected since trapping stopped in 1979. But it is probably safe to assume that few did, considering how quickly the marked ones disappeared. Second, there is no way to distinguish between death and emigration as causes of their disappearance. However, the study area was very large (40 km^2) with traps distributed throughout, and the population was undisturbed, so the turnover of residents was at least natural.

The second method of working out natural lifespan also has its problems, but it takes less time to reach an answer. It depends entirely on an unbiased method of sampling the population, so that weasels of all ages and both sexes are fairly represented (or if not, that the differences between these groups are at least constant); and on a reliable method of determining the ages of the dead animals. It also involves the important

172

assumption that the distribution of ages among the animals killed is the same as in the living population. (The fact that the animals withdrawn from the population were killed in order to find out their ages is irrelevant.) If the samples are valid and the animals correctly classified, a preliminary table can be compiled to show the age structure of the population. In this type of table the data are set out as frequency distributions: so many dead animals of age x, so many different ones of age y, so many of age z, and so on. The difference between this type of table and the other is that this one represents the ages of the standing crop (all the members of that population alive at one time), whereas the other represents the lifespans of individuals observed over several years. This is the method used to construct Table 11.2.

LIFESPAN IN STOATS

Figure 11.2 shows the results of several studies, done in different countries and circumstances, which have calculated the frequency distribution of annual age classes in a population of stoats. In Russia, Holland, Denmark and New Zealand, the ages of stoats killed in the course of routine trapping (for fur, to safeguard protected birds, or for rabies research) were determined; in Sweden and Switzerland, the lives of marked individuals were observed by live-trapping. Despite the variation in methods, study areas, habitats and climates, their results are remarkably consistent.

All the samples agree that by far the largest age-class, on average over all years in all habitats, is the first one, that containing the young of the previous breeding season. The range of variation in this reflects to some extent the stability or otherwise of the populations. At one extreme is Debrot's sample from the Val de Ruz, Switzerland, where the density and age structure varied rather little from year to year and it is fair to pool the data from several years. The young of the year always comprised just over half the total, but ranged only from 55 per cent to 67 per cent; the numbers in the later age-classes drop away in a regular, smooth curve to the oldest class distinguishable, those over four years old. At the other extreme is the sample from the Eglinton Valley, New Zealand, where density varied enormously from year to year (Figure 10.4). The proportion of young of the year averaged over the six years of the study (60 per cent) was not so different from in the Val de Ruz, but it varied from 15 per cent in poor years to 92 per cent after a beech seedfall. In Erlinge's population, the proportion of first-year animals ranged from 31 per cent to 76 per cent, but the proportions of second and third year ones were much as in the Val de Ruz. The age structures of samples whose density was not measured (those from Russia, Holland and Denmark) are hard to interpret, but give the same general picture.

Huge variations in the number of young stoats produced from one year to the next cause changes in the age structure of each annual sample which can often be traced through several following samples (Figure 11.3). For example, in the New Zealand data, the largest cohort of young was produced in 1976, after a heavy seedfall, and the smallest in the following crash season. In the 1977–8 sample the one-year-olds born in 1976 outnumbered the young of the 1977 season. The earlier cohorts are represented by older animals only, so have already lost most of their members. If we had started trapping in 1971, a year of huge abundance of stoats throughout the country, this cohort would certainly have been the largest. That much is obvious even without any estimate of the numbers in the first age class; the bulge of two-year-olds is still evident in the 1973–4 catch.

If the animals were removed for sampling, and especially if the population has been regularly cropped every year, we would expect that the older stoats would disappear sooner than from an undisturbed population. But the regularly culled populations in Russia, Holland and New Zealand included older animals (up to 7–8 years) not recorded in the undisturbed areas in Switzerland and Sweden. The reason is that the kill-trapped samples were large enough to have a high probability of including some of the rare older individuals, while both of the live-trapping studies stopped before the last of the marked young had lived into its undisturbed old age. There is in fact no way to distinguish natural from trap-induced mortality from these figures. Actually, the few older animals make rather little difference to the general age structure of the population and none to its density. By contrast, the variation in the proportion of young is much more significant to both statistics, and is certainly controlled by food supplies rather than by trapping.

When certain stringent conditions are fulfilled, a frequency distribution of age classes can be converted into a life table. One of the purposes of a life table is to estimate the variation in survival rates (and, conversely, the mortality rates) among the age classes in a population. Life tables were invented by the life insurance industry as a means of estimating risk — that is, how long a certain person can be expected to pay the premiums on his life policy before making the claim. Animal ecologists took over the idea when they saw how useful it was as a means of making standardised comparisons within and between populations. There are plenty of books available to explain how to construct and analyse the tables, if we can get that far. The trouble with weasels is that few people have been able to get over the difficulties of constructing the tables in the first place.

The worst problems are the two required assumptions behind a life table, that the rate of increase of the population is zero and the age structure is stationary. Neither is ever true in weasels. The only way to get round them is to use data from marked live animals of known age — a very prolonged and time-consuming business. Erlinge (1983) started live-trapping in the autumn of 1973, and captured, marked and recaptured 75 males a total of 232 times, and 67 females 171 times, over the years 1974–9. Those first marked as juveniles born in the years 1973–6 inclusive, whose age was known with certainty, were followed for as long as they lived on the study area. Of 47 males present on the study area in their first autumn, 28 were still present a year later, and of these, 9 another year later, and so on (Table 11.1). The oldest animals were a male which stayed for 4.5 years, and a female which stayed for 3.5 years. Both were born in 1975, the year of highest numbers and most successful reproduction in that population.

The average expectation of further life on this study area for a newly independent stoat aged 3–4 months was 1.4 years for males and 1.1 years for females. The mortality rate among first-year males was 40 per cent (4 out of 10 disappeared between the ages of 0.25–0.5 years and 1.25–1.5

Figure 11.2. Average age structures of some stoat populations. (a) and (b) Russia, winter only (Stroganov, 1937; Kukarcev 1978); (c) Holland, males only (van Soest and van Bree, 1970); (d) Denmark (Jensen, 1978); (e) Switzerland, live-trapped, annual mean (Debrot, 1984); (f) Sweden, live-trapped, autumn (Erlinge, 1983); (g) Eglinton Valley, and (h) Hollyford Valley, New Zealand (King, unpublished).

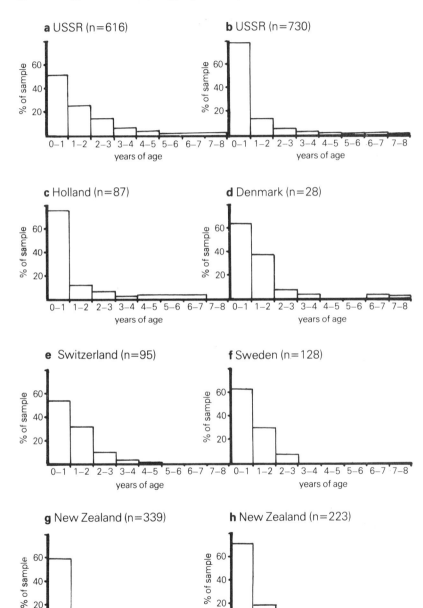

Figure 11.3. When the age distributions for each year are plotted separately, the extra large cohorts of young produced after a good seedfall (chequered columns), e.g. in 1971 and 1976, remain distinguishable in the following year and beyond (data from Eglinton and Hollyford Valleys pooled, from King, unpublished).

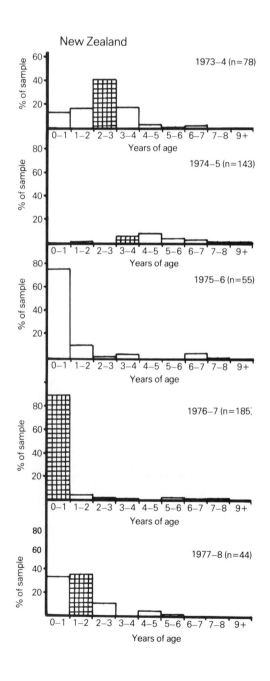

years), and significantly higher (68 per cent) a year later. For females the rates were even higher, in both their first (54 per cent) and second (73 per cent) years. These figures mean that about half the stoats present in autumn will disappear before spring every year, regardless of the autumn density. There will also be additional losses over the summer.

Table 11.1 Life table for stoats in Sweden, observed by live-trapping of marked individuals (from Erlinge, 1983)

Age class[1]	Number alive in age class	Proportion surviving at start of age class	Proportion dying at that age	Mortality rate %
Males				
3–6 months	47	1.00	0.40	40
1.25–1.5 yr	28	0.60	0.41	68
2.25–2.5 yr	9	0.19	0.15	78
3.25–3.5 yr	2	0.04	0.02	50
4.25–4.5 yr	1	0.02		
Females				
3–6 months	48	1.00	0.54	54
1.25–1.5 yr	22	0.46	0.33	73
2.25–2.5 yr	6	0.13	0.11	83
3.25–3.5 yr	1	0.02		

[1] All animals born in the cohorts of 1973, 1974, 1975, and 1976 are considered together. They are grouped as if they had all been born at the same time, and counted every year until the last of the group had died from natural causes.

The only other live population observed in some detail is the one at the Val de Ruz. The study area was rather small, but the population was relatively stable. Debrot did not calculate a conventional life table, but used a different means of arriving at a similar conclusion. He counted all juveniles of the previous year as adults on 1 January, and in the three Januaries of 1979–81 the total number of newly recruited plus older adults averaged 6.2 on the 616 ha study area. They disappeared at an average rate of 68 per cent a year, which means that two out of every three adults present on any given day will have gone a year later. Conversely, the annual replacement rate of adults was 93 per cent. Such a high turnover, Debrot admits, reflects the large dispersal range of the adults compared with the size of the study area, and also explains why most of the marked stoats were recaptured infrequently (average 2.3 times each), and only 7 per cent of adults lived on the study area for more than a year. Some individuals lived (not necessarily only on the study area) to over 4 years old, but the average age of the resident animals was 14.4 months. This is *not* the same statistic as expectation of life at independence, but it emphasises the same point, that most stoats do not live long. In particular, these undisturbed stoats did not live noticeably longer than those collected from regularly culled populations. On a game reserve in Holland, for example, van Soest and van Bree (1970) recorded a mean age of 11.9 months; in Russia, stoats in fur-trapping areas seldom live more than 1–1.5 years (Kopein, 1967).

I have calculated a preliminary life table for stoats from Fiordland by the second method (Table 11.2). Because the rate of increase in a real population of weasels is never zero in any one year, and the age structure varies greatly from year to year, one has to make the apparently reasonable assumption that the average of several years' age distributions approximates the stationary form and can be analysed as if the average rate of increase were zero. Although the sample is large, the results must therefore be regarded as only a first approximation, but they show clearly the enormous mortality of the young stoats — 83 per cent die before the end of their first year — and the relatively good survival of the remaining few over the following several years. Only in their sixth year does the mortality rate start climbing steeply again.

Table 11.2 Preliminary life table for stoats in New Zealand, observed by age-determination of carcasses (from King, unpublished)

Age class[1]	Number alive in age class	Proportion surviving at start of age class	Proportion dying at that age	Mortality rate %
3 months–1 yr	362	1.00	0.83	83
1–2 yr	62	0.17	0.03	16
2–3 yr	52	0.14	0.04	25
3–4 yr	39	0.11	0.05	51
4–5 yr	19	0.05	0.01	26
5–6 yr	14	0.04	0.01	21
6–7 yr	11	0.03	0.02	63
7–8 yr	4	0.01	0.01	75
8–9 yr	1	0.00	0.00	100

[1] Animals born in any year were sampled over several years. The distribution of the ages of the dead animals in the total sample is taken to represent the average distribution of ages of the living animals in the population. For cautions, see text. These are preliminary data only, so the sexes are pooled.

LIFESPAN IN LONGTAILS

Longtails are about the same size or a little larger than stoats in New Zealand, so probably live as long. The only data I have found support this reasonable expectation. Linduska (1947) collected seven years' survival records for various wild mammals on a Michigan farm. Of 73 longtails eartagged, a few were recaptured the year after tagging, but none after two years. Svendsen (1982) mentions that some marked adult longtails lived on his Colorado study area for up to three years.

LIFESPAN IN COMMON WEASELS

So far as we can tell, common weasels live shorter lives than stoats, as we would expect. Populations of common weasels are unpredictable, so no one has attempted to work out age structures by following marked live individuals. The only thing that can be said with certainty is that there is generally a new set of resident common weasels on a study area each season, and that no individual has been known to hold a home range for more than three years. This implies that the average lifespan cannot be much more than a year, and may well be less.

Confirmation of this guess comes from the only two attempts, one in Denmark and one in Britain, to construct a frequency distribution of annual age classes from collections of carcasses (Figure 11.4). Various other studies have used age-classes defined in different ways, which give results of the same general order but usually impossible to compare in detail.

Figure 11.4. As in stoats, the vast majority of common weasels are under a year old, but the oldest of them reach only three years. (a) England, 1968-70 (King, 1980c); (b) Denmark, 1969-70 (Jensen, 1978).

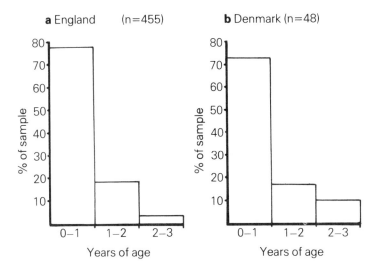

The huge preponderance of first-year animals in both samples confirms our expectations. Common weasels clearly have a short life, up to about three years at most, and by far the greatest majority of them will die long before the end of their first year. The average ages of the individuals collected from the five British estates I sampled (1980c) ranged from 0.79 to 1.16 years, mean 0.88 years, and was about the same in males (0.86 years) and females (0.93 years). The expectation of further life for a young weasel at independence was about 10 months in both sexes. The density of a population will therefore depend very largely on the production and survival of young; and since this varies drastically according to food supplies, the instability of populations of common weasels needs no further explanation.

I calculated a preliminary life table for common weasels on British game estates, on the grounds that fairly wide margins of error might be tolerated in a first attempt (Table 11.3). All the data were pooled, since there were no significant differences between the age distributions for the five sample areas or for the two sexes. The grand total was 455 common weasels, collected at all seasons of the year. The mean annual mortality rate was very high (80 per cent in males, 75 per cent in females), with a well defined peak every year in spring (Figure 11.5). Gamekeepers put most effort into trapping at that season, in the hope of removing predators from the gamebird breeding areas, and it may be this temporary rise in the risk of death that is reflected in the data. On the other hand, spring is a stressful time for weasels anyway, especially if food is short. In Wytham, a protected population never subject to regular trapping, several residents I had been watching for months died or disappeared in spring, often after drastic loss of weight; and the age distribution of weasels from Wytham was not different from those on the game estates.

Table 11.3 Life table for common weasels in Britain, calculated by the method used in Table 11.2 (from King, 1980c)

Age class	Number alive in age class	Proportion surviving at start of age class	Proportion dying at that age	Mortality rate %
Males				
0.25–1.0 yr	339	1.00	0.80	80
1–2 yr	69	0.20	0.18	90
2–3 yr	8	0.02		
Females				
0.25–1.0 yr	116	1.00	0.75	75
1–2 yr	29	0.25	0.20	80
2–3 yr	6	0.05		

Figure 11.5. Seasonal variation in the mortality rate among common weasels collected from English game estates (from King, 1980c).

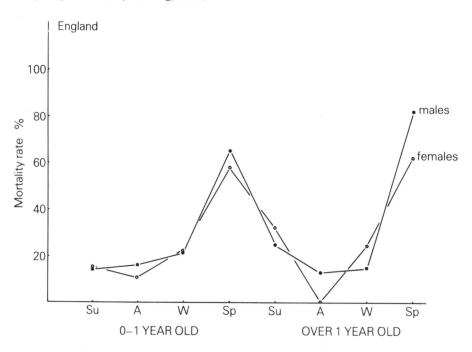

SEX RATIO

In almost any study of trapped weasels, males will be recorded more often than females. The average proportion of males collected in steel traps is usually around 75 per cent in common weasels, and around 60–65 per cent in stoats (King, 1975b). These figures are even higher in spring and summer. Live-trapping or snow-tracking of undisturbed live animals may, over a period (especially in autumn) detect males and females in roughly equal numbers, or even an excess of females (Nyholm, 1959; Raymond and Bergeron, 1982; Erlinge, 1983), but the individuals most often recaptured are always males. But the sex ratio of the young at birth averages 1:1 in all weasels, and there is no sign of a difference in the mortality rates of males and females as large as the difference in capture rates, so what causes the excess of males in the crop?

I have suggested (1975b) that one of the reasons why males are caught more often is that they have more opportunity to be caught. If traps are evenly spread out through a suitable habitat, the larger home ranges of the males will include more traps than the smaller home ranges of females. If the distance between the traps is large, some weasels will not find a trap on their own ground at all, and these are more likely to be females than males. Also, of course, the females of each species are much more likely than males to spend time hunting in burrows or under thick cover where there are no traps. The disparity is increased in spring and summer because many males travel about more widely than usual then, energetically searching for mates, whereas females tend to be less active, and perhaps also more shy of traps, at that season.

These ideas were taken up by Buskirk and Lindstedt (1989). From mathematical simulations of the effects of these and other possible causes of sex bias in trapping mustelids, they concluded that the 'exclusion effect' (some individuals having no traps on their ranges) was a special case applying only if traps are set in a wide-spaced grid pattern. Other factors include the number of traps on each individual's range, and behavioural differences between the sexes in the way they patrol their ground and approach the traps they find. But whatever the reason for the bias, it has important consequences for gamekeepers (Chapter 13).

Since the enormous fluctuations in population density typical of common weasels and stoats in good seasons are due to temporarily improved survival of the young, the ratio of young to adults is distinctly different in high and in low populations. But since the effect is similar in both sexes, and later in life, density variations have little effect on sex ratio at any age (Figure 11.6).

PREDATORS OF WEASELS

Tame weasels of any species, well settled in captivity, can live up to 8–10 years. Why is it that most wild weasels achieve only a tenth or less of their potential lifespan? One possibility is that they suffer from intense persecution from larger predators. Weasels of all species are small enough to be regarded as, or confused with, the normal prey of foxes, cats and mink, owls and hawks. Dead weasels or their remains are sometimes found at the dens of foxes and in the nests of raptors. Weasels are believed

Figure 11.6. Age ratios (a) are greatly affected by sudden changes in density, but sex ratios (b) are not (from King and McMillan, 1982).

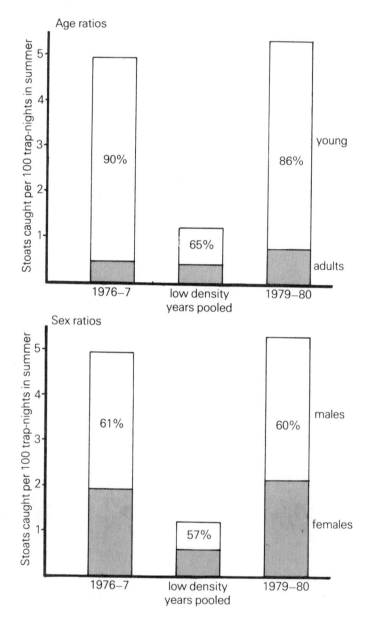

to have somewhat distasteful flesh, so these predators do not necessarily eat a weasel once they have killed it, but that is hardly a comfort. The question is, do these encounters happen often enough to affect the weasel populations?

One researcher who believed they do was Latham (1952). He examined the bounty records of the Pennsylvania Game Commission during the 1930s and 1940s, when hunters and trappers were paid to turn in dead foxes, both red and grey, and weasels of all three species. In the early 1930s the total number of weasels killed per year was over 100,000, and of foxes, under 40,000. Then in the late 1930s and early 1940s the number of weasels declined, reaching under 20,000 by 1946, and the number of foxes over the same period increased to over 80,000, so that their relative proportions in the records were nearly reversed. Between 1946 and 1949 the number of foxes went down again, which Latham attributed to the heavy toll from the bounty hunters; at the same time the weasels were apparently recovering. The inverse relationship was repeated in the relative numbers of foxes and of weasels killed in each county, as shown in Table 11.4. It seems logical to assume, concluded Latham, that foxes reduce and control the numbers of weasels in Pennsylvania.

Table 11.4 Apparent reciprocal distribution of weasels (all three species, but mostly stoats and longtails) in bounty records from Pennslyvania, 1930–51 (from Latham, 1952).

Annual weasel kill per county	weasel/fox ratio
1–99	1:9.33
100–199	1:4.06
200–299	1:2.75
300–399	1:1.86
400–499	1:1.24
500+	1:0.99

Latham's ideas were taken further by Powell (1973), then of Chicago University. Powell used the field data on raptors and their prey collected by Craighead and Craighead (1956) in Michigan in the 1940s. The Craigheads were interested in the ecology of predator-prey relationships in raptors. They attempted to estimate the density and food habits of all the local predators and to census the numbers of their prey available. They reckoned the density of weasels in 1942 was 27–36 per township (36 square miles, 93 km²); Powell took the maximum value of one per square mile, that is, 1/259 ha. From the Craigheads' extensive tables of data on the contents of nearly 5,000 raptor pellets analysed, Powell concluded that the raptors had taken 70 per cent of the summer (post-breeding) weasel population of that year. He then constructed a mathematical model of the weasel-raptor-*Microtus* ecosystem, assuming that (1) the area was large enough to operate as an effectively closed system; (2) weasel populations were not limited by food; (3) the reproduction of weasels and of voles was density-independent; (4) populations of raptors and of voles were linearly related; and (5) all mortality of voles and of weasels was due to predation. A computer was asked to run the model under a variety of starting conditions and ranges of variation in both the weasel and the vole populations. The results always showed that predation kept the weasels below the number that would have been limited by the available voles. Powell concluded that 'under certain conditions, a limiting factor for weasel populations is predation by other predators. This point has been given only limited consideration'.

Some of the rather obvious problems with this model are explicable.

For example, the Craigheads' field data were designed to count raptors, and detected weasels only incidentally, so their estimates of weasel density were certainly too low (Table 10.1). But Powell also ran the model starting from weasel densities that were certainly too high, and told me that the results came out the same. Powell deliberately included assumptions which he well knew were not supported by field evidence, especially that weasel populations are not limited by food, and that weasel mortality is due mainly to predation, but only so as to set the model up to test the question he was asking. The model was designed so that limitation by food and by predation would lead to different outcomes: one set of results would rule out the other, and vice versa. His conclusion was only that predation could sometimes limit weasel populations.

Nevertheless, I am not myself convinced by any data presented so far supposedly showing a real weasel population controlled by larger predators. Latham showed that certain sets of figures are correlated, forgetting that correlation is *not* proof of causation. The connection may easily be due to something else that affects both. For example, his impressive data on the weasel/fox ratio might only show that weasels and foxes have different habitat preferences — the counties supporting large populations of weasels might be less favourable for foxes, and vice versa. Powell's computer model may be interesting and valid as a hypothetical exercise, but the weight of present field evidence is that weasel populations are normally controlled by shortage of food (King, 1983c). Of course raptors kill weasels, perhaps a lot of them at times — e.g. after a vole peak, when weasels and raptors are numerous and voles getting scarce. But the effect of these losses on the weasel population depends on other things besides the number killed (Table 7.1), and anyway, at such times the weasel population will certainly be declining rapidly, whether any are killed by raptors or not (see Figure 13.8). There may indeed be some valid cases, but they do not represent the norm.

To understand the difference between starvation and predation as controlling factors, it helps to distinguish between the hazard and the risk presented by each. The hazard is death from either cause; the risk is the probability of encountering that hazard. Predation is a high hazard for a weasel, but a relatively low risk — at least, one not necessarily encountered every day. Starvation is both a high hazard and a high risk, faced by all weasels every day without fail. In human affairs, people tend to take a chance on a high hazard with a low risk (e.g. flying), and provide for low hazards with a high risk (e.g. denting the car) by insurance. Neither controls the local human population. But in certain parts of Africa in recent years, starvation certainly does.

However, one of the curious quirks of research, and the salvation of many a graduate student, is that it is possible to be led to a valid conclusion for the wrong reasons. Powell's convictions about the effect of raptor predation on the numbers of weasels in ecological time stimulated him to design a series of elegant experiments with trained hawks. They produced a legitimate answer to a long outstanding question in a different field altogether, the effect of raptor predation on the morphology of weasels in evolutionary time. He came up with a simple and convincing explanation for why stoats and longtails have black tips on their tails and least weasels do not.

Even though predation by raptors may not affect populations of weasels, it is a disaster for the individuals caught, and for that reason they avoid open spaces if they can (Figure 11.7, Plate 18). A raptor can swoop down on a fleeing weasel with immense speed, and is unlikely to be deterred by the defensive shriek and 'stink-bomb' which might put off a fox or cat. Only if the talons fail to pierce the thin body of a weasel may the raptor find it has picked up more than it bargained for. Anderson (1966) saw a buzzard swoop, pick up a weasel, and flap away with it; later he saw it fall to the ground with its captive. When he reached the place, there was the bird lying dead on the ground, with its underparts bloody, and the weasel gripping its breast with meshed teeth. Sometimes, raptors survive such an encounter, although without being able to dislodge the weasel's death grip. Svendsen (1982) reports an eagle which was found to have a bleached weasel skull fixed to its neck.

The white winter fur of the northern weasels is probably itself a defence against attack from the air, even though it does not match the snow exactly. For example, one study area near Robinson Lake, Idaho, supported nine longtails and four stoats during the winter of 1950–1. The stoats changed to white, but the longtails did not, and two of them were caught by raptors (Musgrove, 1951). Powell pointed out that many small animals, such as fish and butterflies, have spots of contrasting colour on their hind ends, which are believed to attract a predator's eye and deflect its strike away from vital body parts such as the head and neck. He asked whether the black tail tip of stoats and longtails might have the same

Figure 11.7. A weasel spotted on open ground by a hawk or an owl is nearly defenceless.

function. The black tip is conspicuous at any time, but especially in winter when it remains black after the rest of the coat has turned white. He decided to see whether the black tail tip is an additional hindrance to raptors hunting white weasels on snow.

Powell had three trained red-tailed hawks which could be tethered to a running wire laid out between two perches set up 30 m apart on the flat white-painted roof of the lion house at Chicago Zoo. He presented a series of model weasels to each hawk in turn, pulling them across the hawk's flight path attached to a fishing line looped around two pulleys. He estimated the hawks' attack speed, and adjusted the movement of the dummy so that the hawk could only just catch it. The model weasels were made of white artificial fur in two sizes, one 40 cm long, to represent a male longtail, and the other 17 cm long, representing a male least weasel. Some had a black spot on their backs, some on their tails, and some were plain white. The models were presented in random order to the three hawks until each had seen all six models 12 times (Table 11.5).

Table 11.5 Results of Powell's experiments on the deflective value of the black tail tip to dummy white weasels hunted by hawks against a white background (Powell, 1982).

| Model | NUMBER OF CHANCES MISSED | | | |
	Hawk #1	Hawk #2	Hawk #3	Total
Longtail, no spot	1	1	0	2
Longtail, tail spot	11	4	9	24
Longtail, body spot	2	0	2	4
Least, no spot	9	7	9	25
Least, tail spot	1	0	1	2
Least, body spot	3	0	0	3

The models representing longtailed weasels with tail spots and least weasels with no tail spots — that is, those most like the real thing — were missed by the hawks much more often than the other models. Powell's explanation was that the hawks focussed their attack on the black spot. They nearly always caught either size model if the spot was placed on the body. If the spot was placed on the long thin tail of the larger models, the hawks failed to grasp it, and they also sometimes checked their attack at the last moment, as if they had not seen the rest of the model until then. On the other hand, if the spot was placed on the short tail of the smaller model, they usually caught it because the rest of the body was close enough to be within talon's reach. Larger models with no spots were still visible, even though they were all white against the white-painted concrete roof; but the hawks took fractionally longer to notice and react to the smaller ones with no spots, so often missed them. Powell concluded that the black tail tip on stoats and longtails is a classic predator-deflection mark, and that least weasels do not have it because their tails are too short to hold the mark far enough away from the body.

One might ask, Powell adds, why least weasels do not have longer tails so that a black tip would be a benefit instead of a liability. He suggests that they are too small to keep a longer tail warm during the long northern winters. This is reasonable; and perhaps another reason is that they are less exposed to raptors than are larger weasels, because they spend so much more of their time under cover. However, the snow does not last all year round, and, except in the far north, most weasels are brown for more months of the year than they are white. I would like to see Powell's idea tested with models of brown weasels against various natural backgrounds. Another important factor to consider is the great range in body size of weasels with and without black-tipped tails (Figures 4.5 and 4.6). Some future test should include models representing the races of small stoats that do have short tails with black tips, and the races of large European common weasels that have short tails without black tips. In the meantime, Powell's conclusion on the function of the black tail tip seems secure, and this remains true whether or not predation by raptors has any effect on weasel population dynamics. In nature, predation can have a profound effect on morphology, by determining which animals survive, without affecting density, the total number to survive, at all.

PARASITES AND DISEASES OF WEASELS

Practically all wild mammals, even healthy ones, carry at least a few parasites, internal and/or external. Most are also susceptible to at least some diseases caused by invasive micro-organisms. The degree of inconvenience and debilitation caused varies a great deal. Some parasites are unnoticed; others can cause intense irritation over a long period; a few are fatal. If parasites or diseases could affect weasel populations we should consider them here.

Weasels are known to be susceptible to various diseases, such as tularaemia and distemper (Lavrov, 1944), and murine (but not ovine) sarcosporidiosis (Tadros and Laarman, 1979), but practically nothing is known about the incidence or effects of these conditions. Ringworm, a fungal infection common on hedgehogs and voles in Wytham, was not often passed on to the resident common weasels there (English, 1971).

Bovine tuberculosis is a serious problem for dairy farmers, especially in areas where there are continual 'breakdowns' (reinfections of a cleared herd) from contact with infected wild mammals. Removal of the wild species harbouring the disease becomes a high priority to farmers in such areas. In Britain the main targets are badgers, especially in south-west England; none of the 33 common weasels nor the 33 stoats examined between 1971 and 1985 was positive for TB (MAFF, 1987). In New Zealand the reservoir of infection is held mainly in brush-tailed possums, and stoats can pick it up from them (Coleman, 1975). Although the disease in cattle is generally under control in Britain, it probably cannot be entirely eliminated from wild mammals there. TB certainly could never be eliminated from New Zealand, and cannot even be prevented from spreading further, although stoats probably play little part in helping it.

Skin parasites are common in most mammals. Lice, some ticks, and mites are hard to see, especially the larvae, and all we can say is that weasels do have some. The records are sparse and probably grossly inadequate, but for what they are worth they are listed here. Common weasels have a specific louse, *Trichodectes mustelae*, and are known to carry the mites *Demodex* spp, *Haemaphysalis longicornis* and *Psorergates mustela* (Tenquist and Charleston, 1981). Stoats have a specific louse, *Trichodectes ermineae*, recorded both in Ireland and in New Zealand (Sleeman, 1989; King, 1989). They also carry the mites *Eulaelaps stabulans* and *Hypoaspis nidicorva* (both normally found on birds), *Demodex erminae*, *Gymnolaelaps annectans*, *Haemophysalis longicornis*, and *Listrophorus mustelae*. In Ireland, a comprehensive examination of stoats detected the mite *Neotrombicula autumnalis* (only the larva is parasitic, but one female carried 1,819 of them); the lice *Polyplax spinulosa* (of rats) and *Mysidea picae* (of corvid birds); and the ticks *Ixodes hexagonus* (a nest species; 266 larvae on one female), *I. ricinus* (common on rats) and *I. canisuga* (Sleeman, 1989).

The only two sorts of parasites of weasels that have received considerable attention are the fleas, because they can tell us quite a lot about how weasels hunt and move about their home ranges, and *Skrjabingylus nasicola*, a nematode worm that causes dramatic lesions in the skull.

Fleas

When live-trapped weasels are anaesthetised (Plate 12), the fleas in their fur, which are also anaesthetised, fall out and can be collected by hand. Several field workers undertaking live-trapping studies for quite different reasons have extended their field routine to allow for the collection of fleas during the short time they have an unconscious weasel in their hands. When weasels are collected dead, they often still have some fleas on them, and these are also worth collecting as a routine part of the dissection procedure.

Neither method can be claimed to search the fur thoroughly enough to find all the fleas that might be present, and of course lice and mites are harder still to see. Worse, dead weasels collected in humane traps such as the Fenn will have lost many of the fleas they had, since fleas are not confined to the host's body and will leave a carcass as it cools. These problems aside, the systematic collection of fleas in various places has produced some intriguing sidelights on the natural history of weasels.

The larvae of fleas are free-living scavengers, and they find the best conditions of temperature and food supplies in the nests of small mammals. Fleas evolve along with their hosts, and have developed close relationships with mammals that have substantial nests, occupied or frequently revisited over a long enough time for the fleas to complete their non-parasitic larval stages. Hence mammals with a small home range and a permanent den, such as badgers, moles, shrews and rabbits, have specific fleas; those that move around a lot and have only temporary dens or none at all, such as foxes and hares, have no flea species of their own. Neither do weasels, except in the far North. In temperate lands, they carry only the fleas normally found on other animals. It has always been assumed that weasels pick up fleas from the carcasses that they are eating, and perhaps less often from casual encounters in the grass. But these are probably not the usual ways that weasels acquire their fleas. If they were, the list of the normal hosts of the fleas identified on weasels should closely match the normal diet of weasels, but it does not. The list in Table 11.6 includes fleas specific to hosts that weasels seldom or never eat, such as moles, and some of these in substantial numbers; conversely, there are few fleas specific to hosts frequently eaten, such as rabbits and birds. One species, *Rhadinopsylla pentacantha*, normally found only in the nests of voles rather than on their bodies, turns up on weasels remarkably often.

My explanation (1976) for this strange pattern is that weasels normally pick up their fleas from the burrows that they have run through and the nests they have slept in. These are the places where adult fleas lie in wait, ready to jump onto the first warm furry creature that passes by. Weasels feel the cold badly, and since they do not make their own nests, they have to depend on finding a warm nest to sleep in made by some other animal. They would be very likely to pick up the fleas specific to hosts that make substantial nests of the right size, even though these hosts are seldom eaten. On this theory, common weasels must often borrow the nests of moles, and stoats the nests of rats and squirrels; the fleas of moles, rats and squirrels are found on stoats and common weasels much more often than their hosts are eaten by them. Radio-tracking of stoats in Ireland showed that rats' nests were favourite places to sleep (Sleeman, 1987). On the other hand, the nests of many birds have no roof, so offer little protection from the elements; birds are often eaten, but their fleas are rare on weasels. Irish stoats apparently do eat shrews, yet do not carry shrew fleas, perhaps because a shrew's nest would be too small for even the small Irish stoat to fit into.

There are, of course, other considerations. For example, some fleas are very specific to one particular host and will quickly drop off any other — perhaps this is why so few rabbit fleas are found on weasels. The less fussy ones are likely to stay on the 'wrong' host for a while, especially if they are hungry and actively searching for a meal. This is likely to be a stronger motive for hopping onto a weasel than if they are merely disturbed by a weasel eating the host they are already on.

Skrjabingylosis

Museum curators and researchers dealing with collections of weasel skulls noticed long ago that many specimens were damaged in the post-orbital region, immediately behind the eyes. They had what appeared to be dark patches or swellings with thinned walls, and sometimes these had holes in them, even large openings (Figure 11.8). The cause of the damage became clear when the fresh heads were skinned and the swellings opened. Inside, a mass of bright red worms (Figure 9.11) could be seen crammed into the tiny sinuses in the nasal bone, coiled over each other and pressing hard against the confining skull. The worms were described in 1842 by Leuckart, and are now known by the tongue-twisting name of *Skrjabingylus nasicola* — Skrjabin, for the great Russian parasitologist, and 'nasicola' because of their position. The condition of being infested with these worms is called skrjabingylosis.

These parasites have attracted a lot of attention, for two reasons. First, they are easy to observe in freshly dead mustelids, and very dramatic in appearance and effect. Better still, they can also be studied indirectly from standard museum material. A large collection of skulls allows the incidence and geographical distribution of damage to be calculated with

Table 11.6 Fleas found on common weasels and stoats (columns give total number of fleas found: number of animals inspected, often the same ones on successive days, summed below)

Flea species	Normal host	On common weasels			On stoats		
		England	Scotland	Switz.	N.Z.	U.K.	Eire
Megabothris walkeri	voles	82	67				28
Ctenophthalmus nobilis	voles, mice	48	18	3			
Hystrichopsylla talpae	rodents, insectivores	25	11				
Malareus p. mustelae	voles	26	20	3			
C.bisoctodentatus heselhausi	moles	17	17	2			
Palaeopsylla m. minor	moles	18	16	1			
Rhadinopsylla pentacantha	nests of voles	9		1		2	
Dasypsylla g.gallinulae	birds	5		1			3
Megabothris turbidus	voles	4		1			
Peromyscopsylla spectabilis	voles	1					
Nosopsyllus fasciatus	rats	1		1	662		17
Palaeopsylla s.soricis	shrews		1				
Megabothris rectangulatus	voles		14			1	
Ctenophthalmus agyrtes impavidus				25			
C.b.bisoctodentatus	moles			47			
C.s.solutus				1			
Monopsyllus s.sciurorum	squirrels			6			
Peromyscopsylla bidentata					1		
Leptopsylla segnis	house mouse				8		
Ceratophyllus gallinulae	birds				1		
Parapsyllus nestoris	birds				1		
Orchopeas howardi	squirrels					2	
Spilopsyllus cuniculus	rabbits					1	1
Number of examinations		338	NR	380	1501	NR	122
Reference		King 1976	Mardon & Moors 1982	Debrot & Mermod 1982	King & Moody 1982	Mardon & Moors 1977 King 1976	Sleeman 1989

Figure 11.8. The skulls of weasels commonly show more or less severe distortions and perforations in the post-orbital area, caused by Skrjabingylus *worms (from King, 1977).*

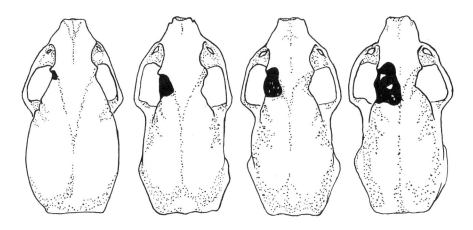

Figure 11.9. Skrjabingylus nasicola *worms (females large, males small) extracted from a moderate-sized lesion in a stoat skull.*

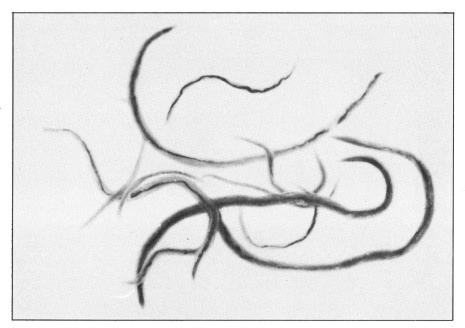

minimum effort. The cheap and simple technique of visual inspection of pre-existing material has ensured many more studies of the damage caused by skrjabingylosis than of the parasite itself. Fortunately, the link between the visible damage and the incidence of infestation is secure (Lewis, 1978). Second, there is the economic aspect. In the far north, weasel furs were once a valuable item of trade, and most of the earliest research on skrjabingylosis was concerned with the effect of the disease on the harvest. Looking at an advanced case, it is hard to avoid the impression that such severe distortion of the skull bones, and consequent pressure on the brain (Figure 11.10), must have some effect on the general health of the afflicted animal, possibly a fatal one. Hence, in the early 1940s Russian biologists interpreted their data to mean that stoats heavily infested with *S.nasicola* were in poorer condition, less fertile, and died sooner than uninfested ones, and that the fur harvest was lower in seasons following widespread infestations (Popov, 1943; Lavrov, 1944). Conversely, there are other places where any species of weasel is regarded as a pest. People concerned with the protection of birds, usually game or endangered native species (see Chapter 13), would welcome any prospect of biological control of weasel populations using a specific and fatal parasite, and encourage research on means of spreading it.

The proportion of skulls visibly damaged by skrjabingylosis is not quite the same as the incidence of the disease in a population, since very early infestations are not detected this way, but nevertheless damage does closely reflect both incidence and severity (the number of worms in each skull). Studies of damaged skulls in museums therefore give an idea of local and regional variation in incidence (Table 11.7). However, these general figures are not very informative. Estimates of incidence are

Figure 11.10. The head of a common weasel cut across in the post-orbital region. 1. Skrjabingylus worms; 2. brain; 3. muscles; 4. skull (to the left of the arrow, the zygomatic arch or cheek bone; to the right, the cranium) (from King, 1977).

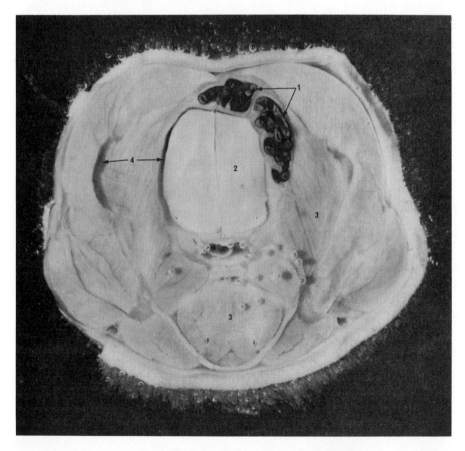

strongly affected by sampling variables such as the season of collection and the age structure of the target population, and the incidence in any one area may vary from year to year (King, 1977; Weber, 1986). Moreover, since the worms tend to damage smaller skulls more severely, the disease is probably detected at an earlier stage in the females than in the males of one species, and more often in common and least weasels than in stoats and longtails. This means that estimates of damage are not strictly comparable in skulls of different sizes.

Table 11.7 Regional variation in incidence of *Skrjabingylus nasicola* in weasels

Species	Country	Incidence	References
Stoats	Britain	17–30%	Lewis, 1967; van Soest *et al*, 1972
	Eurasia	20–50%	Lavrov, 1944; Vik, 1955; Hansson, 1970; van Soest *et al*, 1972; Debrot & Mermod, 1981; Sleeman, 1988
	North America	20–100%	Dougherty & Hall, 1955
	New Zealand	0–40%	King & Moody, 1982
Common and least weasels	Britain	70–100%	King, 1977
	Eurasia	20–60%	Lavrov, 1944; Vik, 1955; Hansson, 1970; van Soest *et al*, 1972
Longtails	North America	0–100%	Dougherty & Hall, 1955
	Manitoba	100%	Gamble & Riewe, 1982

The biology of the parasite was worked out in the laboratory by Dubnitskii (1956). Male and female adults are easily distinguished from their size; the females measure 18–25 mm long, with a diameter of 0.8 mm, and the males about 8–13 mm by 0.5 mm (Figure 11.9). The first-stage larvae, about 300 µm long, travel from the sinuses down the nasal passages to the back of the throat. From there they pass into the gut and to the outside with the faeces. They actively disperse onto nearby grass and leaves, and await their opportunity to invade the soft foot tissues of a slug or a snail. There, after 12–18 days, they pass through an obligatory intermediate second stage. When eaten by a weasel, the third-stage larvae (now grown to 700–750 µm long) pass from the gut into the tissues, through two more moults, and then migrate to the nasal sinuses along the spinal cord as fifth-stage larvae. They grow to adult size and settle in, wriggling around in the confined space and gradually enlarging it, causing the swellings and perforations. How they do this is not quite clear; it could be a matter of simple friction, the rubbing of the worms' hard cuticle against the sensitive bone tissue, or possibly the worms are able to produce some kind of corrosive chemical that interferes with the control of the living bone tissue or erodes it directly. Damage often increases with age, which suggests repeated reinvasions.

The main problem faced by the larvae is how to get from the snail to a weasel. Weasels do not eat snails, or at least, not nearly often enough to account for the high frequency of infestation in some places. Other animals do eat snails regularly, for example, any of the shrews. A larva finding itself inside a shrew will simply retreat into a cyst and wait. The shrew is not needed as part of the parasite's life cycle, but it can act as paratenic (waiting) host, a bridge to the definitive host where the larvae can complete their development into breeding adult worms.

If an infected paratenic host is eaten by a weasel, the cyst opens in the gut and the larva continues on its interrupted journey. Hansson (1967) showed that it was possible to transmit skrjabingylosis into a previously uninfested weasel by feeding it shrews. The suggestion that shrews might be the natural paratenic host was strengthened by the fact that incidence rates are particularly high in places where weasels eat shrews more often than usual. On Terschelling Island, off the coast of Holland, the incidence rate is over 90 per cent, much greater than on the nearby mainland coast (23 per cent), and as there are no voles on the island the Terschelling stoats eat a lot of shrews (van Soest et al, 1972). North American stoats tend to eat shrews more often than their European brethren, and also suffer a generally higher rate of infestation. In western Newfoundland, the incidence of skrjabingylosis in stoats increased dramatically after shrews were introduced to the island (Jennings et al, 1982). However, in most places weasels do not eat shrews, or at least, not often enough, except when their usual resources are extremely scarce. Hansson's experimental animals ate the shrews only with the greatest reluctance. Besides, a few weasels in Newfoundland had skrjabingylosis before the shrews arrived; and there are no shrews in New Zealand, where the parasite arrived with its hosts and has persisted for a hundred years.

The solution to the mystery was found by a doctoral student at Neuchatel and published in a joint paper with his supervisor (Weber and Mermod, 1983). Weber discovered encysted third-stage larvae in the salivary and lacrymal glands of wood mice and bank voles, and also in the muscles and connective tissues of their heads. These small rodents, especially wood mice, do eat snails occasionally; not as a main item of diet, but often enough so that some become carriers of invasive larvae (Figure 11.11). Weber fed infected rodents to six ferrets, which were bred in his laboratory and known to be free of the disease. He checked every day for the development of the adult parasites by inspecting the ferrets' scats in water under a binocular microscope. A host carrying both sexes of worms in the same sinus passes a continual stream of first-stage larvae, which can easily be seen swimming about in the water. Within 24 days, three of the ferrets were infected. The two that had been given the head and front end of the rodents produced larvae first; the one given the hind end only much later; the three given only the viscera (heart, lungs, liver, intestine) remained free. It is a fact that weasels usually begin to eat their prey at the front end, and often leave the viscera. Hence, the larvae not only choose a paratenic host frequently eaten by weasels, but also apparently seem to choose to encyst in the part of the body first eaten by a weasel.

Parasites often show such remarkably close adaptations to the feeding habits of their definitive hosts, for the simple reason that their lives depend on it. Nevertheless, the parasitic way of life is hazardous. Weber calculated that, of every 100 first-stage larvae given the chance to invade a slug, only about 24 reached the infectious third stage, and only six

Figure 11.11. The life cycle of Skrjabingylus nasicola *in weasels. (a) First-stage larvae leave the weasel in the scats. (b) The larvae have to pass through the next two moults in a compulsory intermediate host, a mollusc. (c) Third-stage larvae encysted in the mollusc tissues can reach a weasel directly, but this is rare as weasels seldom eat molluscs. (d) Usually the larvae make use of a paratenic host, a shrew or a mouse which has eaten an infected mollusc. (e) On being eaten by a weasel, the larvae escape from their cysts, pass through another moult, and migrate to the nasal sinuses along the spinal cord (after Weber, 1986).*

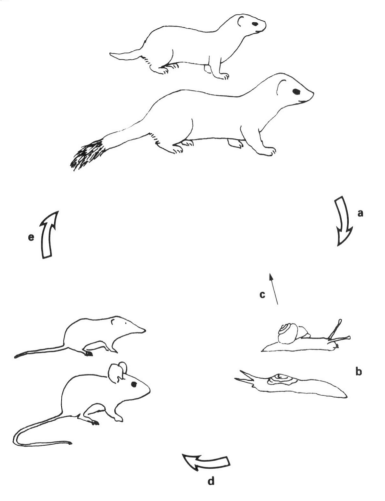

became adult worms (Weber and Mermod, 1985). The losses during the life cycle of the parasite are high even in the ideal conditions in the laboratory; in the wild, they would be much worse. In Weber's study area at the time of his observations, the infestation rate in stoats was 11 per cent; but only 2 (0.3 per cent) of 762 molluscs and 2 (4 per cent) of 48 shrews and small rodents he examined were carrying larvae. The system is wasteful, but it works because the number of larvae produced is so enormous, small rodents are so frequently eaten by weasels, and the time the larvae are prepared to wait in a rodent is so long (at least a year).

Geography and climate also play their part in determining incidence. The disease is generally more prevalent in damper habitats, and absent in deserts. The reason is mainly to do with the conditions that favour the survival of the free larvae and their chances of making the hazardous journey from the weasel's scats to a mollusc's foot. The larvae are very susceptible to drying up, and also to freezing when they are swimming in water (Hansson, 1974); the best conditions, both for the larvae and for the molluscs, are found in a mild and humid climate. In different districts of Sweden and Britain, the frequency of incidence of the disease or the severity of damage it causes increase with the number of rainy days per year, and these correlations need no explanation.

Strangely, the opposite correlation was observed in New Zealand; in the wettest places sampled, all with mean annual rainfall over 3,000 mm, the incidence of skrjabingylosis in stoats was 0–7 per cent, whereas higher local incidences (15–60 per cent) were found only where rainfall was under 1,600 mm. This contradiction was completely inexplicable at the time that study (King and Moody, 1982) was published. Since then, however, Weber's demonstration of the role played by wood mice in the transmission of the disease in Europe suggests a possible solution to the puzzle. Feral house mice are generally less common in the wetter mixed forests of New Zealand, where incidence was low, than in the dryer beech forests and grasslands where incidence was higher. If these mice are the paratenic host transmitting skrjabingylosis to New Zealand stoats, geographical variation in their relative density could explain the unexpected distribution of the disease in that country.

Much work on skrjabingylosis has been done since the early Russian studies that claimed a detrimental effect on infested individuals. On Terschelling Island, stoats tend to be a little smaller than on the mainland, and van Soest *et al* (1972) put this down to the high rate of infestation suffered by the island animals. But they compared only crude averages; to be valid, comparisons must be made only between infested and clean individuals of the same age and sex. Whenever this has been done, there has been no sign that the infested animals were any smaller, lighter or leaner, or died sooner, than the others (King, 1977; King and Moody, 1982).

On the other hand, there seems to be no doubt that incidence does increase after a population decline, both in Russia and in Switzerland. Popov (1943) and Lavrov (1944) attributed the decline to the increased infestation, but Debrot and Mermod (1981) suggest that the relationship works the other way around. In both countries, stoats reach a high density when water voles are abundant (see Chapter 10). Water voles are strictly herbivorous, and are not at all implicated in the transmission of skrjabingylosis. When they are abundant, stoats feed almost exclusively on them, and so run little risk of picking up the parasite. However, when water voles decline, stoats also decline and the survivors are forced to turn to alternative prey, including wood mice, the most likely to be carrying invasive larvae. Hence Debrot documented an increase in infestation during the population decline in the Brévine valley, from 4 per cent when the stoats were feeding almost exclusively on water voles to 50 per cent after the forced change of diet. This attractive idea was confirmed in the Val de Ruz by Weber (1986). Unfortunately, no one seems to have thought of the possible effect on these figures of the change in age structure which also follows a population decline. The higher proportion of older stoats in the post-peak population would in itself cause an increase in incidence, since most data agree that incidence increases with age and weasels have practically no resistance to infestation and no means of repairing the damage (Lewis, 1978). Debrot's hypothesis should be tested; in the meantime, the role of skrjabingylosis in the population dynamics of weasels remains unknown.

Even if the parasite has no effect on populations, it could still affect the behaviour of individuals. The pressure on the brain caused by the distortion of the skull, plus the wriggling of the worms, might be expected to be intensely irritating. Weasels observed behaving strangely in the wild, leaping about and somersaulting, are said to be 'dancing', either in play or as a clever trick to catch birds (see Chapter 6). They are also believed to suffer 'fits', or to 'play dead' after violent exertion (Chapter 8). Perhaps these gyrations and temporary black-outs are merely an understandable response to the extreme discomfort caused by having to carry around such unwelcome and relatively enormous guests in the head. But at present there is no way to prove the point one way or the other.

12

Puzzles: delayed implantation, sexual dimorphism and co-existence

In order to specialise in hunting small rodents, a successful predator must have not only obvious characters such as the ability to enter very small spaces, but also less obvious ones such as some means of surviving and breeding year after year despite huge variations in food supply. Weasels have in fact evolved a whole set of special adaptations to deal with these conditions, which make the weasel way of life possible. Some of the adaptations are long-term, involving physical characters unchangeable in an individual's lifetime — things like the long thin shape of the weasel body, or the details of the reproductive cycle. Some are short-term, including the flexibility of behaviour and reproductive response appropriate in different circumstances. Of course, no-one means to imply that animals are capable of sitting down and working out a plan for survival. It is just that certain sets of characters are likely to favour the animals that happen to have them in a given set of conditions. Over the long term, only the favourable sets of characters survive to be observed. To understand the ways in which weasels have evolved to deal with the hazards of their lives, we need to draw on practically everything we know about weasels presented in this book so far.

HOW SIZE AFFECTS POPULATION DYNAMICS

In the technical literature, the characters which determine the population demography of a species are collectively called its life history strategy. They include, for example, age at first breeding, mating system, litter size, average number of litters per season and per lifetime, amount of parental care invested in each litter, expectation of life at birth, and so on. Life history strategies are determined mainly by two things: body size, and the permanence of the habitat relative to the lifetime of an individual. Small animals can survive in small patches of the environment that would not support larger animals, which tend to range across many different patches. However, since small patches tend to be unreliable, small animals must also be good at dispersing from one patch to the next as local food supplies run out. For example, an overgrown corner of a field containing many field voles provides an excellent temporary home for a common weasel, although after a while it and its young will probably have to move out to find another one. By contrast, the whole field and a large area around it may be the stable and permanent home of generations of badgers (King, 1983c). On the other hand, because small animals generally have small home ranges, they can therefore reach greater population densities than larger animals of a similar kind. For example, common weasels are much more abundant than badgers, and vary in numbers from year to year much more. In one study area in Poland, during a population cycle of field voles, the density of common weasels went from roughly 7 individuals per 100 ha at the vole peak down to just over 2 individuals per 100 ha after the decline, a threefold change; but the density of badgers remained at 2 individuals per 1,000 ha throughout (Goszczynski, 1977).

Small animals living in very variable and unstable habitats tend to accumulate a suite of characteristics collectively known as the opportunistic or 'r-strategy', so named because the net effect of that combination of characteristics is to maximise r, the rate of population increase. Larger animals living in more stable and reliable habitats tend to accumulate the opposite characters, which make up the equilibrium or 'K-strategy'. For them, rate of increase is far less important than producing a few high-quality young, well developed and prepared to compete with others for a place in the adult population. Between the two extreme types are intermediates which have these characters developed to different degrees.

Although the idea of the r-K dichotomy is obviously a gross over-simplification of how real animals work, and is now largely overtaken by more complex theories, nevertheless it is a robust generalisation that has been immensely influential in the past, and there is still much truth in it as a simple way of understanding the differences between animal types. For example, a set of related species can be ranged along a spectrum, from extreme opportunists at one end through all shades of intermediates to extreme equilibrium species at the other. The rank order is determined from the relative importance in each species of the characters which most augment the rate of population increase, which are early maturity, more than one litter per year, large litter size, and more than one litter per female's lifetime, in that order. The six species of British mustelids demonstrate this idea well (King and Moors, 1979a). Common and least weasels are the most opportunistic members of the mustelid family, and stoats and longtails are next; badgers are typical equilibrium species.

Common and least weasels have all the characters of determined opportunists. They tend to mature early, can breed in the season in which they are born, can produce a second or even a third litter in seasons of abundant food, and bear small young with a short life expectancy. Their populations are unstable from year to year and governed mainly by food supplies. The parent animals best represented in the next generation tend to be those that can produce and feed the most young most quickly, so they concentrate on quantity rather than quality. They spend the least possible time on parental care, because, if food is abundant, the effort spent on training one litter could better be spent on producing another one. Besides, training individual young is not a good investment of parental energy for the smaller weasels; chance is probably as important as fighting prowess in determining whether a young common or least weasel will find a suitable home range to settle on, and the more young produced, the greater the chances that one will be successful. On top of that, the mortality rate of adults is so high that few live through more than one breeding season, so there is every reason to make the most of the present one.

Stoats and longtails have the same traits, but to a lesser extent. Young females mature early, but then are prevented by compulsory delayed implantation from producing the litter until they are a year old. Young males cannot mate until ten or eleven months old. Therefore, individuals of both sexes are incapable of producing young in their first year, and only one litter a year is possible in older ones however abundant the food supplies. Hence the rate of population increase in stoats and longtails is considerably less than in common and least weasels. On the other hand, although the mortality of the first year young is very high, those that make it into their second year in an undisturbed population have some chance of living for 3–6 years, and breeding several times (Tables 11.1, 11.2). Their populations are unstable but rather less so than those of common and least weasels, not only because they are longer-lived but also because they can take a wider range of foods, switching from one to another if necessary. They seem to spend rather longer on parental care, partly because they cannot produce another litter until the following year anyway, and perhaps also partly because there is some chance that investment at this stage may be repaid with greater success later. For example, larger than average size is an advantage to a male stoat, because larger males are more likely to be dominant and successful. Among the things that determine whether a male will grow to his full potential size or not may be whether he is well fed by his mother (Ralls and Harvey, 1985; R.A.Powell unpublished). Among litters of weasels brought up in captivity on guaranteed food supplies, the young males grow larger than wild-reared young of the same age (East and Lockie 1965; Hayward, 1983).

DELAYED IMPLANTATION

One of the keys to success for opportunists is that they have the capacity to respond quickly to any local improvement in living conditions. For example, a sudden surge in the population density of voles presents adult weasels with the opportunity to produce more young, and while it lasts it also increases the young weasels' chances of surviving to become adults, and the adults' chances of surviving long enough to breed again. When this happens, common and least weasels can adjust their breeding effort almost immediately; hence the breeding success of common and least weasels is very closely linked to the density of rodents. Common and least weasels have developed the opportunistic way of life to such a fine art that they can thrive in the most dangerous conditions, such as in the fierce cold and regular famines of the far north.

Although most adult stoats and longtails are large enough to survive periods of shortage of small rodents by turning to other prey, their chances of breeding success are also much increased during rodent peaks. Small rodents comprise ideally convenient packages of meat to feed to all young weasels; they are easy to kill, light to carry, and wrapped in a ready-made waterproof packet. Hence the rate of survival of the juvenile stoats and longtails, and the productivity of the adults, are also linked to the density of rodents, just as in the two smaller weasels. Stoats and longtails are therefore also classed as opportunists, even if not quite such specialised ones. But they have one huge disadvantage that common and least weasels do not have; delayed implantation is obligatory, regardless of environmental conditions. It means that stoats and longtails have to wait at least a year before they can increase their breeding effort in response to any extra food available, which by then may well have disappeared. This must be a particularly serious handicap for the smallest races of stoats, which are as dependent on small rodents as are common or least weasels elsewhere, especially those living in the far north. If the capacity to respond rapidly to variations in food supply is important to common and least weasels, then surely it must also be important to stoats and longtails. How then can stoats and longtails survive in the face of such a serious penalty? Indeed, how did such an apparently disadvantageous arrangement become established in the first place?

The Value of Delayed Implantation

Why do stoats have delayed implantation and common weasels do not? Actually, this is really two questions: (1) Is delayed implantation useful to stoats? (2) If it is useful, why do common weasels not have it too? (The question is here confined to stoats and common weasels because they are broadly sympatric and both evolved in Eurasia; there is no necessary implication that the same arguments could be applied to the North American species.)

The ways in which modern animals get their living are, by definition, the ones that work. They are not necessarily the best possible ways, just the best of the ways that have been tried. Delayed implantation must be a useful adaptation for stoats, or it would not have persisted. The mechanism controlling it is extremely complex, precise and consistent, with practically no variation. It is found in virtually all female stoats of all ages every year, in all the temperate habitats carefully studied so far. Clearly, there is never any profit in deviation. It seems obvious that these arrangements are maintained because the advantages of having delayed implantation outweigh the disadvantages.

It is, in fact, easy to think of a list of advantages of having it, and I have suggested some (King 1983b, 1984b). First, the female and her young are all ready for mating at about the same time. This means that any male that can get into a breeding den at the right moment stands to gain several mates all at once. Such extreme polygyny is rare among small carnivores, whose females are usually too widely dispersed for a male to monopolise access to a whole group of them. The precocity of the nestling females makes stoats the outstanding exception to this general rule, and the consequence for the successful male is a huge payoff in future offspring. Better still, only the old female can put up any resistance to his attentions. Second, the young females are fertilised before the family breaks up. This means that they are already assured of a litter next season, even if, by then, prospective mates are few. The blastocysts take very little energy to maintain, so pregnancy does not interfere with normal growth; then, in spring, they are free to concentrate on hunting and on finding and establishing a breeding den.

The trouble about explanations of evolutionary adaptations is that they are always proposed in retrospect. The most famous examples of the type are Rudyard Kipling's *Just So Stories*. Delayed implantation may well have many advantages for stoats; but for all we know, stoats might have been just as successful without it. As in any theoretical problem, answers are easy; the trick is to find the right question. In this case, we need to know not only, why do stoats have delayed implantation, but also, why do common weasels not have it. In response to my suggestions, Sandell (1984, 1985) proposed that the two species have different patterns of reproduction because the keys to success in contemporary times are different for each. For stoats, the most important consideration is to produce the young as early in the season as possible. He assumes that the young need plenty of time to grow before the next winter, yet the adults need to avoid mating too early in spring, while conditions may still be severe. Delayed implantation allows both. For common weasels, the only thing that matters is a high potential rate of increase, i.e., the capacity to turn mouse meat into young weasels faster than anyone else. For this, small size, rapid maturation and no delayed implantation are the best policies. Neither Sandell nor I had much hard evidence to support our suggestions, but it is always legitimate to ask questions.

Stenseth (1985) was stimulated by the exchange between Sandell and me (in the columns of the journal *Oikos*) to produce a model incorporating the different reproductive capacities of the two species (stoat, 6–13 young once a year; common weasel, 4–8 young once or twice a year). He then addressed Sandell's question on whether these differences could be maintained by the action of contemporary natural selection. He concluded that the relative difference in litter size and frequency predicted by his model corresponds to the observed difference in nature — i.e. that Sandell's idea is basically correct. But there are some known errors in his analysis (e.g. he assumes that common weasels always have two litters every year); and there is no evidence that the supposed need of stoats to breed early in the year is sufficiently consistent and compelling to account for the remarkable constancy of delayed implantation that we observe. And there are still many unanswered questions — for example, how do the tiny Canadian stoats manage to continue to behave like stoats when their body size and food resources are those of common weasels? Why must stoats avoid breeding too early in spring when the much smaller least weasels can breed under the snow all winter? There is plenty of scope for future students of weasels to make a contribution to this discussion.

The Origin of Delayed Implantation in Stoats

Of course the adaptation of contemporary animals must be maintained by contemporary advantages; but their origin is a different matter. Modern animals are descended by a continuous process of change from different animals living in the past. Ancestral characters, or modified remnants of them, are often still discernible in contemporary species, constituting what Stephen Jay Gould calls 'the footprints of history'.

I have suggested (see Chapter 2) that weasels evolved, just before and during the Pleistocene, from larger ancestors somewhat similar to martens and polecats. Many of these would already have had delayed implantation, as they still do. (The life histories of only 37 of the 60+

species of mustelids are known in any respect; of these, 17 have delayed implantation: Sandell, 1985.) I suggest that the weasels became smaller in response to the opportunities presented by the evolution of open grasslands inhabited by voles and lemmings. The characters most favoured in predators specialising on these new prey included of course the ability to search efficiently in confined spaces. But even more important was the capacity to breed rapidly in response to sudden increases in food supply and to disperse in response to the decreases. In the process of adapting their population dynamics to the uncertainties of life as a specialist predator of voles, both stoats and common weasels had to develop characters that would substantially increase their reproductive rate. The most effective ways of doing this, especially for small, short-lived animals, are early maturity and more than one litter a year.

Stoats and common weasels look much alike, and it is usually assumed that they are derived from some common ancestor. Suppose that ancestor was a marten-like animal that already had delayed implantation. By abandoning delayed implantation, common weasels could achieve this aim in one stroke. Why, then, did not stoats do the same?

The reason was, I suggest, that stoats developed instead a different, additional character, the extraordinary precocity of the juvenile females. It was the combination of delayed implantation and juvenile precocity which allowed simultaneous mating of adult and young females, which meant enormous potential breeding success for dominant males and certain fertilisation before dispersal for the young females. The addition of juvenile precocity turned delayed implantation into an advantage rather than a handicap, and, allied with the larger litters and longer life expectancy of stoats, made up a set of reproductive characters that succeeded. Females inheriting the combination of juvenile precocity and delayed implantation were at an advantage compared with other females. Consider an imaginary population in which most females died at 2.5 years old and delayed implantation was obligatory. A single heritable change allowing a female to mate as a nestling as well as at one year old would double her lifetime fecundity compared with other females. The advantages of the new arrangement to the female, and perhaps even more importantly to her sons, would ensure that it spread through the population.

I did, of course, consider alternative scenarios. One is that stoats and common weasels descended from an ancestor that did not have delayed implantation, and stoats later acquired it. The trouble with this idea is that stoats would have had to acquire juvenile precocity first, since to add delayed implantation without it would have caused a drastic drop in reproductive rate — the opposite effect to that required. Yet juvenile precocity without delayed implantation would have been suicidal for the young females, which could not possibly bear their litters whilst still nestlings themselves.

My suggestion was first put forward at a meeting in Helsinki in 1982. Soon afterward, Powell (1985) published a comparison between real or reasonable life tables for modern stoats and common weasels and for a hypothetical ancestor, addressing my question on how the modern species evolved. He concluded that, as common weasels have such short lifespans, they could not have evolved their present small size without provision for late summer breeding, first by adults and later, as size decreased, by the rapidly maturing spring-born young. If stoats are descended from a larger ancestor with good adult survival rates and delayed implantation, the reduction in life expectancy which accompanied their decrease in size 'would have required the evolution of juvenile breeding'. In other words, Powell's calculations were saying that the history I had suggested was at least possible.

The only other possiblity I could think of was that stoats and common weasels are not as closely related as they look; perhaps stoats descended from marten-like ancestors that had delayed implantation, whereas common weasels came from polecat-like ones that did not. This idea has something to recommend it; stoats are more similar to martens than to weasels in several curious characters, for example in the shape of the baculum and the temporary neck glands of the juveniles, not to mention delayed implantation and the whole physiological mechanism that controls it. However, this apparently plausible suggestion seems to be contradicted by genetic and cytological evidence that stoats and common weasels are in fact descended from a fairly recent common ancestor (e.g., Mandahl and Fredga, 1980; Obara, 1982).

The history of common weasels and stoats is worth some attention, mainly because the implications of it have a particular fascination. If the two species are descended from a common stock, they pose some interesting questions for the theory of reproductive strategies. If they are from different stocks, then they are a remarkable example of convergence — the tendency for similar-looking animals to evolve, regardless of background, to exploit particular resources.

SEXUAL DIMORPHISM

Male weasels of all species are substantially larger than females (Table 4.1). The reason for this difference was at first considered to have something to do with food. Because the two sexes are so different in size, they tend to eat different things; so, the argument ran, the difference must have arisen so that each could avoid trespassing on the other's supplies. In times of shortage, this trick might be valuable to both. But there is no evidence that this actually happens; indeed, the overlap in the diets of males and females is substantial at all times, but especially when food is short. Fortunately, there is a much better explanation. The current theory is that males and females are different in size for reasons to do with that old driving force, reproduction (Erlinge, 1979b; Moors, 1980), and the differences in their diet are seen as merely the consequences of the general relationship between a predator and its prey.

The population fluctuations of voles and lemmings create alternate feasts and famines over a three or four year period, during which the chances of a female weasel producing surviving young range from very high to practically nil. The population densities of the weasels themselves vary over the same period, during which the chances of a male weasel gaining several mates, or any at all, range from good to bad. The probability of a given individual of either sex meeting a disastrous season, in which successful breeding is impossible, is high; and because they have a relatively short lifespan, the probability of their surviving to a better season is low. The common problem for weasels of both sexes living in such a variable environment is the risk of failing to leave any young at all. Each has met this problem in different ways.

Female weasels always bring up their young alone. In good years there are enough prey available so that these energetic little hunters can rear their entire litter without help, and in the best of the intervening years they can usually manage to produce at least some young. Since a female can have only one litter at a time, and has a rather small chance of having another, her best bet is to invest the maximum possible effort into the one she has, and she does so for the sake of her own future prospects. Of course the task would be easier for her if the male stayed with her and helped protect and provide for the litter. But that would not be a good policy from the male's point of view. In good years the food resources available to the females are sufficient in quantity, distribution and rate of renewal for the females to manage very well alone. In those years the male who has spread his genes liberally around stands to gain many more descendants than the male who has stayed with one mate. The best bet for a male is therefore to invest the minimum possible time in as many litters as possible.

Among mammals in general, those species which normally produce a relatively large litter of blind and helpless young tend to have stable pair-bonds among the adults, whereas those species producing a few well-developed young, born fully furred and with eyes open, tend to be polygamous. Weasels are somewhat unusual in that they have relatively large litters of helpless young, but no pair-bonds at all. The explanation is yet again to do with the consequences of the weasels' specialisation as rodent-hunters. A female cannot afford either to accommodate a growing litter internally for too long after they begin to ruin her svelte outline, or to reduce the number of young she could produce when conditions for breeding are favourable. Her solution is to divide her resources between a large number of small kits, but to avoid carrying them about with her by dropping them in a safe place as soon as they are viable and then bringing food to them.

People do sometimes report seeing male stoats or common weasels taking food to a den, or families of weasels including two adults, but these males are more likely to be motivated by sex than by paternal responsibility. In fact, two breeding dens observed by Erlinge (1979b) had such narrow entrances that no male could enter. But adult female weasels of all species may have a post-partum oestrus, and a female with small young protects her family so fiercely that she becomes temporarily dominant over even the larger males. So a male bringing food to the den is most likely to be attempting to placate the female's hostility in order to gain a mating. Male stoats are especially likely to bring presents, but only for strictly sexual reasons. Because of delayed implantation, the young born this year were fathered last year, very likely by another male, and it is not in any male's interests to invest time and effort into feeding another male's young. On the other hand, he might be willing to invest in the female young as sexual partners for himself, and the potential rewards of gaining access to them are great enough to be worth the investment. Perhaps this explains why male longtails apparently do sometimes help provide for the litter (Gamble, 1980); the young female longtails have to be well grown before they are ready for mating.

Because the roles of male and female weasels in reproduction are totally different, it is not surprising to find that the adaptations that each has evolved are also quite different. Females need to be highly efficient providers of prey for the young, and males need to be dominant in competition with other males for access to the most females. Both aims are critically affected by body size. Small size increases hunting efficiency for a female feeding her young on voles and mice; on the other hand, large size increases a male's chances of success in confrontations with other males. Hence, the balance of size-related advantages favours a different average body size for male and female weasels.

Efficiency in hunting may mean minimising the time taken to collect a certain amount of food, or maximising the amount that can be collected in a given time. Female weasels could do either, according to the need and the conditions. For example, when the young are small, they need the mother with them for as much of the day as possible, to keep them warm and to feed them milk. She would do best to minimise the time spent hunting at that stage. Later, as the young grow and their demands escalate, their growth and future prospects may depend on the extent to which she can supply their needs. They can keep each other warm by then, so the mother would do best to maximise the amount of food she can collect during the time she has the energy to hunt and to avoid chilling while she is out of the nest. It would be interesting to know whether female weasels do switch from the one hunting method to the other as their young grow.

COMPETITION AND CO-EXISTENCE AMONG WEASEL SPECIES

The three species of northern weasels all have a strong family resemblance, and all depend on more or less the same prey. At least two of them may be found in almost all countries north of 40°N, and in some places in North America all three species may be found together. Yet it is one of the basic ideas of ecology that two or more similar species cannot co-exist indefinitely. The theory is that similar species tend to depend on the same resources, harvested in the same way; but unless those resources are so abundant that there is always enough for both, one species will eventually displace the other. Either one will be better at harvesting, so it starves the other out, or one will aggressively drive the other away. The two forms of interaction are known as exploitation or 'scramble' competition, and interference or 'contest' competition. The theory predicts that, unless one of a pair or group of similar species develops some means of evasion (such as hunting at a different time of day or in different habitats), it will be excluded from a habitat by one means or the other, or by a combination of both.

The populations of the various small mammals on which weasels depend fluctuate unpredictably and often independently. In one season there may be abundant prey of all sizes, in the next a shortage of voles, and in the next a shortage of rabbits. Common weasels specialise on field voles, while stoats are large enough to take rabbits or water voles. In a diverse habitat with a variety of prey of different sizes, the two can probably ignore each other for much of the year. But whenever or wherever there is less choice of prey, both must concentrate on anything available, and then competition is inevitable. Because populations of small mammals are so unreliable, this must happen often enough to have a real effect on the distribution and population density of whichever species is less well equipped to meet the conditions of the moment. According to theory, sooner or later one must be eliminated.

Mick Southern always used to say that, although it is fun to discuss theoretical questions in the library at tea time, if you really want to know the answer it is quicker and easier to go out and ask the animals themselves. This is true provided the question is first carefully framed, and then the observations to be made are defined in terms that will give a positive answer. Over the last ten years this process has given us a preliminary idea at least of how stoats and common weasels co-exist.

A Hypothesis

In Aberdeen in 1977, Chris Pounds chose to study co-existence among small mustelids for his doctoral thesis. In Canada in 1973–6, another graduate student, Dave Simms, was thinking along the same lines. Unaware of either, my colleague Phil Moors and I published a paper (King and Moors, 1979b) setting out a hypothesis on how stoats and common weasels could co-exist, hoping that someone would undertake the fieldwork necessary to see whether or not it was right. Pounds was able to test some of our suggestions before he finished fieldwork, and the rest were tested by Erlinge and Sandell (1988).

Our hypothesis was based on the idea of an unstable balance of opposing advantages. Because common weasels are smaller than stoats, they are better able to reach small rodents in their burrows and nests; they can survive in a smaller area, and for long after the rodents have become too scarce to support stoats. Conversely, they can respond more rapidly to a glut of rodents. Common weasels therefore have an advantage over stoats in exploitation competition, although their specialisation also makes them vulnerable to local extinction if the rodents disappear altogether. This certainly happens occasionally, but the vacated area can be recolonised from elsewhere in the next few years. On the other hand, because stoats are larger than common weasels, they are able to turn to larger prey when rodents become scarce; and they will also always win in any territorial dispute, so are better able to evict common weasels from a choice area or steal their catch (Figure 12.1). Stoats therefore have an advantage in interference competition, although only so long as they have access to larger prey. Their slower reproductive rate means they cannot take immediate advantage of a rodent peak, but their wider choice of prey and longer average lifespan means that individual stoats have more chance of surviving to the next breeding season. Hence, each species has a different combination of advantages in foraging and reproduction, and each is best adapted to exploit slightly different conditions. In any one place and time, one may be present and the other locally extinct, but over the long term the two co-exist because in a patchy environment there will always be places and times where common weasels can avoid confrontations with stoats and stoats can avoid over-dependence on rodents. Some habitats, of course, permanantly favour one or the other. The hypothesis predicts that, when they are forced to face up to each other, one or the other always wins, depending on the circumstances; it is the variable environment that permits co-

Figure 12.1. *A common or least weasel is a more efficient hunter of rodents than a stoat, but a stoat will intimidate a common weasel, and steal its prey if it can.*

existence, by constantly changing the balance of the different advantages of each. As examples of how our idea might work, Moors and I cited two cases in which co-existence broke down. In one the outcome favoured common weasels, and in the other it favoured stoats.

The Consequences of Myxomatosis

The arrival of myxomatosis in Britain in 1953–5 constituted the most far-reaching unplanned field experiment in modern times. The consequences for common weasels and stoats were not observed directly, but they were strong enough to make unmistakable ripples in the vermin books of many game estates (Figures 10.3, 10.8). The numbers of each species caught can be compared directly, since both are collected in the same traps by identical methods. The records clearly show that, for at least 15 or 20 years after the epizootic, common weasels flourished, but stoats virtually disappeared.

Moors and I suggested that the reason why myxomatosis had such different consequences for the two small mustelids was that it changed the balance of their relative advantages. When the rabbits disappeared, the broad range of sizes of prey animals available to stoats suddenly narrowed. Stoats lost their main advantage over common weasels, the freedom of choice between large and small prey, and instead found themselves in fierce competition with common weasels for small rodents, and with larger predators for the remaining rabbits. They lost out against both the common weasels, which are much more efficient rodent hunters, and also against the larger predators such as foxes, feral cats and raptors, which would not hesitate to attack a stoat. The result was that the balance of advantages was temporarily tipped in favour of common weasels.

The removal of the enormous grazing pressure formerly exerted by rabbits was immediately obvious in the unprecedented flowering of the countryside in the springs of 1955–6. There was a general shortage of prey at first, because all surviving predators had to concentrate on small rodents; but this did not affect common weasels nearly as much as the larger predators, which can hunt only those rodents that show themselves out of their nests and burrows. Then, in 1956, the populations of small rodents soared, and the common weasels followed them. For the next few years, the ratio of common weasels to stoats killed was reversed, from about 1:2 before myxomatosis to about 2:1 after (Craster, 1970; Hewson, 1972). On one estate in Norfolk, the average number of common weasels killed more than doubled, from 15 per year in the seven years 1947–53 when stoats averaged 650 a year, to 38 per year in the seven years 1957–63, when stoats were at their lowest ebb, 69 a year (King, 1980c). The main reason for their extraordinary increase in numbers was certainly the sudden glut of food, although the removal of interference from stoats (very scarce by then) probably helped. The rabbits were never entirely wiped out, and their slow recovery began to accelerate in the late 1960s. Since the early 1970s, common weasels have been declining and stoats increasing again as things have gradually returned to normal (Tapper, 1982).

Introductions and Distributions on Islands

Rabbits were also the key players in the second example we cited, but which had the opposite result. In the early 1880s the New Zealand Government, pressed by desperate run-holders facing ruin from plagues of rabbits, began advertising for live stoats and common weasels for export. There were about 17,000 keepers employed on the great game estates of Britain at the time, and many took the opportunity to earn some extra pay — e.g. £5 for a pair of common weasels. The animals were easily caught in box-traps, and shipped in small cages. The mortality rate among them, in the traps and on the long voyage under sail, must have been high. Nevertheless, in the first two years of the scheme, 1885 and 1886, 224 stoats and 592 common weasels reached the other side of the world alive and were turned out on the rabbit-infested pastures of the new colony (King, 1984a). Both survived and spread, and now, over a hundred years later, stoats are present in virtually all forested areas. Common weasels, originally imported in much greater numbers, are now among the rarest of all New Zealand's mammals.

Moors and I suggested that the reason why the two small mustelids reacted so differently to their new environment was that the radically unfamiliar conditions in New Zealand changed the balance of their relative advantages. Although rabbits and rats are abundant in New Zealand, smaller prey are scarce. There are no voles, and feral house mice are the only rodents under 50 g (see Chapter 5). Because common weasels are so strongly specialised on small rodents, especially voles, they were, and are, greatly handicapped by the absence of voles in New Zealand. Their main advantage over stoats, their greater efficiency as specialist rodent-hunters, is of no use to them where rodents are always hard to find; and the alternative small prey, mostly large native insects and lizards, seem to be insufficient substitutes. Stoats, on the other hand, have the range of large and small prey that they prefer, and hardly any larger predators to avoid. The consequence was that the balance of advantages was permanently tipped in favour of stoats.

Common weasels are never likely to be abundant in New Zealand, but even after a hundred years' disadvantage they are not yet extinct either. The reason they have survived is probably that the two main islands of New Zealand are very large and diverse, giving them plenty of room to disperse in search of good patches and to avoid stoats. But matters were different on Terschelling, a much smaller island (110 km^2) off the Dutch coast. In 1931, about 104 common weasels and 9 stoats were released there in an attempt to control huge numbers of water voles. As in New Zealand, many more common weasels were released than stoats; but by 1934 the common weasels had disappeared, while the stoats were well established. The size distribution of prey available on Terschelling is much better for common weasels than is that in New Zealand, which suggests that they might have survived but for interference from stoats; but on such a small island they could not escape it.

Our hypothesis also offers an explanation for the puzzling distribution of stoats and common weasels on the offshore islands of Britain. Eleven of these islands, including relatively small ones (to 60 km^2) are or have been occupied by stoats, but only four by common weasels, all of them over 380 km^2 or connected to the mainland by bridges. This is odd, because common weasels are smaller and might be expected to survive better than stoats in a restricted area. We suggest that common weasels cannot survive at all on small islands without voles, and on small islands with voles but without stoats they are still, due to shortage of prey, too vulnerable to local extinction to last long. On larger islands they might be better off, except that they are vulnerable to interference from stoats unless the island is diverse or easily recolonised. Terschelling, one of the few islands on which we know that both arrived in numbers sufficient to found a population, is much smaller than the Isle of Wight, the smallest British island on which both may be found together. Ireland is much larger than Wight, and the absence of common weasels there is a mystery. Our suggestion (1979b) is that they were there in earliest post-glacial times, along with a whole fauna of hardy northern species including stoats and lemmings, but that they disappeared later when the lemmings became extinct and were not replaced by voles.

Testing the Hypothesis

Pounds (1981) radio-tracked both stoats and common weasels in the farmlands and sand dunes near Newburgh, Aberdeen. He found that both preferred to hunt in the same habitats, the field margins and rough grasslands where small mammals were most abundant. Both stoats and common weasels could be found in such places at any time. Overall, there was a constant ratio of 5 stoats to 10 common weasels over an area of 54 km^2, which implies, since stoats are twice the size of common weasels, that both species were making roughly equal demands on the prey resources available. Competition seemed to be unavoidable, especially in spring when the numbers of small mammals were at their annual low after seven months (October–April) of unreplaced losses.

Pounds watched both species at a distance (30–50 m) with strong binoculars, using infra-red lights after dark, and followed them on hunting expeditions. Both hunted at any time of day or night. The diameters of the local field vole burrows averaged 23 mm, and Pounds estimated that female weasels could get into any but the narrowest ones. Males could get into the larger ones with a squeeze, but stoats of both sexes were excluded from all burrows. By scat analysis Pounds showed that field voles were the most important prey of common weasels all the year round, and also of stoats in autumn; for the rest of the year stoats concentrated on rabbits. There were differences in emphasis, but still the overlap in diet was substantial, especially between male weasels and female stoats. There were no obvious ways by which the two species could be partitioning their common prey resources, either in space or time. Pounds reckoned that competition for food between the two must be serious, and that no other consideration (e.g. shortage of den sites, predation by man or other larger predators) was anything like as significant to them. Nevertheless, he concluded that, most of the time, the exploitation advantage of the common weasels' ability to hunt in tunnels was sufficient to ensure their survival; and the stoats' ability to hunt alternative prey over a larger area was sufficient to compensate for their restricted access to rodents.

The other side of our hypothesis was that we predicted that stoats would be able to evict common weasels from choice hunting areas. In fact, of course, there need not be any open aggression — the parties need not even meet face to face; the effect would be the same so long as a common weasel always knows when there is a stoat about, and is scared enough of meeting it to move elsewhere rather than risk an encounter. Pounds pointed out that both species routinely mark their home ranges with scent signals, and these could be quite enough on their own to have the required effect, perhaps reinforced occasionally by an actual meeting. Pounds carefully refrained from speculating any further, but he reported that, in the 1,300 hours of radio-tracking he logged, he recorded no direct encounters between free-living stoats and common weasels. His experiments with captive animals in enclosures and in cages in the field strongly suggested that common weasels could detect the presence of a stoat, and would avoid it if they could, although he reckoned the effect in the wild would be very limited in time and extent. Female weasels, which might be considered most vulnerable to interference from stoats, were actually least concerned by them, because they could always escape to a rodent tunnel.

Although Erlinge and Sandell (1988) made much use of enclosures, in which animals cannot be guaranteed to behave naturally, their observations complement Pounds' field work in two out of three respects. First, they showed that common weasels really are scared to death of face to face encounters with stoats. When both were released into the enclosure (30 m²), the weasel always fled to a refuge box, while the stoat took over the open area, moving about confidently, ignoring the weasel with lordly disdain. The weasel remained hidden but alert (Plate 19), watching the stoat and ready to react with threats if ever it approached the refuge. If the stoat settled down somewhere quietly, the weasel cautiously emerged and began to make desperate attempts to escape. Then Erlinge and Sandell showed that weasels would avoid a trap that had previously been occupied by a stoat, and still reeked of stoat scent, whereas a stoat treated weasel-scented traps the same as any others.

Finally, Erlinge and Sandell looked for field evidence to support their observations in the enclosure. They searched back through years of trapping records (1973–84) to see whether there was any evidence of reciprocal distribution of the two species in their study area. The two species were considered to be in potential contact if one was caught within 200 m of a site, and within two months before or after the date, on which the other had been caught. In habitats that were potentially suitable for both, they recorded 21 weasels caught in places without stoats, but only 6 in places with them. Erlinge and Sandell concluded that common weasels will avoid areas occupied by stoats, although they will use them when the stoats are absent.

This result disagreed quite specifically with Pounds's radio-tracking observations. I decided to try to repeat the test for reciprocal distribution, using the detailed trapping records kept by three gamekeepers at North Farm, Sussex, in 1974 and 1975, and kindly lent to me by The Game Conservancy. The keepers had a network of about 300 permanent Fenn trap sites spread evenly over about 1,500 ha, mostly along field boundaries and tracks, as mapped by Tapper (1982). These are kill-traps, so each individual was removed as soon as it was caught, but the scent-marks left by resident mustelids continue to proclaim home range boundaries for long after the owner has gone.

The entire area, except in the centres of open fields, was suitable habitat for both species. First I marked the trap sites where stoats were caught; then I marked all captures of common weasels, distinguishing those that could have been in contact with a stoat by Erlinge and Sandell's definition. The common weasels clearly did not avoid the areas occupied by stoats; over a quarter of them (64 of 246) were potentially 'in contact', and 15 were caught in the same trap as a stoat within 30 days.

This is, of course, a very rough method of estimating the relative distributions of the two species over such a large area, and even if the results had shown the mutual avoidance claimed, there would be no way to tell why. 'Unfavoured' areas could be unoccupied by common weasels not only because stoats were there but also because hunting conditions were better elsewhere, or simply because the density of common weasels was low in that year. The only reliable method of tackling the problem is the way Pounds did it, by direct observation, and his conclusion was that, if the habitat is favourable to both, both will use it. There may well be mutual avoidance, but it must be on a rather fine scale in normal conditions, and would become a critical factor only in places (such as on small islands) where food is severely limited and confrontations inescapable.

Relationships among the North American species might be different. There are several reports of locally reciprocal distribution among sympatric weasels, e.g. stoats moving out when longtails arrived (Fitzgerald, 1977; Simms, 1979a; Gamble, 1980). These are not necessarily cases of mutual avoidance; the simpler alternative explanation is that the two species prefer different habitats. However, the distribution of North American weasels has one curious feature. Stoats and common weasels are found together from the Arctic right down to around 40°N on both sides of the Atlantic, but the longtails of North America live only south of about 55°N. If they are capable of displacing the smaller species by aggressive interference, why do longtails not extend into the forests and grasslands further north? The answer may lie in a thoughtful hypothesis by Simms (1979b), which was put forward quite independently of ours, but has some intriguing similarities with it. Simms pointed out that the small stoats of the snowy north feed primarily on voles. They are well adapted to hunt in rodent tunnels and are strongly specialised as underground or undersnow predators. Longtailed weasels are larger and have more general food habits. Simms suggested that longtails are confined to the south by the prolonged snow cover of the north, because they are less efficient in hunting through the confined under-snow spaces than smaller weasels, and the only alternative is to compete with the larger predators such as foxes and martens which hunt above the snow. Conversely, stoats are confined to the north by interference competition from longtails. In fact, longtails can and do hunt under the snow at times; there must be more to it than that. Gamble (1981) immediately pointed out that the key to the longtail's success is its ability to switch to alternative prey when rodents are scarce. There are few other prey in boreal forests, and it is this poor diversity of prey that keeps the longtails in the south, regardless of snow or other weasels.

Co-existence and Distribution of Weasel Species

These ideas were formulated at a time when the theory of competitive exclusion was one of the central, indisputable ideas of ecology. For example, most people generally accepted that the reason why a group of similar-looking animals, such as the weasels, are graded by size is so that they can avoid competition. It is true that smaller weasels specialise on field voles, whereas larger ones take prey the size of rabbits or water voles. The trouble is, these are differences of degree, not of kind, because in fact the larger weasels do eat a great many field voles, and the smaller ones are still capable of taking rabbits. Besides, computer simulation models constructed to imitate the competitive interactions of weasels, and analyses of the dynamics of communities including weasels, imply that local co-existence of two species cannot be long-term; when it is possible at all, it can be only temporary (Powell and Zielinski, 1983). Yet at least two species of weasels have in fact lived together in Eurasia and North America for thousands of years.

Some ecologists now see the theory of competitive exclusion as not very useful in explaining the real world, because its assumptions are too restrictive to be realistic outside the laboratory, and its reasoning is suspected of being circular. After all, every species is by definition slightly different from every other, every patch of habitat is in practice unique in some respect, and very few environments are truly in stable equilibrium. On the other hand, opportunistic species such as the weasels never do live in equilibrium conditions, so any theory based on that assumption simply cannot be applied to them. The point made by Powell and Zielinski is that the co-existence of weasel species actually depends on lack of equilibrium. It is the fluctuations in food supply and the patchy distribution of habitats that lead to the frequent local extinctions and recolonisations of weasel populations. Given enough space and time, these in turn permit the longterm survival of more than one variation on the weasel way of life.

13 Weasels and man

Human attitudes to wild creatures are not, as we would like to think, reasonable. There is hardly any better demonstration of this than the way people think about weasels. Contradictions and misconceptions are the stuff of common knowledge, mostly because, until recently, not much was known about weasels, so people simply projected their own ideas onto the real animals. There are two main streams of opinion, held by people with different interests. Both start from what seems to be an obvious fact; weasels are highly efficient killing machines specialising on small mammals and birds. Both assume therefore that predation by weasels is capable of controlling local populations of these animals. One group concludes that all weasels must therefore be killed on sight in order to protect birds, especially game birds. The other group concludes that all weasels must therefore be preserved, and even spread around, in order to protect farms and plantations from the ravages of pest mammals such as rodents and rabbits.

WEASELS AS PESTS OF GAME BIRDS

Game Preservation in the Last Century

The privately owned sporting estate, and the modern range of sporting firearms, evolved together during the nineteenth century. Game birds were required in large numbers, especially for 'driven' shoots. They were (and are) the legal possession of the landowner, who was usually disinclined to share them with natural predators. The policy of the time was to increase the harvest available to the shooters by indiscriminate suppression of all predatory mammals and birds. Gamekeepers were supplied with guns, poisons, and the newly-developed steel spring (gin) traps. They proudly displayed their catches on 'gibbets' as evidence of their hard work, and some even turned this deadly trade into an art form (Figure 13.1). The number of keepers employed increased steadily from 15,000 in 1871 (the earliest available figure) to a peak of over 23,000 in 1911 (Potts, 1986). At that time about half the land area of Britain suitable for shooting was covered by more or less intensive predator control operations, and almost any mammal or bird that got its living

Figure 13.1. The skills of the traditional gamekeeper are neatly carved on the handle of this walking stick, which I spotted at the Scottish Game Fair in 1968. At left, a stoat is poised to run through a tunnel to a waiting gin trap; at right, a rabbit is already caught in one.

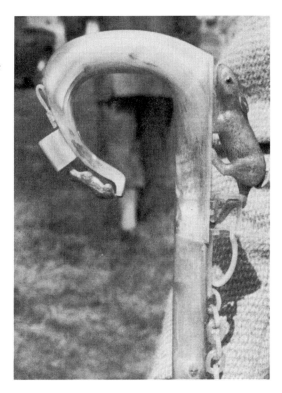

even partly by hunting was at risk of its life. The effects on predators were of two main kinds.

Several species of carnivores and raptors, which had previously been widespread, disappeared from most of Britain. The pine marten and the wild cat vanished from England and most of Scotland during the first half of the nineteenth century, and the polecat during the second half (Langley and Yalden, 1977). Five species of hawks and eagles were completely eliminated by 1916, and three others reduced to remnants. This was not due to any contemporary losses of the habitat of these species. Massive deforestation had already reduced the natural forest cover of Britain to its all-time low (probably to under 4 per cent of the total land area) by the mid-eighteenth century. The most serious declines of martens, polecats and raptors started some 50–100 years later, and they coincided rather with the reforestation programmes which started about 1750. Even game authorities now generally accept that the decline of the rarer predators in the last century was due mainly to direct persecution by man (Tapper, 1982).

At the same time, huge numbers of foxes, otters, badgers, stoats and common weasels were also killed, but none of them suffered the same catastrophic decline, except perhaps locally and temporarily. This is because foxes and otters were also conserved for hunting: at least some badgers could remain secure in their underground setts during the era before power-driven cyanide gassing equipment; and stoats and common weasels are simply extremely resistant to control.

The reason for their resilience is one of the consequences for weasel populations of the opportunistic way of life. Weasels have very variable productivity and constantly high natural mortality. Births and deaths are seldom in equilibrium, so local variation in density is expected, and frequent local extinctions normal. But at the same time, they are also very resistant to total extinction, because there is always a favourable patch somewhere where a few have survived hard times, and these are good at recolonising abandoned areas when things improve. Weasels generally do not need legal protection, and in the British Isles they do not have it (Stuttard, 1986) except for the stoats of Eire. By contrast, equilibrium species such as martens, otters and the large raptors tend to have steadier, lower productivity and, when undisturbed, fairly stable populations with relatively low mortality among the adults. They cannot compensate for any sudden increase in mortality, so they are slow to recover from heavy losses, and are particularly vulnerable to both local and total extinction. They certainly needed the legal protection which was granted just in time to save many of them from oblivion. These ideas explain why it is nearly always the larger ones among a given kind of animals that first become threatened by persecution (unless they have some refuges or are locally protected), while smaller ones survive (King and Moors, 1979a).

In the conditions of the time, the old policy of enhancing game bags by rigorous predator control alone was highly successful. The small fields, networks of hedges, regular crop rotation and absence of chemical pesticides provided the best possible conditions for the nesting and survival of partridges and pheasants. Both flourished greatly, and were shot in numbers that seem unbelievable to today's sportsmen. Nowadays, game estates are fewer and smaller. Systematic predator control is practised on only about 12 per cent of suitable land, and the number of gamekeepers has fallen by 80 per cent, to about 5,000. Pine martens, polecats, wild cats, buzzards and hen harriers are all extending their ranges, as the twentieth-century concept of conservation slowly takes over from the nineteenth-century concept of game preservation. Old attitudes towards predators (the only good weasel is a dead one) are changing to a more informed and discriminating assessment; long lines of decomposing 'vermin' on gibbets are now seen as a bad advertisement for the keeper's work, and distracts attention from the real good that keepers do for conservation in the countryside; and research now plays a key part in determining management policies on game estates. Particularly intensive research has been done on the ecology of the grey partridge in England, including some estimate of the part played in it by stoats and common weasels.

The Partridge Survival Project

The grey partridge is (or was) one of the most important of the English game birds. Bag records from long-established estates, some going back for 150 years, show that populations of the grey partridge reached their greatest densities between 1870 and 1914 — that is, during the heyday of traditional game management by intensive predator control. The early records of the National Game Census, for the peace-time years between 1933 and 1960, showed that about 18–20 birds on average were shot on every square kilometre of the estates participating in the recording scheme. Then there was a sudden decline, so intense that the mean bag for 1971–9 was only 3.7 birds/km^2. The reasons for this decline were sought in a series of studies of partridge ecology and especially by the Game Conservancy's Partridge Survival Project (Potts, 1986).

Among the prime suspects were, of course, the predators, so it was obvious that studies of the predators that kill partridges should be included in the programme right from the beginning. Potts began the work convinced that this opinion was wrong, and set up the study expecting it to show that predation did not control the population density of partridges. Over an area of 13.1 km^2 of the South Downs at North Farm, Sussex (described in Chapter 7), Potts and his team monitored a continuous effort to control all predators of partridges other than the protected raptors. On other parts of the study area, predators were not systematically controlled. The team then monitored the reproductive performance of partridges on the areas with and without predators. They also measured various other things, such as the extent of nesting cover and yearly variations in food supplies and in the weather, that could also affect the birds' success.

For the predator control work, gamekeepers at nearly the customary density for traditional partridge shoots (one per 4 km^2) employed up to 300 permanent Fenn traps (Plate 20), plus guns and some poison. The main predators of partridge eggs, the carrion crows and magpies, were practically eliminated. The main predators of the sitting hens were removed at the best possible rate — foxes at an average of 3.2 adults/km^2/year, stoats at 3.7/km^2/year, and feral cats at about 1/km^2/year. This effort was systematic and intensive enough to achieve considerable success in removing predators, at least temporarily. For example, although the traps for stoats were set all the year round, the most determined effort was made in spring, when game bird nests are most vulnerable. The records showed (Figure 13.2) a steep decline in the number of stoats killed per 100 traps over the first six months of the year. The team concluded from this that the resident population was largely removed each spring, although it was replaced later in the year as the season's crop of young stoats dispersed.

Partridge chicks feed on the ground, and are very vulnerable to predators, including weasels. Tapper (1976) collected 151 common weasels and 46 stoats from the study area during the critical months of May, June and July of the years 1971–74. Of all the items he identified in their guts, 2.1 per cent in the common weasels and 6.8 per cent in the stoats were game birds. In order to estimate the possible contribution made by common weasels to the average season's chick mortality, he reasoned as follows:

The important period when game chicks are available is June and July (about 60 critical days). Captive [common] weasels eat an average of seven 4 g meals a day . . . and, if we assume that weasels feed entirely on game-bird chicks, they would probably have to make three kills a day to maintain this consumption, i.e. 180 kills during the 60 day period. In this study 3/132 food items found in weasels taken during those 60 days were game-bird chicks, and at this rate an average weasel on this study area would kill about four game-bird chicks per summer . . . The density of chicks at hatching is about 94/100 ha. The survival rate of these chicks . . . is approximately 37 per cent in an

Figure 13.2. The number of stoats caught per month in the intensive spring campaign at North Farm, Sussex (from Tapper et al, 1982).

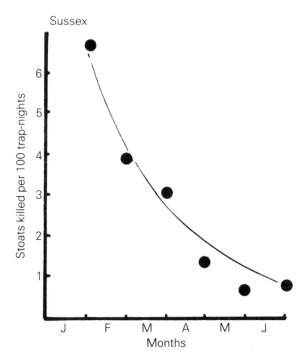

average year . . . i.e. 55 birds die/100 ha. If weasels were to account for all this loss their density would have to be 14 animals/100 ha.

This is a possible figure, although perhaps a little high. Tapper applied the same reasoning to the data for stoats, except that he assumed they took larger chicks. If stoats were responsible for the total loss, they would have to eat 11 chicks each per summer and live at a density of 5/100 ha. This figure is entirely reasonable (Table 10.2). He concluded, with reservations, that

> These calculations make it clear that weasels and stoats could be an important factor when mortality in game-birds is being considered.

But knowing whether or not predation accounts for observed losses tells us little about what those losses might be in the absence of predators. Therefore, the extent to which such hypothetical calculations are realistic in any given year depends a lot on other circumstances.

Partridge chicks feed entirely on insects for the first 2–3 weeks of their lives. More than 70 per cent of the chicks that fail to reach adult size die during this early period, and this mortality is related to the abundance of insects and to the weather. In a good year for insects, the young partridges which are not killed by predators are likely to survive, because they have enough food at this critical stage: but in a bad year for insects, it does not matter if most of the chicks are killed by predators, for they probably would not have survived anyway. Hence, the effects of predation are not the same every year, and calculations of the value of removing predators have to take into account umpteen other factors. They soon become so complicated that the only way to deal with them is to set up a computer model.

The first thing the computer wants to know is what controls the population. Potts identified three sources of density-dependent losses (those whose action is directly related to the number of animals present); the density of breeding females in spring, the proportion of pairs with a brood in early summer, and the proportion of the total population shot in autumn. The first and, especially, the second of these losses can be reduced by effective removal of predators. Losses of adult birds in early spring are not too serious unless very severe, because those killed can be replaced by immigrants during the partridges' annual competition for territories. If there are more than the maximum number of birds present, some will be evicted from the estate anyway. But losses of sitting hens are crucial, because by that stage they cannot be replaced, and if many are killed there will be a serious reduction in productivity for the season.

In addition, the mortality of the chicks is another important loss, but because it is related to the abundance of insects and to the weather, rather than to the density of partridges, it is density-independent. Its action does not slacken off as the number of partridges declines; it acts blindly, and if it continues at a high rate there is nothing to stop it driving the population to extinction. Removal of predators that eat chicks does not improve the survival of chicks in poor years, although density-dependent processes later in the cycle can in some years compensate for a poor season for production of chicks, especially if predators are removed.

After ten years of fieldwork, plus endless patient study of an enormous volume of contemporary and historical data on partridges, Potts came to the conclusion that the main cause of the decline in Sussex was the high mortality of the chicks, due to the destruction of their food supplies by agricultural pesticides. The only hope of restoring numbers is to reduce the effects of pesticide spraying at the field margins. But this policy would be effective only if nesting success was improved at the same time. The decline due to pesticides was accelerated by predation during the nesting season, which does strongly affect the density of partridges, especially the number of surplus birds available for shooting.

Potts's most interesting find concerns the relationship between nesting cover and predator control. Ever since the work of the influential American ecologist Paul Errington in the 1930s, game managers have believed that the population density of most animals is set by the extent of their preferred habitat. He believed that predation is relatively unimportant except to 'the doomed surplus' individuals unable to find a secure home base. The logical conclusion from this idea is that habitat improvement is a much more important means of increasing game than predator control, or even the only one worthwhile. But Potts argues that, although it is true that predation is not important all the year round, it is very important during the nesting season. The long-term decline in partridges coincides with an 80 per cent reduction in gamekeepering since 1911 and a 40 per cent loss of hedges since the 1930s, both of which greatly increase the hazards of nesting for the sitting females.

Potts concluded that the most urgent need is to curtail the spraying of toxic chemicals at field margins, since no other measure can have more than a temporary effect if chick mortality remains high. After that, habitat improvements such as provision of more and better nesting cover will increase the number of partridges only if predators are controlled as well, at least in the nesting season (Figure 13.3). The effect is most decisive where there is already enough cover to support nests at a density of 25/km^2 or above. Without gamekeeping, the success of these nests is only about 10 per cent, mostly because predators can more easily find and kill the sitting birds the more there are of them. Gamekeepering increases nesting success to 60–70 per cent, and results in up to three times more birds in the autumn population. In nature, these extra birds would be the 'doomed surplus' which would be removed by overwintering mortality or by emigration of birds the following spring; but on a game estate nature is managed so as to direct the largest possible proportion of this surplus (now called the 'maximum sustainable yield') into the shooter's bags.

Figure 13.3 The conclusion of G.R. Potts's work on the ecology of the grey partridge is a computer model, which predicts that the highest populations will be found where nesting cover has been increased, provided predators are removed as well (from Anon, 1979).

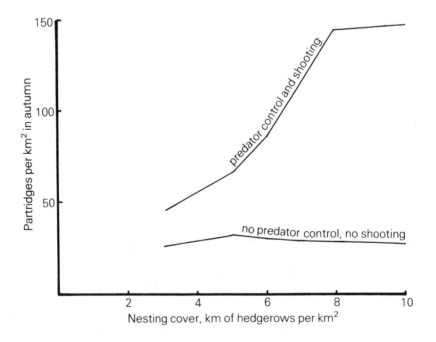

Stoats and common weasels are not the most important predators of partridges, but they are not to be ignored either. On one estate in Norfolk in 1944, all the losses in one small area (Figure 13.4) were attributed to the work of a single stoat which was seen at one of the nests. On open farmland, stoats usually move along the field boundaries, and this effectively channels predator and prey together, greatly increasing the chances of contact. Stoats can also steal whole clutches of eggs and carry them away to cache for later. Cringle (1968), helping two keepers to dig

out rabbits in autumn, found a stoat's larder about a foot underground —
two or three dozen partridge eggs packed neatly at the end of the burrow.
They had been carried some distance, since the keepers knew that the
nests that had been robbed were all along the hedgebank up to 100 m
away, but not one of the eggs was damaged. A year later, Cringle saw a
stoat carrying a tern's egg by walking on three legs and holding the egg
against its chin with the fourth. Stoats can certainly also destroy the
chicks, but what makes them dangerous is that they can kill the sitting
hen. Predation by stoats can therefore make an important contribution in
the long term, since losses of sitting birds are more directly damaging
than losses of eggs or chicks. By contrast, common weasels take only
chicks, so their effect is short term and not necessarily damaging; it is
also much reduced during the years that voles are abundant (Figure
13.6). It is perhaps inevitable that common weasels should also be blamed
for damage done only by the stoat, even though there is a good case for
arguing that common weasels should be conserved rather than controlled. For example, Muller-Using (1965) advocates the use of box traps with
an escape hole that would let the smaller common weasels out.

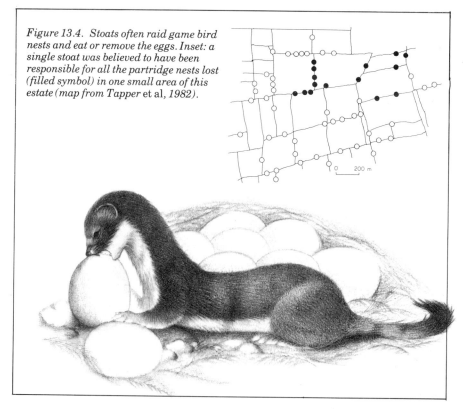

*Figure 13.4. Stoats often raid game bird
nests and eat or remove the eggs. Inset: a
single stoat was believed to have been
responsible for all the partridge nests lost
(filled symbol) in one small area of this
estate (map from Tapper et al, 1982).*

Weasels and Other Game Birds

Predators in general may take a heavy toll of game birds, and weasels
often make some contribution to the losses. For example, of 59 waterfowl
nests observed by Teer (1964), three were destroyed by longtails. The
nests themselves were undamaged, but there were paired punctures on

the remaining eggs exactly corresponding to the size and position of a weasel's canine teeth. Stoats are important predators of willow grouse in northern Norway, especially in years when rodents are scarce. Myrberget (1972) calculated the rate of predation, mostly due to stoats, over the ten years 1960–9. In four years when rodents were abundant, the average loss of eggs was 11 per cent, and of chicks 38 per cent; but in three years when rodents were low, the losses of eggs reached 23 per cent and of chicks 54 per cent. The worst losses were in the crash year of 1967 (36 per cent of grouse eggs taken), and other birds suffered too; yet on a nearby island where there were no stoats, relatively few eggs were lost.

Artificially reared game birds are especially vulnerable, and most gamekeepers have a fund of eloquent eyewitness accounts. For example, one keeper had been unable to prevent continuing losses of pheasant chicks from the rearing field, or to find what had happened to them, until one morning when he was moving the coops. He went to fire a heap of old straw, but caught a slight movement and, instead, began to turn the heap over while a mate stood by with a gun. Under the straw was a mole's nest containing a score of dead chicks, each of which must have been carried or dragged some 150 m across the grass or through a mole run. 'I will not remark on my companion's language when, first-class shot though he was, he missed the [common] weasel with both barrels' (Tower Bird, 1967). Stoats also take their share of pheasant nests (Figure 13.5), though their contribution to the toll is small compared with that of foxes and crows.

Figure 13.5. The proportion of pheasant nests destroyed by various predators, according to the Game Conservancy's nest recording scheme, 1977–9 (from Anon, 1981).

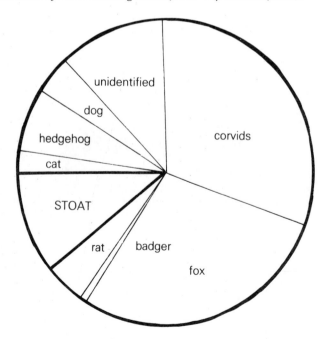

WEASELS AS PESTS OF PROTECTED WILD BIRDS

Birdwatching is an immensely popular hobby, and dozens of new books about birds appear year after year. Appeals for conservation funds do well if linked to a particularly attractive bird, at least partly because people tend to feel protective towards birds and respond quickly when they are under threat. If the threat has reddened teeth and claws, the reaction can be extreme and sometimes irrational.

In most of Eurasia and North America, weasels and wild birds have lived together for a very long time. Weasels certainly do raid birds' nests and kill many of the young and adults, especially of the smaller species. Certainly the common weasels I was watching in Wytham did their share. I often caught a known resident in spring with yellow yolk stains all down its white chest, and eggshells and feathers were very common in their scats at that time. The natural history literature is full of accounts of such raids. To quote only one example: Clowes (1933) describes how, when he was watching gulls on a rugged headland, a female stoat appeared and surveyed the scene. Satisfied, she purred, and three young appeared 'as if from the earth'. She found a rock pipit's nest, took a nestling and disappeared with it, returning three times and darting off again, each time with a young bird. Similar stories are legion. But these losses are, over the long term, sustainable. The hazard of predation is integrated with all the other hazards faced by those birds, and allowed for by the actuarial processes of evolution. Likewise, the numbers of weasels are adjusted year by year by their food resources, including the supplies of birds and their nests. Lasting damage is done only when weasels suddenly arrive in a place where this mutual adaptation has never had time to get established. The most likely such place is an island.

The inshore islands of the northern hemisphere are not very different from the mainlands, and those separated by only shallow (<100 m) channels have been connected to the mainland during periods of low sea level in the past. The larger ones are inhabited by weasels, and many of the smaller ones are visited from time to time; weasels in general, especially stoats, are good swimmers. From eyewitness accounts, and from the distribution of stoats on offshore islands, it seems quite certain that a stoat can fairly easily reach islands within a kilometre of the mainland (King and Moors, 1979b; Taylor and Tilley, 1984). The swimmer cannot know whether the effort is going to be worthwhile, although sometimes it is lucky. G.C. Phillips watched a stoat swimming 'a determinedly straight course' for a quarter of a mile to an island in Baltimore Bay (south-west Ireland) that still had healthy rabbits after the mainland stock had been virtually wiped out by myxomatosis (unpublished observation quoted by King and Moors, 1979b). On the other hand, the stoat seen by Morton Boyd (1958) on Eilean Molach, 200 m from the shore of a Scottish loch, would not have stayed long on an islet of less than a tenth of a hectare.

Islands without mainland predators are often important nesting sites for seabirds, but their eggs and chicks are generally too big for even the hungriest weasel to tackle. So the consequences of a weasel arriving on one of the northern hemisphere islands are usually not too serious. Any birds temporarily displaced after such a visit can usually recolonise later from the mainland. Matters would be very different, however, if any weasels were to reach an island further offshore or in the open ocean, which has never been connected to a continental mainland. History does not prepare the inhabitants of such a place to deal with predators, and the consequences are likely to be catastrophic. The best-documented example of this tragic process is New Zealand.

The New Zealand archipelago has a total land area about the same as Britain, but it has been isolated in the south-west Pacific for some 60 million years — that is, since before any of the modern mammals evolved. In the absence of terrestrial hunters (the carnivores and snakes), many of the longest-established birds of New Zealand found it safe to live, feed and nest on the ground, and in the course of time many of them became large, flightless, slow-breeding and unique. Only a mere thousand or so years ago, a series of invasions began, bringing to the islands increasing numbers of people plus alien mammals and birds. The intruders arrived with stunning speed, numbers and superiority, and they overwhelmed the previously undisturbed native fauna with devastating effect. Altogether, *at least* 153 separate populations of native birds have become drastically reduced or totally lost since about 1000 AD (King, 1984a). The losses of native lizards and insects must have been even greater. These grim figures do not mean that the colonising peoples and their animal companions were unusually rapacious; only that long-isolated island faunas are extremely susceptible to invasion, and losses of endemic species cannot be made good from elsewhere.

The new arrivals included large numbers of stoats and common weasels. Within a very short period both species, but especially stoats, spread throughout the country. Stoats are now present in virtually all forests, including in all the national parks. Public attitudes towards them are universally hostile, especially in areas where the destruction of the ancient endemic birds was recent enough to have been witnessed by the parents or grandparents of the local people. Because stoats are very obviously efficient predators, they are commonly and indiscriminately blamed for all losses of native fauna, both historical and contemporary; however these are quite different processes.

It is easy to acquit stoats of involvement in most of the historical extinctions, not because they were not capable, but because they had no opportunity. They arrived rather late in the story (after 1884), after the native species had suffered attack from Polynesian rats and human hunters for a thousand years and also from cats, European rats and dogs for a hundred, not to mention rapid and drastic habitat modification. Moreover, stoats never reached many of the offshore islands from which dozens of unique populations have disappeared. It was the sailors and their companions (rats and cats) that had the luck to find the last colonies of tame, defenceless and meaty birds. So stoats could not be held responsible for more than about 4 per cent of the 135 populations of birds that have become extinct, and at most about 60 per cent of the 18 that are now threatened — and even those were probably at least as much affected by rats as by stoats. However, the question of the extent to which stoats threaten the contemporary rare and endangered species, not to mention the ordinary common bush birds, is entirely different, and much more difficult to answer.

The first and most obvious approach to the question, analysis of what stoats eat, has been done on a large scale (Figure 5.2). Stoats in New

Zealand do indeed eat a great many birds, although not more than on English game estates; and anyway, such information is no help in trying to assess the effect of that many birds being removed from a given population. The only thing that can be said from studying the stoats themselves is that there are certain places and times when stoats are potentially a real threat. In beech forests after a heavy seedfall, mice become hugely abundant very suddenly (Figure 10.4). Changes in the abundance of a particularly favoured prey often reduce the extent to which stoats eat other prey. In the northern hemisphere, a surfeit of rodents 'buffers' the local birds from the attentions of predators, so good seasons for rodents tend to be easy ones for the birds (Figure 13.6a,b). In New Zealand forests in autumn, stoats do normally switch to mice (their favourite food), when the mice have produced their season's crop of young, and at the same time, they eat fewer birds. But in summer, young birds are especially vulnerable to predation, and extra supplies of mice at that season do not reduce the effects of predation by stoats on birds. In Fiordland National Park during the 1970s the stoats each continued to eat birds in the summer after a seedfall as often as they ever did (Figure 13.6c). Since there were so many more stoats about at that time than usual, it follows that the post-seedfall mouse summers could well be particularly bad times for the local birds. This suggestion has not yet been tested, although the parallel effect on the mice is apparently substantial (Figure 7.2).

Rather more can be discovered by observing the problem from the birds' point of view. At Kaikoura, an intensively-studied patch of bush in the South Island, stoats and common weasels together accounted for 77 per cent of known nest losses of bush birds over three seasons, affecting native (101 nests) and introduced (48 nests) species equally (Moors, 1983a,b). Unfortunately, that information on its own does not tell us whether predation is affecting the numbers of those birds. Potts's partridge model is an example of how much additional information is needed, and nothing like it is available for any New Zealand species. The nearest approach is a study of the South Island robin, done over several years at Kaikoura and on three predator-free offshore islands (Flack and Lloyd, 1978; Hunt and Gill, 1979). It showed that the mainland robins survive by making a huge effort to compensate for their losses. By comparison with the island birds, which are still presumably in more or less their natural state, the mainland birds have much larger breeding territories (1–5 ha, instead of 0.2–0.6 ha); they start breeding much earlier and finish much later; their productivity is higher (clutch size 3 instead of 2, 3 broods reared per season instead of one, and 3.0 juveniles fledged per pair per season instead of 0.14–1.1); nest failure due to predators averages 55 per cent per season instead of <10 per cent; and annual adult mortality is 23–37 per cent instead of 17 per cent. Despite this enormous extra effort, the mainland birds live at a much lower density (1–2 pairs/10 ha, instead of 25 pairs/10 ha), and not all available breeding habitat is used every season. These robins are, or were then, able to compensate, but elsewhere they and many other species could not. Most of those are now extinct; a few hang on as the endangered species of today, very liable to join the list of extinctions tomorrow.

Conservation authorities in New Zealand have always been very conscious of the historical effects of introduced predators on the native

Figure 13.6. In England, as in Europe and North America generally, abundant rodents 'buffer' birds against predation by weasels, both in open farmland (a) and in woodland (b). The opposite is true in New Zealand beech forests (c) where stoats eat birds frequently whatever the density of mice (from Tapper, 1979; Dunn, 1977; King, 1983a).

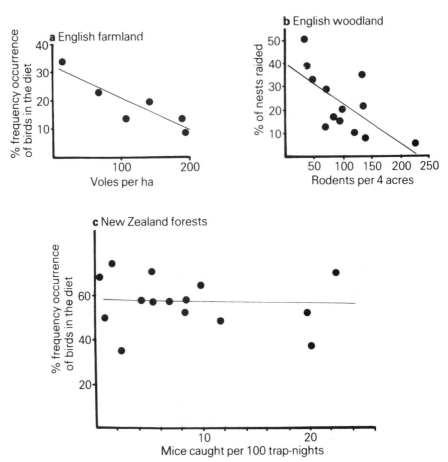

fauna, but uncertain as to how to protect the contemporary species from predation — or, indeed, whether it is now too late to offer any protection. Stoats are probably the most abundant carnivores in the remaining forests, and throughout the 1970s a real effort was made to find a workable management policy for them. The conclusion was, briefly, that although introduced predators (including stoats) have certainly been damaging in the past, most of the remaining mainland bush birds have either accommodated themselves to the new conditions or have already gone, to extinction or to permanent exile on safe refuges offshore. Only two species of native birds classified as endangered need protection on the mainland (the takahe and the North Island kokako), and even these are threatened more by other dangers than by stoats. They and all other surviving native birds of New Zealand live in habitats that are to various degrees reduced and dissected by human activities (especially extensive deforestation) and also modified and invaded by a whole range of introduced aliens. It may be illegal to kill or possess any of the threatened native birds, but it is not illegal to fell the remaining forests. Not all birds are particularly vulnerable to predation, but all are vulnerable to the loss of their habitat. The benefits of removing stoats to protect native fauna without also protecting and improving the habitat are debatable. But if that habitat protection can be assured, especially in areas where threatened birds still survive, then by analogy with the partridge work we may hope that some carefully planned stoat control work could be worthwhile.

THE TECHNOLOGY OF TRAPPING FOR CONTROL

If there are times and places where it is worth trying to control a local population of weasels in order to protect birds, then it makes sense to work out the most humane, economical and efficient method. Effective control of an animal population is not merely efficient killing, although it may involve that. It is the translation of ecology into management policy.

The first prerequisite for intelligent application of ecology to a weasel-control problem is to gather reliable information about the relationship between the weasels and the birds. It is pointless to kill weasels to protect birds unless predation by weasels actually is damaging them. Obviously, a control programme cannot be called successful if the weasels are eliminated but the losses continue, because they are really caused by something else. Conversely, if predator control is to be credited with improving life for the protected species, care must be taken to remove all cause for suspicion that any improvement observed could be due to something else. The second prerequisite is to understand the normal population ecology of weasels, and how to disrupt it. Finally, it is prudent to monitor the effectiveness of a programme, and abandon it if it is having no impact on the target population.

Control of a population can be indirect, by manipulating its habitat and food supplies, or direct, by removing more animals each season than can be replaced. The scope for deliberate indirect control of weasels is limited, although it has happened several times as a side-effect of some other process. Myxomatosis removed the main prey of British stoats, and thereby achieved a spectacular reduction in their numbers; a similar though more moderate effect was noticed in New Zealand when real control over rabbits was first achieved (by aerial poisoning) from the 1950s onwards.

Weasels are naturally resistant to control, because of their normally high mortality rates and their skill at recolonisation. In order to remove more weasels than can be replaced, a huge proportion of the target population has to be removed (probably over 80 per cent), and those that are removed will be replaced very quickly. On any large or inaccessible area, or where a weasel has only a low chance of finding a trap or being shot, this is usually impossible; attempts at 'control' usually turn into harvesting, which takes a yield but does not affect density. For example, on a 5,000 ha stretch of coastal sand-dunes in Holland, managed as a game reserve for pheasants, a force of 13 gamekeepers reaped a relatively constant harvest of stoats averaging 210 ± 32 per year, every year from 1952 to 1966. According to Heitkamp and van der Schoot (1966), there could have been about 75 stoat territories over the whole reserve, on each of which an average of 4.5 young might be born, giving an annual increment of about 340 stoats a year. Since the keepers removed only 210 (58 per cent) of that number, some unknown proportion of the surplus must have been left to die naturally. A century of such efforts on the game estates of Europe has had no long-term effects on the distribution of stoats and common weasels, for reasons easily understandable from their population biology.

On the other hand, on an intensively keepered estate such as North Farm, matters are rather different. The traps there are set out at the rate of 300 over 1,300 ha, i.e. averaging about 200 m apart in all directions. They are placed along the hedgerows and field margins where common weasels and stoats are bound to find them. The traps are not baited, largely because the sites are so attractive; weasels are not only naturally curious, they also like to keep under cover, and a good site that happens to be on a regular runway under a hedge will go on catching each successive local resident in turn. When such a system is operated by experts, a real reduction in numbers of stoats is possible, even if only temporary (Figure 13.2). On North Farm most resident stoats and common weasels are removed by June, although by September they are replaced by immigration from surrounding untrapped areas (Tapper, 1979; Tapper *et al*, 1982). The concentration of the keeper's trapping effort in spring produces a distinct seasonal peak in the mortality rate of common weasels (Figure 11.5), although it does not necessarily increase the general level of *annual* mortality. Either way, the danger period has passed by June, and in any case affects mostly males. There is plenty of opportunity to replace the losses, especially in vole peak years. Over the course of a year, many more weasels will be taken from an estate than could live there all at once.

The Fenn trap (Figure 13.7, Plate 20), developed in Britain during the 1950s, is extremely efficient and widely used. There are various useful manuals on how to use it, such as the one published by the Game Conservancy (Anon, 1981). In New Zealand, where gin (leghold) traps are still legal, I was able (1981b) to test the manufacturer's claim that the Fenn is more humane than the gin trap, and much better for collecting undamaged carcasses for research. Significantly fewer of the stoats caught in Fenn traps had gross external injuries (broken legs or teeth, crushed or severed feet), fewer were still alive when the traps were checked; and fewer had empty guts or fleas (i.e. they had died sooner and been cold for longer) compared with those caught in gin traps. Stoats held alive by one leg will chew through their own foot in order to escape, and others may be caught with well-healed injuries (missing toes or tails, deformed leg bones) showing that they had escaped from a previous trap. Most such cases were recorded in areas where gin traps are still commonly used for possum hunting, or in Fenn traps incorrectly placed with the spring crosswise in the tunnel. In many other countries leghold traps are illegal, and these data support the contention that they should be outlawed everywhere.

The way the traps are set out may decisively influence the number, sex ratio and proportion of the total population captured, and the cost (in time and effort) of the operation. Spacing, baiting, number of days set, visiting schedule and so on, are all important. To see how great these effects could be on the success of the programme, we tried some field experiments with Fenn traps in Fiordland National Park.

Figure 13.7. (Top) the Fenn trap has a safety catch (arrowed) to hold the jaws open whilst the treadle is set. (Centre) when the trap is positioned and the treadle poised, the safety catch can be removed with minimal danger to the fingers. (Bottom) the Fenn is designed to be set in a tunnel or under cover where it will not threaten ground-feeding birds (from King and Edgar, 1977).

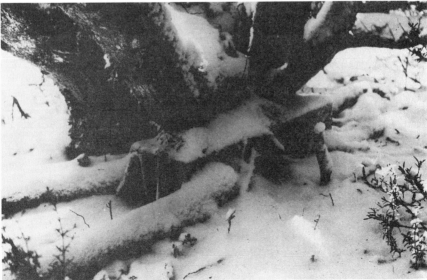

Take, for example, the effect of trap spacing on the sex ratio of the catch. Trapping for control needs to concentrate on catching females, especially as nearly all female stoats are already pregnant with the following year's litter. The further apart the traps were set, the more the number caught per km fell and the more the proportion of males increased (Table 13.1). The removal of even large numbers of males makes little difference to the number of young born the next spring, whereas all females that escape trapping can produce a litter even if every male in the area is killed. There is a much greater chance of catching males in spring anyway (see Chapter 8). Put another way, wide-spaced traps cause less mortality among females than males, and enhances the ability of the population to recover. Clearly, only close-set traps can be effective. No wonder the North Farm gamekeepers achieved such impressive results.

Table 13.1 The effect of the spacing between Fenn traps on the number of male and female stoats caught (data from experimental studies in southern New Zealand in 1972–6, reported in King, 1980d)

| | Distance between traps, m | | | | |
	100	200	400	800	2100
Number of traps	22	22	22	22	19
Length of line (km)	1.8	4.0	8.0	16.0	42.0
Total number of stoats caught	14	25	36	65	123
Sex ratio (percentage males)	29	32	44	42	76
Stoats caught per 100 trapnights	0.47	0.59	0.87	1.45	1.13
Stoats caught per km of trapline	7.8	6.3	4.5	4.1	2.9

Rather similar reasoning applies to common weasels too. I collected (King, 1975b) casual records of common weasels caught in Longworth traps set for rodents, and they were much more often females than males. The difference is not due to any attribute of the traps, but to the fact that traps set for small rodents are always laid out closer together than steel traps set by gamekeepers. Obviously, traps for either species set too far apart are pretty useless.

The field trials also showed that more stoats were caught on the first few days after the traps were set, and more if the traps were baited. I concluded that the most efficient way to run a trap-line in those forests was to set the traps close together for a few days, bait them well and inspect them daily, and then spring them closed and do something else for the rest of the month. The number of stoats we caught fell by about 60 per cent by the end of a 14-day session, although immigrants soon replaced those caught by the beginning of the next month's trapping.

However efficient the traps, it is impossible to catch all the stoats living in one area, because there is a lot of variation between individual animals. In another experiment with live-traps, my field assistant Chris McMillan marked a large number of stoats with eartags. Of one group of 21, tagged on or before 15 January and known to be present on the same area on or after 25 January, 9 were not caught on any of the 7 days on which the traps were set between 15 and 25 January. In other words, a full third of the 21 stoats known to be present were not recaptured in a whole week's trapping (King and McMillan, 1982). Another astonishing fact that emerged from this work was that young male stoats are able to travel extraordinary distances (20 km or more) within a few weeks of independence (see Chapter 9). We reckoned it was unlikely that we had caught more than about half the number of stoats present in the forest, even though we had expended the greatest practicable effort on the trapping work. Yet 50 per cent is not enough to make any difference to the number remaining, and in fact, most of those killed would probably have died anyway from some other cause, and been replaced from elsewhere. The intensity of trapping required to kill more stoats than are removed by natural processes involves a prohibitive commitment of labour for a temporary result, and a decline in the numbers of stoats after that effort is not necessarily proof of the effectiveness of control.

Clearly, it is impossible to control the number of stoats in the inaccessible forests of New Zealand. When the number of stoats soars after a beech seedfall, public criticism is often directed at national parks rangers, who are expected to 'do something' to protect native birds. It may be true that the influx is damaging, at least temporarily, but the sudden increase in numbers of stoats (mostly young ones) will soon be cut down by natural causes. Control work undertaken at that time merely brings forward an already inevitable decline (Figure 13.8). Meanwhile, the resident adult stoats are virtually secure, because in such rugged country it is not possible to set traps at the density required to achieve the effect shown in Figure 13.2. I consider that well planned, carefully timed trapping could form part of a comprehensive management policy for a few threatened mainland species; but otherwise, their only hope of survival is on predator-free offshore islands. General, low-intensity precautionary trapping to protect non-threatened species is a waste of effort.

This conclusion is not universally accepted in New Zealand, and there is still a strong antipathy towards stoats there, especially among visitors to national parks. But at least it might help to divert scarce conservation funds away from trapping programmes that can do no good and towards

Figure 13.8. In two Fiordland valleys, attempts to curtail an expected influx of young stoats (at great effort and expense) merely hastened their inevitable natural disappearance (from King and MacMillan, 1982).

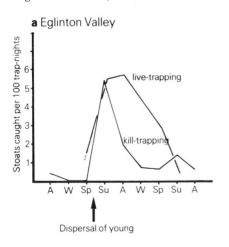

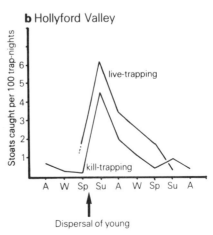

the really important work of habitat protection. Our work on trapping techniques was worth doing, even for what could be seen as negative results.

WEASELS AND THE CONTROL OF PEST MAMMALS

Common weasels are the smallest and probably the most numerous carnivores in the Holarctic, and, weight for weight, they eat the most. The daily food requirement of a biomass of, say, 50 kg of common weasels would be much greater than that of an equivalent weight of foxes: 50 kg of common weasels eating 35 per cent of their body weight in food per day (Table 2.2) would need 1,750 grams of food (88 'mice') whereas 50 kg of foxes, at 8 per cent per day, would need only 400 grams (20 mice). Better still, when rodents are abundant, weasels do not kill only what they need for the day: they kill as many as they can and store up the surplus for future use. If the prey were, say, field voles causing damage to crops, the weasel would be a much better friend to the farmer than the fox. It is therefore assumed by some that weasels in general have the power to 'keep the rodents down' (plus any other small mammals that can cause a nuisance, such as rabbits) and that therefore farmers and foresters should actively encourage weasels to live on their land.

Norman and Stuart Criddle (1925) were among the earliest champions of weasels, arguing against the common perception, picked up from the folklore of Europe and 'the game mentality', of the weasel as a savage killer of game birds and poultry. They listed many field observations of all three species of weasels in Canada in the early years of this century, mostly describing weasels hunting rodents or rabbits. They pointed out that, in nine years out of ten the longtail will find sufficient food in the fields and woods, and only in the tenth turn temporarily to domestic fowls. A thousand mice may have been killed in the meantime, but the destruction of half a dozen hens is enough to label the weasel a pest. Surely, they add, this is a remarkably small payment for the great good done by weasels in killing rodents, and ample evidence that weasels should be protected.

Field observers can easily find evidence to support this attitude. Lippincott (1940) described how he had tracked a weasel through the woods and farmlands round his home near Philadelphia. All along the two mile trail, the weasel took no notice of rabbit sign or grey squirrel tracks or roosting pheasants. It stopped only to flush out a rat from a pile of corn shocks and two meadow voles from under a low tree, and to try to get into two other mouse holes which were too frozen for even its slim body to enter. On another occasion Lippincott was surprised to see meadow voles running across the lawn beside his house, till he found a small weasel busy flushing them out of nearby weeds. Later the same day he saw three meadow voles scurry across the road, with a brown streak in furious pursuit. He concluded that, even if a weasel does take a few ducklings in the springtime, he still prefers to have a weasel about the place than hordes of rodents. Other American authors have also pointed out the absurdity of killing weasels on sight even where there is no bounty on them; that weasels probably kill hens only when barnyard rats are scarce, and the rats may well have killed more hens themselves. They support the same idea that weasels perform a valuable service to farmers (Quick, 1944; Hamilton, 1933).

Whether or not this argument is actually correct has never been tested. Logically, it is quite untenable, for the same reason that no one attempts to to judge the financial position of a company only from the debit columns of its balance sheet. The effect of predation by weasels on rodents is the difference between the rate at which weasels remove rodents and the rate at which rodents are replaced (Table 7.1), and this is impossible to figure out from casual field observations. But the logical conclusion of the idea that weasels 'keep the rodents down' has been put into practice several times. It is that it should be possible to enlist the help of weasels to reduce high numbers of pest mammals in field crops and forest plantations, or at least to control the damage done by pests. For this purpose, weasels have been released in various places, with mixed results.

One of the earliest known deliberate introductions was in the Shetland Islands, to which stoats were taken in the seventeenth century or earlier, but the consequences went unrecorded. The best-documented case is that of New Zealand, where ferrets, stoats and common weasels were deliberately introduced in the mid-1880s, in order to control rabbits. They failed. With hindsight we can see now that this could never have worked, but at the time it seemed a good idea. There are many examples of successful biological control of pests by invertebrate predators — such as the immediate repression of scale insects by the vedalia beetle in the citrus orchards of California. This most spectacular success happened almost overnight in 1889; it must have greatly encouraged the continued importation of mustelids into New Zealand, which was going on at the same time. Vedalia beetles saved the citrus farmers; so why did mustelids fail to save the sheep farmers?

The answer is that vedalia beetles have advantages over their prey not shared by mustelids. These include a reproductive rate nearly matching that of the scale insects, efficient aerial searching, no territorial restrictions, and absolutely no risk in killing immobile, conveniently clumped prey. When the scale insects increase in numbers, the vedalia can respond immediately, and when a beetle is stuffed full it simply produces more mouths to continue feeding. These characters make the beetles super-efficient shoppers (Table 7.1). By contrast, there is a huge disparity in the reproductive rates of stoats and rabbits; searching on and under the ground is inefficient, and confined to the stoat's own home range; and adult rabbits run, hide, and when found are risky prey for stoats (Figure 6.2). Even when a stoat is stuffed full it cannot produce any more mouths to feed on rabbits till the following year, so it usually goes to sleep. These differences help to explain why stoats never had any hope of controlling the numbers of rabbits over an area as large as the two main islands of New Zealand (114,000 km^2 and 157,000 km^2). Rather, as the history of myxomatosis shows, the converse is true: rabbits control stoats (Figure 10.3).

In Canada, deer mice and Oregon voles are considered serious pests in forestry, because they eat great quantities of conifer seed and bark young trees, so interfering with the regeneration of logged forests. In one short experiment at Maple Ridge, British Columbia in the autumn of 1978, seven of the small Canadian stoats were captured and released on a one-hectare experimental plot, while the numbers of mice and voles were monitored both there and on a control plot (Sullivan and Sullivan, 1980). The hope was that stoats at such a high local density would reduce the number of rodents on the experimental area. Unfortunately, they did not. Deer mice remained high on both areas, and voles declined on both. But there was no evidence that the stoats had stayed where they had been released: seven could not live together on one hectare at any season, especially not in autumn when the young are dispersing. In fact, two of the stoats returned to their original home ranges, up to 4 km away. It is clearly pretty unrealistic to expect predators to stay put and clear rodents from an unfenced area of mainland, just to oblige the owners of the forest.

If, however, both stoats and their prey are confined together on a smaller island or in an enclosure, the outcome can be very different. The island of Terschelling, off the coast of Holland, measures about 110 km². During afforestation in 1910–30, pines, oaks and alders were planted on 600 ha (about 5 per cent) of the island. The ditches dug to drain the plantations provided ideal conditions for water voles, and from about 1920 the high numbers of voles began to damage trees and gardens. Bounties, mouse typhoid and poison failed to control them, so in 1931, stoats and common weasels were introduced. By 1937, the stoats had established a fluctuating but permanent population; the water voles (and the common weasels) were extinct (van Wijngaarden and Bruijns, 1961).

This success was repeated in even shorter time on the much smaller Danish island of Strynoe Kalv (46 ha), south of Funen (Kildemoes, 1985). High numbers of water voles were destroying the dikes and damaging crops. Beginning in October 1979, the numbers of water voles were assessed by trapping sessions of 5–6 days in October, March, May, June and August for two years. In May 1980, six male stoats were released, evenly distributed along a 2 km dike. The numbers of both water voles and of ground-nesting birds on the island were regularly monitored until October 1981. In the first breeding season, 1980, there was no effect on the birds and not a lot on the voles. In the following year, water voles were very scarce, even though breeding conditions elsewhere in Denmark were favourable in 1981. Some birds were fewer than usual, but could soon be replaced from neighbouring islands.

More often, however, weasels usually fail to do what is expected of them by those who still believe that they 'keep the rodents down'. That does not mean that the combined force of all the local predators has no effect on rodents or game birds; it certainly may (Chapter 7). It is just that, in temperate lands, weasels usually make only a modest contribution to the total effect. The reason is that natural predators are not normally geared to control the numbers of their prey, only to harvest them. Any predator can control its prey only if it eats more prey animals than are produced as they increase, and fewer than are still surviving as they decrease (Table 7.1). This is not what weasels do. Because the rate of reproduction of any weasel is slower than that of rodents, and there is a practical limit to the number of rodents an individual weasel can kill in a day, weasels cannot hope to match their consumption to the numbers of prey, so they cannot prevent an increase, nor start a decline, unless the rodents have already ceased to add recruits to their population. During and after the decline, the 'overshoot' of predators caused by the lag of their response ensures that their predation is disproportionately heavy at the time it should be slackening. This is why predation by weasels has such a destabilising effect on northern populations of lemmings and voles (Chapter 7).

On top of this, the population dynamics of weasels are almost entirely controlled by the density of prey, whereas the density of prey is affected by many other things besides predation — particularly food supplies and social behaviour. So, contrary to appearances, weasels do not have the whip hand: rather, it is the other way about. The very mechanics of weasel predation make it impossible for them to 'keep the rodents down', and this is why attempts to use weasels as a control agent on mainland areas have failed. The only way to get round this is to remove their power of choice. Hunting gets more difficult as the prey decline, and the last few are the hardest of all to catch. The weasels' natural inclination to move away when the prey get scarce can be frustrated only on small islands. There, it is a matter of hunting the last few or starving; weasels have the same instinct for self preservation as the rest of us, so, not surprisingly, they oblige.

14 General summary

Weasels are descended from Pleistocene ancestors whose passport to success was their ability to enter the burrows of small rodents. This is an efficient hunting strategy everywhere, and in cold climates is the only way a small, energetic, non-hibernating animal can escape freezing to death. Contemporary weasels need to be the right size to tackle contemporary prey, and to compete with other weasels of the same species for greatest success in the production of young. The best size to be varies from one place to another, and is different for males and females; hence there is huge variation in the absolute and relative sizes of male and female weasels in different places.

Weasels are specialist predators of small mammals, and their fortunes are closely tied to those of the local population of rodents. Weasels are completely at home in deep snow, which inhibits the hunting of larger predators. In the severe climates of the far north and at high altitude, voles and lemmings are the principal or only source of food for much of the year. Under a deep, prolonged snow cover, weasels have the field to themselves, but they cannot emigrate, hibernate or turn to other prey when the voles decline. The pressure of predation by weasels on non-breeding populations of voles can be very substantial. Their impact then is to deepen and lengthen the declines, whereas by the time the voles begin to breed again, the weasels are few and powerless to prevent their increase. On the other hand, in patchy temperate habitats where food supplies are more varied, stable and available all year, weasels are the smallest members of a diverse local community of predators. There they generally have rather little effect on any one species of prey, and make only a minor contribution to the large effect exerted by all the local predators together. Only in special circumstances can weasels actually control populations of prey in temperate habitats — that is, only on prey that are especially vulnerable (e.g. unusually conspicuous, not breeding, or confined to an enclosure or a small island).

It is clear from observing the activities of weasels around their home ranges that they concentrate on the habitats and the areas where there is most food. Patches of cover favoured by small rodents are vitally important to weasels, and all viable home ranges have some; the best is rank grassland, thick hedges and stone walls, stacks of hay, brush, logs or stones, and the banks of streams and bogs. By contrast, disturbed agricultural land, such as grazed pasture and stubble, and open-floored woodland with little understorey, are avoided. In a sufficiently mixed landscape, if a weasel can find all it needs within a short distance from a few closely spaced good dens, it will tend to be fairly sedentary, especially in winter.

When food is abundant in spring, female weasels of all species can raise large litters, and female common and least weasels can also produce extra summer litters. The size of the summer surge in weasel density depends very largely on the breeding success of the females, and the survival of the young, over the previous few months. In good years the season's cohort of young enormously outnumbers the surviving adults; in poor years they scarcely equal them; in disastrous years there are hardly any young at all. The breeding success of the females, and hence the annual variation in summer density, depends almost entirely on food supplies in spring, and this is true in all species of weasels; but the relationship between food and breeding success is not the same in weasels that have delayed implantation and in those that do not. Mortality is always very high, regardless of density and food supplies, and affects both sexes and all ages more or less indiscriminately. Population declines in weasels are usually caused, not by increases in mortality but by failures in recruitment.

In normal times on any mainland or very large island, predation by weasels alone is neither a great benefit to agriculture nor a menace to the conservation of game. Stoats, but not common weasels, are a nuisance on game estates, though much less so than are crows or foxes; conversely, stoats have had some success in eradicating water voles from small islands, but they totally failed to rid New Zealand of rabbits or Canadian pine forests of rodents.

The weasels are an especially challenging group of animals for taxonomists and ecologists interested in theories explaining sexual dimorphism and the co-existence of related species. The natural history of the weasels is largely the story of how these adaptable little animals profit from the advantages, and cope with the drawbacks, of their diminuitive stature.

Bibliography

Allen, D.L. (1938) 'Ecological studies on the vertebrate fauna of 500-acre farm in Kalamazoo County, Michigan', *Ecol. Monogr.*, 8, 347–436.

Anderson, E. (1966) 'Weasel kills buzzard', *The Countryman* Spring 1966, 122.

Anon. (1960) 'Vermin bag records', *I.C.I. Game Services, Ann. Rep. 1959*, 56.

—— (1979) *Annual Report, 1978*, The Game Conservancy, Fordingbridge

—— (1981) *Predator and Squirrel Control*, The Game Conservancy, Fordingbridge.

Aspisov, D.I. and Popov, V.A. (1940) 'Factors determining fluctuations in the numbers of ermines', in King, C.M. (1980a), 109–31.

Barrow, C. (1953) 'Weasel and waterhen', *The Countryman* Spring 1953, 115.

Bishop, S. (1923) 'Note on the nest and young of the small brown weasel', *J. Mamm.*, 4, 26–7.

Blomquist, L., Muuronen, P. and Rantanan, V. (1981) 'Breeding the least weasel (*Mustela rixosa*) in Helsinki Zoo', *Zool. Garten NF Jena*, 51, 363–68.

Brinck, C., Erlinge, S. and Sandell, M. (1983) 'Anal sac secretion in mustelids: a comparison', *J. Chem. Ecol.*, 9, 727–45.

Brown, J.H. and Lasiewski, R.C. (1972) 'Metabolism of weasels: the cost of being long and thin', *Ecology*, 53, 939–43.

Brugge, T. (1977) 'Prooidierkeuze van wezel, hermelijn en bunzing in relatie tot geslacht en lichaamsgrootte, *Lutra*, 19, 39–49.

Buckingham, C.J. (1979) *The activity and exploratory behaviour of the weasel* Mustela nivalis, PhD thesis, Exeter University.

Bullock, D. and Pickering, S. (1982) 'Weasels (*Mustela nivalis*) attacking a young and adult brown hare (*Lepus capensis*)', *J. Zool. Lond.*, 197, 307–8.

Burns J.J. (1964) 'Movements of a tagged weasel in Alaska', *Murrelet*, 45, 10.

Burt, W.H. (1960) 'Bacula of North American Mammals', *Misc. Publ., Mus. Zool., Univ. Mich.*, 113, 1–76.

Buskirk, S.W. and Lindstedt, S.L. (1989) 'Sex biases in trapped samples of Mustelidae', *J. Mammal.* 70: 88–97.

Cahn, A.R. (1936) 'A weasel learns by experience', *J. Mamm.*, 17, 286.

Casey, T.M. and Casey, K.K. (1979) 'Thermoregulation of arctic weasels', *Physiol. Zool.*, 52, 153–64.

Chernov, Yu. I. (1985) *'The Living Tundra'*, Cambridge University Press, Cambridge.

Choate, J.R., Engstrom, M.D. and Wilhelm, R.B. (1979) 'Historical biogeography of the least weasel (*Mustela nivalis campestris*) in Kansas, USA', *Trans. Kans. Acad. Sci.*, 82, 231–34.

Clowes, E.F. (1933) 'Stoat feeding young on rock pipits', *Irish Nat. J.*, 4, 217–8.

Coleman, J. (1975) 'Tuberculosis in opossums', *What's New in Forest Research*, 27, 1–4.

Corbet, G.B. (1978) *'The Mammals of the Palaearctic Region: a Taxonomic Review'*, British Museum of Natural History, London.

Corbet, G.B. and Harris, S. (1990) *The Handbook of British Mammals*, 3rd edition, Blackwell Scientific Publications, Oxford.

Coues, E. (1877) *Fur-bearing mammals: A monograph of the North American Mustelidae*, Government Printing Office, Washington.

REFERENCES

Craighead, J.J. and Craighead, F.C. (1956) *Hawks, Owls and Wildlife*, Stackpole Co. and Wildlife Management Institute.

Craster, J. (1970) 'Stoats and weasels: a new contrast', *The Field*, 22 October, 786–7.

Criddle, N. and Criddle, S. (1925) 'The weasels of southern Manitoba', *Can. Field. Nat.*, 39, 142–8.

Cringle, P. (1968) 'Marshland incidents', *Shooting Times*, 9 March 1968.

Day, M.G. (1963) *An ecological study of the stoat* (Mustela erminea L.) *and the weasel* (Mustela nivalis L.) *with particular reference to their food and feeding habits*, PhD. thesis, Exeter University.

—— (1966) 'Identification of hair and feather remains in the gut and faeces of stoats and weasels', *J. Zool. Lond.*, 148, 201–17.

—— (1968) 'Food habits of British stoats (*Mustela erminea*) and weasels (*Mustela nivalis*), *J. Zool. Lond.*, 155, 485–97.

Deanesley, R. (1935) 'The reproductive processes of certain mammals. Part 9 – Growth and reproduction in the stoat (*Mustela erminea*), *Phil. Trans. R. Soc., Ser. B.*, 225, 459–92.

—— (1943) 'Delayed implantation in the stoat (*Mustela mustela* [sic])', *Nature*, 151, 365–6.

—— (1944) 'The reproductive cycle of the female weasel (*Mustela nivalis*)', *Proc. Zool. Soc. (Lond.)* 114, 339–49.

Debrot, S. (1981) 'Trophic relations between the stoat (*Mustela erminea* L.) and its prey, mainly the water vole (*Arvicola terrestris* Scherman)', in J.A. Chapman and D. Pursley (eds), *World Furbearer Conf. Proc.*, 1259–89.

—— (1983) 'Fluctuations de populations chez l'hermine (*Mustela erminea* L.)', *Mammalia* 47, 323–32.

—— (1984) 'Dynamique du renouvellement et structure d'age d'une population d'hermines (*Mustela erminea*)', *Rev. Ecol. Terre Vie* 39, 77–88.

Debrot, S. and Mermod, C. (1981) 'Cranial helminth parasites of the stoat and other mustelids in Switzerland', in J.A. Chapman and D. Pursley (eds), *World Furbearer Conf. Proc.*, 690–705.

—— —— (1982) 'Quelques siphonaptères de mustélidés, dont *Rhadinopsylla pentacantha* (Rothschild, 1897), nouvelle espèce pour la Suisse', *Rev. Suisse Zool.* 89, 27–32.

—— —— (1983) 'The spatial and temporal distribution pattern of the stoat (*Mustela erminea* L.)', *Oecologia* 59, 69–73.

Debrot, S., Weber, J-M., Marchesi, P. and Mermod, C. (1985) 'The day and night activity pattern of the stoat (*Mustela erminea* L.)', *Mammalia* 49, 13–17.

Delattre, P. (1983) 'Density of weasel (*Mustela nivalis* L.) and stoat (*Mustela erminea* L.) in relation to water vole abundance', *Acta Zool. Fenn.* 174, 221–2.

—— (1984) 'Influence de la pression de prédation exercée par une population de belettes (*Mustela nivalis* L.) sur un peuplement de Microtidae', *Acta. Oecol. Gen.* 5, 285–300.

Devan, R. (1982) *'The ecology and life history of the longtailed weasel* (Mustela frenata). Unpublished PhD thesis, University of Cincinatti.

Devos, A. (1960) '*Mustela frenata* climbing trees', *J. Mammal.* 41, 520.

Don Carlos, M.W., Petersen, J.S. and Tilson, R.L. (1986) 'Captive biology of an asocial mustelid: *Mustela erminea*', *Zool. Biol.* 5, 363–70.

Dougherty, E.C. and Hall, E.R. (1955) 'The biological relationships between American weasels (genus *Mustela*) and nematodes of the genus *Skrjabingylus* Petrov 1927 (Nematoda: Metastrongylidae), the causative organisms of certain lesions in weasel skulls', *Rev. Iberica de Parasit., Granada (Espana), Tomo Extraordiaro*, March 1955.

Drabble, P. (1977) *'A Weasel in my Meatsafe'*, Michael Joseph, London.

Dubnitskii, A.A. (1956) 'Study of the cycle of development of the nematode *Skrjabingylus nasicola*, a parasite of the frontal sinuses of mustelids', in King (1975c), 235–41.

Dunn, E. (1977) 'Predation by weasels (*Mustela nivalis*) on breeding tits (*Parus* sp.) in relation to the density of tits and rodents', *J. Anim. Ecol.* 46, 633–52.

East, K. and Lockie, J.D. (1964) 'Observations on a family of weasels (*Mustela nivalis*) bred in captivity', *Proc. Zool. Soc. Lond.* 143, 359–63.

—— —— (1965) 'Further observations on weasels (*Mustela nivalis*) and stoats (*Mustela erminea*) born in captivity', *J. Zool. Lond.* 147, 234–8.

Easterla, D.A. (1970) 'First records of the least weasel, *Mustela nivalis*, from Missouri and southwestern Iowa', *J. Mamm.* 51, 333–40.

Edson, J.M. (1933) 'A visitation of weasels', *Murrelet* 14, 76–7.

English, M.P.E. (1971) 'Ringworm in groups of wild mammals', *J. Zool. Lond.* 165, 535–44.

Erlinge, S. (1974) 'Distribution, territoriality and numbers of the weasel *Mustela nivalis* in relation to prey abundance', *Oikos* 25, 308–14.

—— (1975) 'Feeding habits of the weasel *Mustela nivalis* in relation to prey abundance', *Oikos* 26, 378–84.

239

—— (1977a) 'Spacing strategy in stoat *Mustela erminea*', *Oikos* 28, 32–42.

—— (1977b) 'Home range utilisation and movements of the stoat, *Mustela erminea*', *Int. Congr. Game Biol.* 13, 31–42.

—— (1977c) 'Agonistic behaviour and dominance in stoats (*Mustela erminea* L.)', *Z. Tierpsychol.* 44, 375–88.

—— (1979a) 'Movements and daily activity pattern of radiotracked male stoats, *Mustela erminea*', in C.J. Amlaner and D.W. Macdonald (eds), *A. Handbook on Radiotelemetry and Radio Tracking*, Pergamon Press, Oxford, 703–10.

—— (1979b) 'Adaptive significance of sexual dimorphism in weasels', *Oikos* 33, 233–45.

—— (1981) 'Food preference, optimal diet and reproductive output in stoats *Mustela erminea* in Sweden', *Oikos* 36, 303–15.

—— (1983) 'Demography and dynamics of a stoat *Mustela erminea* population in a diverse community of vertebrates', *J. Anim. Ecol.* 52, 705–26.

—— (1987) 'Why do European stoats *Mustela erminea* not follow Bergmann's Rule?', *Hol. Ecol.* 10, 33–9.

Erlinge, S., Göransson, G., Hansson, L., Högstedt, G., Liberg, O., Nilsson, I.N., Nilsson, T., von Schantz, T., and Sylvén, M. (1983) 'Predation as a regulating factor on small rodent populations in southern Sweden'. *Oikos* 40, 36–52.

Erlinge, S., Göransson, G., Högstedt, G., Jansson, G., Liberg, O., Loman, J., Nilsson, I.N., von Schantz, T., and Sylvén, M. (1983) 'Can vertebrate predators regulate their prey?', *Am. Nat.* 123, 125–133.

Erlinge, S., Göransson, G., Högstedt, G., Jansson, G., Liberg, O., Loman, J., Nilsson, I.N., von Schantz, T., and Sylvén, M. (1988) 'More thoughts on vertebrate predator regulation of prey', *Am. Nat.* 132, 148–54.

Erlinge, S., Jonsson, B. and Willstedt, H. (1974) 'Jaktbeteende och bytesval hos småvesslan', *Fauna Flora* (Stockholm) 69, 95–101.

Erlinge, S. and Sandell, M. (1986) 'Seasonal changes in the social organisation of male stoats *Mustela erminea*: an effect of shifts between two decisive resources', *Oikos* 47, 57–62.

—— —— (1988) 'Co-existence of stoat (*Mustela erminea*) and weasel (*Mustela nivalis*): social dominance, scent communication and reciprocal distribution', *Oikos* 53, 242–6.

Erlinge, S., Sandell, M. and Brinck, C. (1982) 'Scent-marking and its territorial significance in stoats, *Mustela erminea*, *Anim. Behav.* 30, 811–18.

Fairley, J.S. (1971) 'New data on the Irish stoat', *Irish Nat. J.* 17, 49–57.

—— (1981) 'A north-south cline in the size of the Irish stoat', *Proc. R. Ir. Acad. B* 81, 5–10.

—— (1984) *An Irish Beast Book*, 2nd edition, Blackstaff Press, Belfast.

Fitzgerald, B.M. (1977) 'Weasel predation on a cyclic population of the montane vole (*Microtus montanus*) in California', *J. Anim. Ecol.* 46, 367–97.

—— (1981) 'Predatory birds and mammals', in L.C. Bliss, J.B. Cragg, D.W. Heal and J.J. Moore (eds), *Tundra Ecosystems: A Comparative Analysis*, Cambridge University Press, 485–508.

Flack, J.A.D. and Lloyd, B.D. (1978), 'The effects of rodents on the breeding success of the South Island robin', in P.R. Dingwall, I.A.E. Atkinson and C. Hay (eds), *The Ecology and Control of Rodents in New Zealand Nature Reserves*, Department of Conservation, Wellington, 59–66.

Flintoff, R.J. (1933) 'Stoats and weasels, brown and white', *Northwestern Nat.* 8, 36–45.

—— (1935) 'Stoats and weasels, brown and white', *Northwestern Nat.* 10, 214–29.

Florine, C. (1942) 'Weasel in a pocket gopher burrow', *J. Mammal.* 23, 213.

Flowerdew, J.R. (1972) 'The effect of supplementary food on a population of woodmice (*Apodemus sylvaticus*)', *J. Anim. Ecol.* 41, 553–66.

Formosov, A.N. (1946) 'Snow cover as an integral factor of the environment and its importance in the ecology of mammals and birds', *Boreal Inst. for Northern Studies, Univ. Alberta, Occ. Publ.* 1, 1–141.

Forsyth, J.F. (1967) 'Stoated rabbits', *Shooting Times* 18 March 1967 p. 327.

Frank, F. (1974) 'Wurfzahl und Wurffolge beim nordischen wiesel (*Mustela nivalis rixosa* Bangs 1896), *Z. Saug.* 39, 248–50.

Gaiduk, V.E. (1977) 'Control of moulting and winter whitening in the ermine (*Mustela erminea*)', in King (1980a), 56–61.

Gamble, R.L. (1980) *The ecology and distribution of* Mustela frenata longicauda *Bonaparte and its relationships to other* Mustela *species in sympatry.* M.S. thesis, University of Manitoba.

—— (1981) 'Distribution in Manitoba of *Mustela frenata longicauda* Bonaparte, the longtailed weasel, and the interrelation of distribution and habitat selection in Manitoba, Saskatchewan and Alberta', *Can. J. Zool.* 59, 1036–39.

Gamble, R.L. and Riewe, R.R. (1982) 'Infestations of the nematode *Skrjabingylus nasicola* (Leukart 1842) in *Mustela frenata* (Lichtenstein) and *M. erminea* (L.) and some evidence of a paratenic host in the life cycle of this nematode', *Can. J. Zool.*, 60, 45–52.

Gewalt, W. (1959) 'Optisches Differenzierungsvermögen einiger Musteliden', *Zool. Beitr.* (Berl.) 5, 117–75.

Gillingham, B.J. (1984) 'Meal size and feeding rate in the least weasel *Mustela nivalis*', *J. Mammal.* 65, 517–19.

Glover, F.A. (1942) *A population study of weasels in Pennsylvania*, M.S. thesis, Pennsylvania State College (parts published in *Penn. Game News* in 1942 and 1943).

Golley, F.B. (1960) 'Energy dynamics of a food chain of an old-field community', *Ecol. Monogr.* 30, 187–206.

Gorman, M.L. (1976) 'A mechanism for individual recognition by odour in *Herpestes auropunctatus* (Carnivora: Viverridae)', *Anim. Behav.* 24, 141–5.

—— (1984) 'The response of prey to the stoat (*Mustela erminea*) scent', *J. Zool. Lond.* 202, 419–23.

Goszczynski, J. (1977) 'Connections between predatory birds and mammals and their prey', *Acta Theriol.* 22, 399–430.

Grue, H. and King, C.M. (1984) 'Evaluation of age criteria in New Zealand stoats (*Mustela erminea*) of known age', *N.Z.J. Zool.* 11, 437–43.

Gulamhusein, A.P. and Tam, W.H. (1974) 'Reproduction in the male stoat, *Mustela erminea*', *J. Repro. Fert.* 41, 303–12.

Gulamhusein, A.P. and Thawley, A.R. (1974) 'Plasma progesterone levels in the stoat', *J. Reprod. Fert.* 36, 405–408.

Haley, D. (1975) *Sleek and Savage: North America's Weasel Family*, Pacific Search Books, Seattle.

Hall, E.R. (1951) 'American weasels', *Univ. Kansas Publ.: Mus. Nat. Hist.* 4, 1–466.

Hamilton, W.J. (1933) 'The weasels of New York', *Am. Midl. Nat.* 14, 289–344.

Hansson, I. (1967) 'Transmission of the parasitic nematode *Skrjabingylus nasicola* (Leuckart 1842) to species of *Mustela* (Mammalia)', *Oikos* 18, 247–52.

—— (1970) 'Cranial helminth parasites in species of Mustelidae: II. Regional frequencies of damage in preserved crania from Denmark, Finland, Sweden, Greenland and the northeast of Canada compared with the helminth invasion in fresh mustelid skulls from Sweden', *Ark. Zool.* 22, 571–94.

—— (1974) 'Seasonal and environmental conditions affecting the invasion of mustelids by larvae of the nematode *Skrjabingylus nasicola*. *Oikos* 25, 61–70.

Hansson, L. and Henttonen, H. (1985) 'Gradients in density variation of small rodents: the importance of latitude and snow cover', *Oecologia* 67, 394–402.

Harting, J.E. (1894) 'The weasel', *Zoologist* 52, 417–23, 445–54.

Hartman, L. (1964) 'The behaviour and breeding of captive weasels (*Mustela nivalis* L.)', *N.Z.J. Sci.* 7, 147–56.

Hayward, G.F. (1983) *The bioenergetics of the weasel*, Mustela nivalis, D. Phil. thesis, Oxford University.

Hayward, G.F. and Phillipson, J. (1979), 'Community structure and functional role of small mammals in ecosystems' in D.M. Stoddart (ed) *Ecology of small mammals*, Chapman and Hall, London, 135–211.

Heffner, R.S. and Heffner, H.E. (1985) 'Hearing in mammals: the least weasel', *J. Mammal.* 66, 745–55.

Heidt, G.A. (1970) 'The least weasel, *Mustela nivalis* L. Developmental biology in comparison with other North American *Mustela*. *Mich. State Univ., Publ. Mus. (Biol. Ser.)* 4, 227–282.

—— (1972) 'Anatomical and behavioural aspects of killing and feeding by the least weasel, *Mustela nivalis* L., *Proc. Ark. Acad. Sci.* 26, 53–4.

Heidt, G.A., Petersen, M.K. and Kirkland, G.L. (1968) 'Mating behaviour and development of least weasels (*Mustela nivalis*) in captivity', *J. Mammal.* 49, 413–19.

Heitkamp, P.H. and van der Schoot, P.J. (1966) 'De hermelijnen, *Mustela erminea* L., in het Noord-Hollands Duinreservaat', ITBON internal report, 1–22.

Henttonen, H., Oksanen, T., Jortikka, A. and Haukisalmi, V. (1987) 'How much do weasels shape microtine cycles in the northern Fenno-scandian taiga?', *Oikos* 50, 353–65.

Heptner, V.G., Naumov, N.P., Yurgenson, P.B., Sludski, A.A., Chirkova, A.F. and Bannikov, A.G. (1967) [*Mammals of the Soviet Union* Vol. 2], Moscow (chapters on weasel and stoat translated by British Library, RTS 6458).

Herter, K. (1939) 'Psychologische Untersuchungen an einem Mauswiesel (*Mustela nivalis* L.)', *Z. Tierpsychol.* 3, 249–63.

241

REFERENCES

Hewson, R. (1972) 'Changes in the number of stoats, rats and little owls in Yorkshire as shown by tunnel trapping', *J. Zool. Lond.* 168, 427–9.

Hewson, R. and Healing, T.D. (1971) 'The stoat, *Mustela erminea*, and its prey', *J. Zool. Lond.* 164, 239–44.

Hewson, R. and Watson, A. (1979) 'Winter whitening of stoats (*Mustela erminea*) in Scotland and northeast England', *J. Zool. Lond.* 187, 55–64.

Hill, M. (1939) 'The reproductive cycle of the male weasel (*Mustela nivalis*)', *Proc. Zool. Soc. Lond. (Ser. B)* 109, 481–512.

Hirschi, R. (1985) 'A mother's work is never done', *BBC Wildlife* 3, 222–6.

Howard, P. (1988) 'New words for old', *The Times*, 30 March 1988.

Huff, J.N. and Price, E.O. (1968) 'Vocalisations of the least weasel, *Mustela nivalis*', *J. Mammal*, 49, 548–50.

Huggett, A.St.G., and Widas, W.F. (1951) 'The relationship between mammalian foetal weight and conception age' *J. Physiol.* 114, 306–317.

Hunt, D.M. and Gill, B.J. (eds) (1979) 'Ecology of Kowhai Bush, Kaikoura', *Mauri Ora* Special Publ. 2, 1–54.

Hunter, T.S. (1969) 'Aggressive sparrows', *Country Life*, 25 September 1969.

Hutchinson, G.E. (1959) 'Homage to Santa Rosalia, or, why are there so many kinds of animals?', *Am. Nat.* 93, 145–59.

Hutchinson, G.E. and Parker, P.J. (1978) 'Sexual dimorphism in the winter whitening of the stoat, *Mustela erminea*, J. Zool. Lond. 186, 560–3.

Jedrzejweska, B. (1987) 'Reproduction in weasels, *Mustela nivalis* in Poland, *Acta Theriol.* 32, 493–6.

Jennings, D.H., Threllfall, W. and Dodds, D.G. (1982) 'Metazoan parasites and food of short-tailed weasels and mink in Newfoundland, Canada', *Can. J. Zool.* 60, 180–3.

Jensen, B. (1978) 'Resultater af fangst med kassefaelder', *Nat. Jutlandica* 20, 129–36.

Kidd, N.A.C. and Lewis, G.B. (1987) 'Can vertebrate predators regulate their prey? a reply', *Am. Nat.* 130, 448–53.

Kildemoes, A. (1985) 'The impact of introduced stoats (*Mustela erminea*) on an island population of the water vole, *Arvicola terrestris*', *Acta Zool. Fenn.* 173, 193–5.

King, C.M. (1973) 'A system for trapping and handling live weasels in the field', *J. Zool. Lond.* 171, 458–64.

—— (1975a) 'The home range of the weasel (*Mustela nivalis*) in an English woodland', *J. Anim. Ecol.* 44, 639–68.

—— (1975b) 'The sex ratio of trapped weasels (*Mustela nivalis*)', *Mamm. Rev.* 5, 1–8.

—— (1975c) *Biology of Mustelids: some Soviet research*, British Library, Boston Spa.

—— (1976) 'The fleas of a population of weasels in Wytham Woods, Oxford', *J. Zool. Lond.* 180, 525–35.

—— (1977) 'The effects of the nematode parasite *Skrjabingylus nasicola* on British weasels (*Mustela nivalis*)', *J. Zool. Lond.* 182, 225–49.

—— (1979) 'Moult and colour change in English weasels (*Mustela nivalis*)', *J. Zool. Lond.* 189, 127–34.

—— (1980a) *Biology of Mustelids: some Soviet research*, Vol. 2, DSIR Bulletin 227, Wellington.

—— (1980b) 'The weasel (*Mustela nivalis*) and its prey in an English woodland', *J. Anim. Ecol.* 49, 127–59.

—— (1980c) 'Population biology of the weasel *Mustela nivalis* on British game estates', *Hol. Ecol.* 3, 160–8.

—— (1980d) 'Field experiments on the trapping of stoats (*Mustela erminea*), *N.Z.J. Zool.* 7, 261–6.

—— (1980e) 'Age determination in the weasel (*Mustela nivalis*)', *Z. Saug.* 45, 153–73.

—— (1981a), 'The reproductive tactics of the stoat, *Mustela erminea*, in New Zealand forests', in J.A. Chapman and D. Pursley (eds). *World Furbearer Conf.*, 443–68.

—— (1981b) 'The effects of two types of steel traps upon captured stoats (*Mustela erminea*)', *J. Zool. Lond.* 195, 553–4.

—— (1982a) 'Stoat observations', *Landscape*, Wellington, 12, 12–15.

—— (1982b) 'Age structure and reproduction in feral New Zealand populations of the house mouse (*Mus musculus*), in relation to seedfall of southern beech', *N.Z.J. Zool.* 9, 467–80.

—— (1983a) 'The relationships between beech (*Nothofagus* sp) seedfall and populations of mice (*Mus musculus*), and the demographic and dietary responses of stoats (*Mustela erminea*), in three New Zealand forests', *J. Anim. Ecol.* 52, 141–66.

—— (1983b) 'The life history strategies of *Mustela nivalis* and *M. erminea*', *Acta Zool. Fenn.* 174, 183–4.

REFERENCES

—— (1983c) 'Factors regulating mustelid populations', *Acta Zool. Fenn.* 174, 217–20.

—— (1984a) *Immigrant Killers. Introduced Predators and the Conservation of Birds in New Zealand*, Oxford University Press, Auckland.

—— (1984b) 'The origin and adaptive advantages of delayed implantation in *Mustela erminea*', *Oikos* 42, 126–8.

—— (1985) 'Interactions between woodland rodents and their predators', *Symp. Zool. Soc. Lond.* 55, 219–47.

—— (1989) 'The advantages and disadvantages of small size to weasels, *Mustela* species', in J.L. Gittleman (ed), *Carnivore Behaviour, Ecology and Evolution*, Cornell University Press, Ithaca, 302–34.

—— (1990) (ed) *The Handbook of New Zealand Mammals*, Oxford University Press, Auckland.

King, C.M. and Edgar, R.L. (1977) 'Techniques for trapping and tracking stoats (*Mustela erminea*): a review, and a new system', *N.Z.J. Zool.* 4, 193–212.

King, C.M. and McMillan, C.D. (1982) 'Population structure and dispersal of peak-year cohorts of stoats (*Mustela erminea*) in two New Zealand forests, with especial reference to control', *N.Z.J. Ecol.* 5, 59–66.

King, C.M. and Moody, J.E. (1982) 'The biology of the stoat (*Mustela erminea*) in the National Parks of New Zealand', *N.Z.J. Zool.* 9, 49–144.

King, C.M. and Moors, P.J. (1979a) 'The life history tactics of mustelids, and their significance for predator control and conservation in New Zealand', *N.Z.J. Zool.* 6, 619–22.

—— —— (1979b) 'On co-existence, foraging strategy and the biogeography of weasels and stoats (*Mustela nivalis* and *M. erminea*) in Britain', *Oecologia* 39, 129–50.

Kopein, K.I. (1965) 'The biology of reproduction of ermine in Yamal', in King (1980a), 62–9.

—— (1967) 'Analysis of the age structure of ermine populations', in King (1975c), 158–69.

—— (1969) 'The relationship between age and individual variation in the ermine', in King (1980a), 132–8.

Kraft, V.A. (1966) 'Influence of temperature on the activity of the ermine in winter', in King (1975c), 104–7.

Kratochvil, J. (1977a) 'Sexual dimorphism and status of *Mustela nivalis* in Central Europe (Mammalia, Mustelidae)', *Acta Sci. Nat. Brno* 11, 1–42.

—— (1977b) 'Studies on *Mustela erminea* (Mustelidae, Mammalia) I. Variability of metric and mass traits', *Folia Zool.* 26, 291–304.

Kukarcev, V.A. (1978) 'The structure of an ermine (*Mustela erminea*) population at different densities', *Int. Congr. Theriol,* 2 (Brno) Abstracts, 328.

Kurtén, B. (1960) 'Chronology and faunal evolution of the earlier European glaciations', *Comment. Biol. Soc. Sci. Fenn.* 21, 1–62.

—— (1968) *Pleistocene Mammals of Europe*, Weidenfeld and Nicholson, London.

Kurtén, B. and Anderson, E. (1980) *Pleistocene Mammals of North America*, Columbia University Press, New York.

Langley, P.J.W. and Yalden, D.W. (1977) 'The decline of the rarer carnivores in Great Britain during the nineteenth century', *Mamm. Rev.* 7, 95–116.

Latham, R.M. (1952) 'The fox as a factor in the control of weasel populations', *J. Wildl. Mgmt.* 16, 516–7.

Lavrov, N.P. (1944) 'Effect of helminth invasions and infectious diseases on variations in numbers of the ermine, *Mustela erminea* L.', in King (1975c), 170–87.

Lewis, J.W. (1967) 'Observations on the skull of Mustelidae infected with the nematode, *Skrjabingylus nasicola, J. Zool. Lond.* 153, 561–4.

—— (1978) 'A population study of the metastrongylid nematode *Skrjabingylus nasicola* in the weasel, *Mustela nivalis, J. Zool. Lond.* 184, 225–9.

Lightfoot, V.M.A. and Wallis, S.J. (1982) 'Predation of small mammals inside Longworth traps by a weasel', *J. Zool. Lond.* 198, 521.

Linduska, J.P. (1947) 'Longevity of some Michigan farm game mammals', *J. Mammal.* 28, 126–9.

Linn, I. and Day, M.G. (1966) 'Identification of individual weasels *Mustela nivalis* using the ventral pelage pattern', *J. Zool. Lond.* 148, 583–5.

Lippincott, J.W. (1940) 'I trap no more weasels', *Penn. Game News* 10 (12), 6, 25.

Lockie, J.D. (1966) 'Territory in small carnivores', *Symp. Zool. Soc. Lond.* 18, 143–65.

Lockie, J.D., Charles, W.N. and East, K. (1962) 'Weasel and stoat', *Nature Conservancy Ann. Rep. for 1962,* 83–4.

Lockie, J.D. and Day, M.G. (1963) 'The use of anaesthetics in the handling of stoats and weasels', in O.G. Jones (ed) *Symposium on Small Mammal Anaesthesia*, Pergamon Press, Oxford, 187–9.

Lokemoen, J.T. and Higgins, K.F. (1972) 'Population irruption of the least weasel (*Mustela nivalis*) in east central North Dakota', *Prairie Nat.* 4, 96.

McLean, S.F. Jr., Fitzgerald, B.M. and Pitelka, F.A. (1974) 'Population cycles in Arctic lemmings: winter reproduction and predation by weasels', *Arctic & Alpine Res.* 6, 1–12.

Madison, D.M., Fitzgerald, R.W. and McShea, W.J. (1984) 'Dynamics of social nesting in overwintering meadow voles (*Microtus pennslyvanicus*): possible consequences for population cycling', *Behav. Ecol. Sociobiol.* 15, 9–17.

Maher. W.J. (1967) 'Predation by weasels on a winter population of lemmings, Banks Island, Northwest Territories', *Can. Field. Nat.* 81, 248–50.

Mandahl, N. and Fredga, K. (1980) 'A comparative chromosome study by means of G,C and Nor-bandings of the weasel, the pygmy weasel and the stoat (Mustelida, Carnivora, Mammalia)', *Hereditas* 93, 75–83.

Mardon, D.K. and Moors, P.J. (1977) 'Records of fleas collected from weasels (*Mustela nivalis* L.) in northeast Scotland (Siphonaptera: Hystrichopsyllidae and Ceratophyllidae)', *Ent, Gaz.* 28, 277–80.

Marshall, W.H. (1963) 'The ecology of mustelids in New Zealand', *DSIR Info. Ser.* 38, 1–32.

Mead, R.A. (1981) 'Delayed implantation in mustelids, with special emphasis on the spotted skunk', *J. Rep. Fert.* Suppl. 29, 11–24.

MAFF (Min. Ag. Fish Food) (1987) *Bovine tuberculosis in badgers*, 11th report, 27.

Moors, P.J. (1974) *The annual energy budget of a weasel* (Mustela nivalis *L.) population in farmland*, Ph.D. thesis, University of Aberdeen.

—— (1975) 'The food of weasels (*Mustela nivalis*) on farmland in northeast Scotland', *J. Zool. Lond.* 177, 455–61.

—— (1977) 'Studies of the metabolism, food consumption and assimilation efficiency of a small carnivore, the weasel (*Mustela nivalis* L.), *Oecologia* 27, 185–202.

—— (1980) 'Sexual dimorphism in the body size of mustelids (Carnivora): the roles of food habits and breeding systems', *Oikos* 34, 147–58.

—— (1983a) 'Predation by stoats (*Mustela erminea*) and weasels (*Mustela nivalis*) on nests of New Zealand forest birds', *Acta Zool. Fenn.* 174, 193–6.

—— (1983b) 'Predation by mustelids and rodents on the eggs and chicks of native and introduced birds in Kowhai Bush, New Zealand', *Ibis* 125, 137–54.

Morozova-Turova, L.G. (1965) 'Geographical differences in weasels in the Soviet Union', in King (1975c), 7–29.

Mortimer Batten, H. (1936) 'Weasels and stoats – do they mesmerise their prey?', *The Field*, August 29, 504.

Morton Boyd, J. (1958) 'Mole and stoat on Eilean Molach, Loch Ba, Argyll', *Proc. Zool. Soc. Lond.* 131, 327–8.

Müller, H. (1970) 'Beiträge zur Biologie des Hermelins, *Mustela erminea* Linné 1758', *Saug. Mitt* 18, 293–380.

Müller-Using, D. (1965) 'Die Bedeutung von *Mustela nivalis* für das Niederwild', *Int. Congr. Game Biol.* 6, 55–7.

Mumford, R.E. (1969) 'Longtailed weasel preys on big brown bats', *J.Mammal.* 50, 360.

Murie, A. (1935) 'Weasel goes hungry', *J. Mammal.* 16, 321–2.

Musgrove, B.F. (1951) 'Weasel foraging patterns in the Robinson Lake area, Idaho', *Murrelet* 32, 8–11.

Myrberget, S. (1972) 'Fluctuations in a north Norwegian population of willow grouse', *Int. Orn. Congr*, 15, 107–20.

Nams, V. (1981) 'Prey selection mechanisms of the ermine (*Mustela erminea*)', in J.A. Chapman and D. Pursley (eds) *World Furbearer Conf.*, 861–82.

Nasimovich, A.A. (1949) '[The biology of the weasel in the Kola Peninsula in connection with its competitive relations with the ermine]', *Zool.Zhurn.* 28, 177–82 (translation in Elton Library, Oxford).

Noback, C.V. (1935) 'Observations on the seasonal hair moult of the New York weasel', *Bull. N.Y. Zool. Soc.* 38, 25–7.

Northcott, T.H. (1971) 'Winter predation of *Mustela erminea* in northern Canada', *Arctic* 24, 142–4.

Nyholm, E.S. (1959) 'Stoats and weasels and their winter habitats', in King (1975c), 118–31.

Obara, Y. (1982) 'Comparative analysis of karyotypes in the Japanese mustelids, *Mustela nivalis namiyei* and *M.erminea nippon*, *J. Mamm. Soc. Japan* 9, 59–69.

Oehler, C. (1945) 'Temperament of the New York weasel', *J. Mammal.* 25, 198.

Oksanen, T., Oksanen, L. and Fretwell, S.D. (1985) 'Surplus killing in the hunting strategy of small predators', *Am. Nat.* 126, 328–46.

Osborn, D.J. and Helmy, I. (1980) 'The contemporary land mammals of Egypt (including

Sinai): *Mustela nivalis, Fieldiana: Zool.* n.s. 5. 405–9.

Osgood, F.L. (1936) 'Earthworms as a supplementary food of weasels', *J. Mammal.* 17, 64.

Parovshchikov, V.Y. (1963) 'A contribution to the ecology of *Mustela nivalis* Linnaeus, 1766 of the Arkhangel'sk north', in King (1975c), 84–97.

Pearce, J. (1937) 'A captive New York weasel' *J. Mammal.* 18, 483–88.

Pearson, O.P. (1985) 'Predation', in R.H. Tamarin (ed) *Biology of New World* Microtus, *Spec. Publ. Am. Soc. Mam.* 8, 535–66.

Petrov, O.V. (1962) 'The validity of Bergmann's Rule as applied to intraspecific variation in the ermine', in King (1975c),30–38.

Polder, E. (1968) 'Spotted skunk and weasel populations den and cover usage by northeastern Iowa', *Proc. Iowa Acad. Sci.* 75, 142–6.

Polderboer, E.B. (1942) 'Habits of the least weasel (*Mustela rixosa*) in northeastern Iowa', *J. Mammal.* 23, 145–7.

Polderboer, E.B., Kuhn, L.W. and Hendrickson, G.O. (1941) 'Winter and spring habits of weasels in central Iowa', *J. Wildl. Mgmt.* 5, 115–9.

Popov, V.A. (1943) 'Numerosity of *Mustela erminea* Pall. as affected by *Skrjabingylus* invasion', *C.R. Acad. Sci.* 39, 160–2.

Potts, G.R. (1986) *The Partridge: Pesticides, Predation and Conservation*, Collins, London.

Potts, G.R. and Vickerman, G.P. (1974) 'Studies on the cereal ecosystem', *Adv. Ecol. Res.* 8, 107–97.

Pounds, C.J. (1981) *Niche overlap in sympatric populations of stoats* (Mustela erminea) *and weasels* (Mustela nivalis) *in northeast Scotland*, Ph.D. thesis, University of Aberdeen.

Powell, R.A. (1973) 'A model for raptor predation on weasels', *J. Mammal.* 54, 259–63.

—— (1978) 'A comparison of fisher and weasel hunting behaviour', *Carnivore* 1, 28–34.

—— (1979) 'Mustelid spacing patterns: variations on a theme by *Mustela*', *Z. Tierpsychol.* 50, 153–65.

—— (1982) 'Evolution of black-tipped tails in weasels: predator confusion', *Am. Nat.* 119, 126–31.

—— (1985) 'Possible pathways for the evolution of reproductive strategies in weasels and stoats', *Oikos* 44, 506–8.

Powell, R.A. and Zielinski, W.J. (1983) 'Competition and co-existence in mustelid communities', *Acta Zool. Fenn.* 174, 223–7.

Pruitt, W.O.Jr. (1978) *Boreal Ecology*, Arnold, London.

Quick, H.F. (1944) 'Habits and economics of the New York weasel in Michigan', *J. Wildl. Mgmt.* 8, 71–8.

—— (1951) 'Notes on the ecology of weasels in Gunnison County, Colorado', *J.Mammal.* 32, 281–90.

Ralls, K. and Harvey, P.H. (1985) 'Geographic variation in size and sexual dimorphism of North American weasels', *Biol. J. Linn. Soc.* 25, 119–67.

Raymond, M. and Bergeron, J-M. (1982) 'Réponse numérique de l'hermine aux fluctuations d'abondance de *Microtus pennsylvanicus*', *Can. J. Zool.* 60, 542–9.

Raymond, M., Bergeron, J-M. and Plante, Y. (1984) 'Dimorphisme sexuel et régime alimentaire de l'hermine dans une agrosystème du Québec', *Can. J. Zool.* 62, 594–600.

Reichstein, H. (1957) 'Schädelvariabilität europäischer Mauswiesel (*Mustela nivalis* L.) und Hermeline (*Mustela erminea* L.) in Beziehung zu Verbreitung und Geschlecht', *Z.Saug.* 22, 151–82.

Robitaille, J-F. and Baron, G. (1987) 'Seasonal changes in the activity budget of captive ermine, *Mustela erminea* L.', *Can. J. Zool.* 65, 2864–71.

Rothschild, M. and Lane, C. (1957) 'Note on change of pelage in the stoat (*Mustela erminea* L.)', *Proc. Zool. Soc. Lond.* 128, 602.

Rowlands, I.W. (1972) 'Reproductive studies in the stoat', *J.Zool. Lond.* 166, 574–6.

Rubina, M.A. (1960) '[Some features of weasel (*Mustela nivalis* L.) ecology based on observations in the Moscow region]', *Byull. Mosk. Obshch. Ispyt. Prir., Ot. Biol.* 65, 27–33 (translation in British Library, RTS 2292).

Rust, C.C. (1962) 'Temperature as a modifying factor in the spring pelage change of short-tailed weasels', *J. Mammal.* 43, 323–8.

—— (1965) 'Hormonal control of pelage cycles in the short-tailed weasel (*Mustela erminea bangsi*)', *Gen. Comp. Endocr.* 5, 222–31.

—— (1968) 'Procedure for live-trapping weasels', *J. Mammal.* 49, 318–9.

Rust, C.C. and Meyer, R.K. (1969) 'Hair color, molt and testis size in male short-tailed weasels treated with melatonin', *Science* 165, 921–2.

Salomonsen, F. (1939) 'Moults and sequence of plumages in the Rock Ptarmigan (*Lagopus mutus* (Montin)), *Dan. Natur. For. Vidensk. Med.* 103, 1–491.

REFERENCES

Sandell, M. (1984) 'To have or not to have delayed implantation: the example of the weasel and the stoat', *Oikos* 42, 123–6.

—— (1985) *Ecology and behaviour of the stoat* Mustela erminea *and a theory on delayed implantation*, Ph.D. thesis, University of Lund.

—— (1986) 'Movement patterns of male stoats *Mustela erminea* during the mating season: differences in relation to social status', *Oikos* 47, 63–70.

Sanderson, G.C. (1949) 'Growth and behaviour of a litter of captive longtailed weasels, *Mustela frenata*', *J. Mammal.* 30, 412–6.

Schmidt-Nielsen, K. (1984) *Scaling: why is animal size so important?*, Cambridge University Press, Cambridge.

Segal, A.N. (1975) 'Postnatal growth, metabolism and thermoregulation in the stoat', *Soviet J. Ecol* 6, 28–32.

Shelden, R.M. (1972) 'The fate of short-tailed weasel, *Mustela erminea*, blastocysts following ovariectomy during diapause'. *J. Reprod. Fert.* 31, 347–52.

Short, H.L. (1961) 'Food habits of a captive least weasel', *J. Mammal.* 42, 273–4.

Simms, D.A. (1978) 'Spring and summer food habits of an ermine (*Mustela erminea*) in the central Arctic', *Can. Field Nat.* 92, 192–3.

—— (1979a) 'Studies of an ermine population in southern Ontario', *Can. J. Zool.* 57, 824–32.

—— (1979b) 'North American weasels: resource utilisation and distribution', *Can. J. Zool.* 57, 504–20.

Sleeman, P. (1987) *The ecology of the Irish stoat*, Ph.D. thesis, National University of Ireland.

—— (1988) '*Skrjabingylus nasicola* (Leukart) [Metastrongylidae] as a parasite of the Irish stoat', *Ir. Nat. J.* 22, 525–27.

—— (1989) 'Ectoparasites of the Irish stoat', *Med. Vet. Entomol.* 3. (in press).

Sonerud, G.A. (1988) 'What causes extended lows in microtine cycles? Analysis of fluctuations in sympatric shrew and microtine populations in Fennoscandia', *Oecologia* 76, 37–42.

Southern, H.N. (1970) 'The natural control of a population of tawny owls (*Strix aluco*), *J. Zool. Lond.* 162, 197–285.

Southern, H.N. and Lowe, V.P.W. (1982) 'Predation by tawny owls (*Strix aluco*) on bank voles (*Clethrionomys glareolus*) and wood mice (*Apodemus sylvaticus*), *J. Zool. Lond.* 198, 83–102.

Stenseth, N.C. (1985) 'Optimal size and frequency of litters in predators of cyclic prey: comments on the reproductive biology of stoats and weasels', *Oikos* 45, 293–6.

Stephen, D. (1969) 'Miniature maneaters', *The Scotsman* 25 October 1969.

Stoddart, D.M. (1976) 'Effect of the odour of weasels (*Mustela nivalis* L.) on trapped samples of their prey', *Oecologia* 22, 439–41.

Stolt, B-O. (1979) 'Colour pattern and size variation of the weasel, *Mustela nivalis*, in Sweden', *Zoon* 7, 55–62.

Stronganov, S.U. (1937) 'A method of age determination and an analysis of the age structures of ermine populations (*Mustela erminea* L.)', in King (1980a), 93–108.

Stuart, A.J. (1982) *Pleistocene Vertebrates in the British Isles*, Longman Group, London.

Stubbe, M. (1970) 'Zur Evolution der analen Markierungsorgane bei Musteliden', *Biol. Zentralblatt* 89, 213–23.

—— (1972) 'Die analen Markierungsorgane der *Mustela*-Arten', *Zool. Garten N.F.* Leipzig 42, 176–88.

Stuttard, R.M. (ed) (1986) *Predatory mammals in Britain*, 4th edition, British Field Sports Society, London.

Sullivan, T.P. and Sullivan, D.S. (1980) 'The use of weasels for natural control of mouse and vole populations in a coastal coniferous forest', *Oecologia* 47, 125–9.

Sumption, K.J. and Flowerdew, J.R. (1985) 'The ecological effects of the decline in rabbits (*Oryctolagus cuniculus* L.) due to myxomatosis', *Mamm. Rev.* 15, 151–86.

Svendsen, G.E. (1976) 'Vocalisations of the longtailed weasel (*Mustela frenata*)', *J. Mammal.* 57, 398–99.

—— (1982) 'Weasels, *Mustela* species', in J.A. Chapman and G.A. Feldhamer (eds) *Wild Mammals of North America*, Johns Hopkins University Press, Baltimore.

Swanson, G. and Fryklund, P.O. (1935) 'The least weasel in Minnesota and its fluctuations in numbers', *Am. Midl. Nat.* 16, 120–6.

Tadros, W. and Laarman, J.J. (1979) 'Muscular sarcosporidiosis in the common European weasel *Mustela nivalis*', *Z. Parasit.* 58, 195–200.

Tapper, S.C. (1976) 'The diet of weasels, *Mustela nivalis* and stoats, *Mustela erminea* during early summer, in relation to predation on gamebirds', *J. Zool. Lond.* 179, 219–24.

—— (1979) 'The effect of fluctuating vole numbers *(Microtus agrestis)* on a population of weasels *(Mustela nivalis)* on farmland', *J. Anim. Ecol.* 48, 603–17.

—— (1982) 'Using estate records to monitor population trends in game and predator species, particularly weasels and stoats', *Int. Congr. Game Biol.* 14, 115–20.

Tapper, S.C., Green, R.E. and Rands, M.R.W. (1982) 'Effects of mammalian predators on partridge populations', *Mamm. Rev.* 12, 159–67.

Taylor, R.H. and Tilley, J.A.V. (1984) 'Stoats *(Mustela erminea)* on Adele and Fisherman Islands, Abel Tasman National Park, and other offshore islands in New Zealand', *N.Z. J. Ecol.* 7, 139–45.

Teer, J.G. (1964) 'Predation by longtailed weasels on eggs of blue-winged teal', *J. Wildl. Mgmt.* 28, 404–6.

Tenquist, J.D. and Charleston, W.A.G. (1981) 'An annotated checklist of ectoparasites of terrestrial mammals in New Zealand', *J. Roy. Soc. N.Z.* 11, 257–85.

Teplov, V.P. (1948) 'The problem of sex ratio in ermine', in King (1975c), 98–103.

Ternovsky, D.V. (1983) '[The biology of reproduction and development of the stoat *Mustela erminea* (Carnivora, Mustelidae)]', *Zool. Zhurn.* 62, 1097–1105 (translated by Department of Internal Affairs, Wellington, New Zealand).

'Tower Bird' (1967) 'Weasels' *Shooting Times*, 6 May 1967.

Tumanov, I.L. and Levin, V.G. (1974) 'Age and seasonal changes in some physiological characters in the weasel *(Mustela nivalis* L.) and ermine *(Mustela erminea* L.)', in King (1980a), 192–6.

Vaisfeld, M.A. (1972) 'Ecology of the ermine in the cold season in the European north', in King (1980a), 1–10.

van Soest, R.W.M. and van Bree, P.J.H. (1969) 'On the moult in the stoat, *Mustela erminea* Linnaeus 1758, from the Netherlands', *Bijdr. Dierk.* 39, 63–8.

—— —— (1970) 'Sex and age composition of a stoat population *(Mustela erminea* Linnaeus 1758) from a coastal dune region of the Netherlands', *Beaufortia* 17, 51–77.

van Soest, R.W.M., van der Land, J. and van Bree, P.J.H. (1972) 'Skrjabingylus nasicola (Nematoda) in skulls of *Mustela erminea* and *Mustela nivalis* (Mammalia) from the Netherlands', *Beaufortia* 20, 85–97.

van Wijngaarden, A. and Bruijns, M.F.M. (1961) 'Die hermelijnen, *Mustela erminea* L., van Terschelling', *Lutra* 3, 35–42.

Vernon-Betts, R.J. (1967) 'Weasels' running battle', *The Field* 15 June 1967.

Vershinin, A.A. (1972) 'The biology and trapping of the ermine in Kamchatka', in King (1980a), 11–23.

Vik, R. (1955) 'Invasion of *Skrjabingylus* (Nematoda) in Norwegian Mustelidae', *Nytt. Mag. Zool.* 3, 70–8.

Watzka, M. (1940) 'Mikroskopisch-anatomische Untersuchungen über die Ranzzeit und Tragdauer des Hermelins *(Putorius [sic] ermineus)]*', *Z. Mikroskop.-Anatom. Forsch.* 48, 359–74.

Weber, J-M. (1986) *Aspects quantitatifs du cycle de* Skrjabingylus nasicola *(Leukart, 1842), nematode parasite des sinus frontaux des mustelides,* Ph.D. thesis, University of Neuchatel.

Weber, J-M. and Mermod, C. (1983) 'Experimental transmission of *Skrjabingylus nasicola*, parasitic nematode of mustelids', *Acta. Zool. Fenn.* 174, 237–8.

—— —— (1985) 'Quantitative aspects of the life cycle of *Skrjabingylus nasicola*, a parasitic nematode of the frontal sinuses of mustelids', *Z. Parasit.* 71, 631–8.

Wojcik, M. (1974) 'Remains of Mustelidae (Carnivora, Mammalia) from the late Pleistocene deposits of Polish caves', *Acta Zool. Cracov.* 19, 75–90.

Wood, K. (1946) 'Five o'clock killer', *Fauna* Philadelphia, 8, 44–6.

Wright, P.L. (1942) 'Delayed implantation in the longtailed weasel *(Mustela frenata)*, the short-tailed weasel *(Mustela cicognanii)* and the marten *(Martes americana)*', *Anat. Rec.* 83, 341–53.

—— (1947) 'The sexual cycle of the male longtailed weasel *(Mustela frenata)*', *J. Mammal.* 28, 343–52.

—— (1948) 'Breeding habits of captive longtailed weasels (*Mustela frenata)*', *Amer. Midl. Nat.* 39, 338–44.

—— (1950) 'Development of the baculum of the longtailed weasel', *Proc. Soc. Exp. Biol. Med. N.Y.* 75, 820–2.

—— (1963) 'Variations in reproductive cycles in North American mustelids', in A.C. Enders (ed) *Delayed Implantation*, Univ. Chicago Press, 77–97.

Index